The
Sociology of

KNOWLEDGE

---

in America

ઌ

1883 - 1915

The
Sociology of
KNOWLEDGE
in America

❧

1883 - 1915

ELLSWORTH R. FUHRMAN

University Press of Virginia

Charlottesville

The publication of this volume is sponsored by the VPI Educational Foundation, Inc.

THE UNIVERSITY PRESS OF VIRGINIA

Copyright © 1980 by the Rector and Visitors of the University of Virginia

First published 1980

Fried. 20,00 /18.00 /10 /16/81

Library of Congress Cataloging in Publication Data

Fuhrman, Ellsworth R
    The sociology of knowledge in America, 1883-1915.

    Bibliography: p.
    Includes index.
    1. Sociology—United States—History. 2. Social structure.
3. Knowledge, Sociology of. I. Title.
HM22.U5F84   301'.0973   79-14829
ISBN 0-8139-0785-3

Printed in the United States of America

For

KRISTEL

Whether a proposition can turn out false after all depends on what I make count as determinants for that proposition.... Doubting and non-doubting behavior. There is the first only if there is the second.... "An empirical proposition can be tested" (we say). But how? and through what? What *counts* as its test?—"But is this an adequate test?"...As if giving grounds did not come to an end sometime. But the end is not an ungrounded presupposition: it is an ungrounded way of acting.

—Ludwig Wittgenstein *On Certainty*

The only possible strategy when facing a situation of total or near-total bewilderment is a monistic one: choose some point, and try to recover a coherent picture by building anew, using it as a base. The choice of base may have to be in some measure arbitrary, and it may even be tentative; it must be arbitrary in as far as the state of hazed confusion precludes the possession of clear, reliable principles which would single out the base in an objective, rational manner.... Such monism is absolutely essential for our life.

—Ernest Gellner *Legitimation of Belief*

Contents

Preface

In these pages I have tried to present and to analyze the writings of six early American sociologists—William Graham Sumner, Lester Frank Ward, Franklin Henry Giddings, Albion Woodbury Small, Edward Alsworth Ross, and Charles Horton Cooley. In particular, my interest is to show that these writers displayed an intellectual concern with the relationship between social structure and the production, distribution, and consumption of ideas. In more traditional terms, this branch of sociology has been called *Wissenssoziologie,* or the sociology of knowledge. Since the sociology of knowledge makes the assumption that a relationship exists between social structure and ideas, it seems appropriate to indicate the social background of this work insofar as I am aware of such influences.

As a graduate student, I was often surprised and dismayed at the amount of intellectual effort given to discussing European sociological theorists, at the expense of considering the American sociological tradition. For a long time, I simply assumed that American social theories must not be worthy of examination. In addition, and simultaneously, I was made aware of competing sociological theories—exchange, conflict, phenomenology, ethnomethodology, critical theory, Marxism, etc.—which led me to wonder whether there were agreed-upon grounds for comparing the predictive, interpretive, and evaluative aspects of sociological theory. It soon became apparent to me that such a common ground *did not* exist. In my intellectual meanderings, I turned to metasociology, the sociology of sociology, and the sociology of knowledge, believing intuitively that these branches of sociology would provide a more adequate basis for comparing the competing theories mentioned above, exchange, conflict, etc. However, even these metasociological branches of sociology, which explicitly claimed to be interested in the assumptions and social bases of intellectual discourse, also manifested assumptive disagreements. In part, then, a solution of the sort I had in mind did not seem available. However, this search for a solution did convince me that the problems which concerned me were not idiosyncratic, but were a part of sociology, in particular, and of the larger social world I inhabited, in general.

At the same time, the social and political atmosphere of this country was not one which led to trust. As a part of the World War II population explosion, I had been exposed to the cold war and to the threat of nuclear annihilation. The death of the Kennedy brothers and of Martin Luther King, as well as high unemployment, helped forge an attitude of distrust and scepticism. The student movements, the corruption in high political offices, and the uncertain status of the Vietnam conflict also contributed to a distrust of accepted ways of thinking and acting. One did not need to be a sociologist to look *beyond* the face value of both public and private statements. This intellectual and social milieu, I believe, helped to shape the character of this work, which combines my interest in American sociological theory with my curiosity about the assumptions of intellectual discourse.

This work is not, strictly speaking, a sociology of knowledge study of early American sociologists, although I have given some attention to the general milieu in which they wrote as well as to their biographies. In particular, I indicate in the first chapter that there are at least two distinct sociology of knowledge traditions (i.e., social-technological and critical-emancipatory) which make different assumptions about the nature of knowledge and its relationship to social structure. The major part of this study, then, focuses on the social-technological sociology of knowledge tradition exhibited in their writings. However, I also attempt to show more generally that the various traditions within the sociology of knowledge rest on disputable assumptions. As such, the sociology of knowledge cannot be used to discredit other theories and simultaneously declare the cognitive superiority of its own vision. On this point, I briefly examine the assumptions of the critical-emancipatory tradition for the purpose of showing that it may provide an appropriate grounding for the sociology of knowledge, since it expresses a self-conscious interest in its own assumptions. This work, of course, can only be a preliminary inquiry into the assumptions of sociological theory and the more general issue of the cognitive limits of sociology.

I would like to thank David Westby of Pennsylvania State University for his encouragement and guidance throughout the development of this project, particularly in its earliest stages. Charles Page of the University of Massachusetts graciously provided a critical reading of the entire manuscript and made many valuable suggestions. In addition, I would like to thank Don Martindale of the University of Minnesota for his support and comments and William C. Havard, Jr. for his encouragement. I also would like to acknowledge here my former teachers David Westby, Alex Simirenko, George Theodorson, and Robert Bealer. Joseph Blake, Jack Dudley, Patricia Kluck, James Skipper and William Snizek, my colleagues, have supported and commented on various aspects of this work and deserve a note of thanks. I also would like to thank Clifton D. Bryant for making available the necessary administrative and clerical help. In addition, many thanks to Cindy Crawford and Tracey Shelor for the typing and retyping of this manuscript. I also would like to thank my two graduate assistants, Deborah Brooks, and, in particular, Alan Stump for his help in the preparation of this manuscript. Finally, a special note of thanks goes to Richard Hoffman for seeing this work through its final production and for making the process of publication more intellectually satisfying.

E.R.F.
Blacksburg, Virginia

Introduction

For two hundred years, sociological thought has contributed to the secularization and industrialization of the Western world. As a distinct form of consciousness, it helps remove religious symbols and institutions from the dominant sectors of society (particularly economic and political organizations).[1] Sociological thinking is a questioning, skeptical form of consciousness, taking little for granted as it appears phenomenally.

To ask sociological questions, then, presupposes that one is interested in looking some distance beyond the commonly accepted or officially defined goals of human actions. It presupposes a certain awareness that human events have different levels of meaning, some of which are hidden from the consciousness of everyday life. It may even presuppose a measure of suspicion about the way in which human events are officially interpreted by the authorities, be they political, juridical or religious in character.[2]

When thought was released from its theological bond, intellectuals had to search for secular answers to religious questions about man's essential nature, the meaning of life, and the nature of knowledge (epistemology). Once social thought was extricated from biblical exegesis, tradition, revelation, and the exhortations of divine principles, it was forced to explain not only man's place in nature but also how human consciousness is possible at all. Philosophers answered this question in a variety of ways.[3] In some instances they viewed sense perception as the foundation of knowledge. In others, they thought the mind was the cornerstone of all conceptualizations. Sociologists rejected the philosophers' abstract, formal categories: knowledge was social in its origin. In this context the sociology of knowledge as a tradition of thought came into being.

Historically, the sociology of knowledge was characterized by a questioning, skeptical frame of mind in general. It is a perspective critical of received notions about relationships between knowledge and social conditions. In particular, the central concern of the sociology of knowledge is explaining the knowledge systems of special social groups (i.e., elites), or more recently of whole cultures.[4] Its explanatory pattern is secularized—knowledge is no longer sanctioned by God or his divine interpreters; it is created and held by men. Men can be and are held accountable for their thoughts in ways which the divinity never can be.

The decline of cognitive authority in the modern world was recently chronicled by Ernest Gellner in his *Legitimation of Belief.* Gellner argues that even modern philosophy and "its epistemological stress gain in plausibility when read *not* as descriptive or explanatory accounts of what knowledge is really like, but as a formulation of norms which are to govern and limit our cognitive behavior."[5] He goes on to indicate that cognitive appeals can be made to: (1) something outside us which is larger and more objective, and (2) anthropocentric validation, some premises internal to man. The first type of appeal runs the risk of justifying belief in the existence of and the accessibility to the norm outside us. The latter claim is fine when things are stable; when conflict occurs and humans are not agreed, however, then anthropocentric appeals lack a persuasive common ground.

The sociology of knowledge as a subdiscipline in sociology has been concerned with the social grounds of various ideas. In this sense, part of its concern is not only with the social origins of ideas but also with the courts of appeals involved in cognitive claims to superiority. The sociology of knowledge, insofar as it can be construed as a branch of skepticism, undermined the coginitive authority of philosophers as well as that of sociologists themselves. For example, Göran Therborn has recently argued that:

What the present study indicates, then, is neither convergence nor synthesis, but a *transcendence of sociology,* similar to Marx's transcendence of classical economics, and the development of historical materialism as the science of society. To indicate a task, however, is not to accomplish it. The extent to which these possibilities prove capable of realization will not depend on intra-scientific events alone. The rise and formation of the social sciences were determined by the class struggles of particular historical societies, and so, no doubt, will be their further or arrested development. Thus the question of a future development of social sciences in the direction of historical materialism remains open—above all to those of us who are committed to working for it.[6]

Therborn argues for the cognitive superiority of historical materialism, but not based on the intrascientific testing of empirical propositions alone. His appeal to cognitive authority—which is, in part, extra scientific by positivist standards—depends on the class struggle and those committed to it. Ironically, Karl Mannheim sought a different way to ground his claim to cognitive superiority—the free-floating intelligentsia.[7] The sociology of knowledge, which sought the social origins of other belief systems, inevitably was concerned with the secular grounding of its own arguments. There were a great many attempts to root arguments in a transcendental authority which was *this worldly*—some norm endorsing other.[8] The form and content of these arguments differed (i.e., self-evident truths, intuition, laws, facts, reason, praxis), yet the pervasive idea remained the same. They were attempts to ground cognitive claims in such a way that the bases of the claim will be unassailable from other groups' competing arguments.[9] The sociology of knowledge was, in part, a response to diverse and competing arguments in the cognitive realm. It attempted to show the social origins of these competing claims and yet to ground itself in some unassailable sphere of its own. Whether this can be done or not will be taken up in the last chapter.

Interestingly enough, the sociology of knowledge as a distinct intellectual tradition was regarded by some as a movement primarily confined to Europe.[10] Secularization was not a process confined to western Europe alone, however; America also experienced an industrial revolution. Insofar as the sociology of knowledge can be understood as a response to industrialization and secularization, one would expect it to appear in America as well as in Europe, and indeed, this is the case. Early American sociologists showed a concern with the relationships between ideas and social structure. Yet there has been little or no research directed toward identifying the sociology of knowledge in America.

This neglect, in part, stemmed from some American sociologists' refusal to take ideas—particularly those called ideological—seriously. Indeed, American sociologists tend to ignore the fact that their ideas may be, in part, ideological. Recently, however, some American sociologists have declared an interest in the role of ideas in sociology, particularly the ideas that sociologists create.[11] The most important question that emerged from their analyses was: Does sociology (read: do sociologists) contribute to the predominance of repressive or of liberative forces in society? The sociology of knowledge is reflexively applied to itself (sociology of sociology).

An important and related subtheme also emerges: Can sociologists lay claim to the notion that they, and they alone, can represent the interests of humanity? Both St. Simon and Comte believed this to be the case. Yet Marx challenged their claim and was, in turn, challenged by later critical theorists.[12] The counterclaims brought by each group are part of the current effort to rethink the social ground of sociology. This thinking anew has led to a revived interest in exploring the history of sociological theory.[13] This interest leads to a concern for both the assumptions and the social bases of intellectual discourse. Sociology clearly rests on assumptions and utilizes arguments of various sorts to justify its claim to cognitive authority. Yet, those who call themselves sociologists clearly differ about what they are doing and why they are doing it.[14]

This work is part of that larger concern with the ideological and social bases of sociological thought. Specifically, it explores the writings of six pioneer American sociologists: William Graham Sumner (1840-1910), Lester Frank Ward (1841-1913), Franklin Henry Giddings (1844-1931), Albion Woodbury Small (1854-1926), Edward Alsworth Ross (1866-1951), and Charles Horton Cooley (1864-1929). These men are important because they set the intellectual tone for the foundation of a sociology of knowledge tradition in America. They occupied positions at the important centers of graduate training: Brown, Yale, Columbia, Wisconsin, Chicago, and Michigan. In addition, they each served as president of the American Sociological Association. This work explores how this first generation of American sociologists handled the relationship between ideas and social structure. It will show that their claim to objectivity and concern for the whole of society was, in part, ideological. They had their own interests to protect.

There is some intellectual advantage also in examining the writing of the six men mentioned above. Sociology was not well developed as a discipline in the United States at this time. These sociologists had to make clear their claim to cognitive authority. They had to prove that the ideas of the socialists and the traditions of the humanities were not adequate for an understanding of the modern world. Unlike present sociologists, the pioneers' claim to importance was *not* self-evident. The sociology of knowledge which they developed was clearly conservative in nature. They were critics of laissez-faire capitalism and, in particular, of past political philosophies which viewed the state as an isolated institution.

They were not, however, critics of the existing political economy (i.e., adherents of commodity production). They argued that the major thing wrong with the modern capitalist world was its individualistic philosophy (although Sumner is an exception here). These sociologists (except for Sumner) argued that society was unhealthy and that it contained no natural healing elements.[15] We needed, according to them, a science which showed the proper relationship of the individual to the larger community. As sociologists, they leaned toward an analysis of values and sentiments. Although they were critics of a certain form of capitalism, they never attached themselves to the labor movement in spirit or in practice. They were against that kind of commitment.

Even more decisive for our argument is the basis from which these men made their claim to cognitive authority. It was not an authority based on radical change of the existing capitalist world. These men based their claim to superiority on the ideas of accumulation of facts, disinterested pursuit of knowledge, and discovery of laws. Ironically, these claims are just as suspect as those of the socialists they sought to criticize. The sociologists offered a promissory note to be delivered in the future.

The analysis of these theorists requires an analytic framework within which to scrutinize their writings. For this analysis, I have decided to examine the sociology of knowledge in their writings, and sociology of knowledge practitioners, it will be recalled, are primarily interested in the correspondence between social structures and ideas. By observing the way in which these early American sociologists examined the social origins of ideas other than their own, we may be better able to scrutinize their claim to cognitive superiority.

Chapter one indicates that at least two political themes were articulated within a European sociology of knowledge tradition: "social-technological" and "critical-emancipatory."[16] These two models generate the criteria for examining the writings of early American social theorists.[17] The second chapter examines some of the major social-historical characteristics of the period in which these men wrote—the Progressive era. Chapters three thru eight explore the writings of the individual theorists. The final chapter summarizes the writings of these men in relation to each other as well as to the social-technological political theme developed in the first chapter. In addition, it argues that the sociology of knowledge cannot transcend its own embeddedness in the social world. It, too, has certain interests to protect.

The
Sociology of

KNOWLEDGE
---
in America

‏❧‏

1883 - 1915

I / Critical-Emancipatory and Social-Technological Themes in the Sociology of Knowledge

Introduction

Before we can analyze the sociology of knowledge implicit and explicit in the writings of six early American sociologists, we must first know what will count as the sociology of knowledge and what will not. Moreover, as indicated above, the sociology of knowledge can itself take diverse forms. Therefore, some classificatory scheme, no matter how rudimentary, is necessary for the task set out here.

In addition to the attempts to explain the sociology of knowledge in national terms, taxonomic schemes grounded in other considerations have been advanced.[1] There has been a tendency in the literature on the sociology of knowledge to equate it with a generalized approach in which distinct political preconceptions are submerged.[2] A few attempts have been made to grasp the philosophical assumptions,[3] and a number of inquiries have been undertaken into the various Marxist and other permutations.[4] All of these are valuable contributions, but they overlook, in part, the distinctive political aspects of these various formulations. It is my purpose in this section to draw out those political distinctions which may transcend national boundaries in the same manner as did those in Karl Mannheim's work, *Ideology and Utopia*. Mannheim was concerned with delineating the variegated ideological and utopian elements of political thought. He was interested in analyzing the stages of utopian thinking in ideal typical formulations. For example, the liberal-humanitarian type of utopian mentality is rooted in the conception of idea. Ideas were goals projected into the future and did not belong to the Platonic realm of essences. In liberal-humanitarian thought, ideas were goals which served as a measuring device in the realm of everyday political affairs. Mannheim notes that in France the term idea (goals) took on an extreme rational meaning and led to political action in the form of the French Revolution. In Germany, however, ideas were turned inward and took a subjective tone. "Here the road to progress was not sought in external deeds or in revolutions, but exclusively in the inner constitution of man and its transformations."[5] Although Mannheim was aware of the differences in liberal-humanitarian and utopian thinking, his major concern was to document the international political similarities rather than simply the differences.

Like Mannheim, I intend to create two themes, which shall be designated the critical-emancipatory and the social-technological orientations in the sociology of knowledge. Moreover, my express interest is to seek out the implicit normative political structure that operates in sociological theorizing about the relationship between ideas and social structure. In particular, I take it as axiomatic that sociologists acquire value dispositions long before they enter the discipline. Social theory not only conceptualizes and classifies social facts but also judges them. The kinds of assumptions that sociologists make before they begin to theorize are varied. These assumptions range from metaphysical types (e.g., the universe is causally maintained) to those that are highly personal and possibly idiosyncratic, and they do help to shape the nature of the theorizing attempt. As well as indicating what needs to be examined, assumptions form the background of social theory and vocabulary to be utilized in such an examination. According to Hermann Strasser, social theorizing proceeds in three steps:

The normative perspective, often pre-scientifically acquired, will ultimately determine a theory's social and political fate. Together with the second step, model definition and model selection, a general image of the main outline of some social phenomenon is provided. Our pre-scientific interests as members of some society guide our acquisition of knowledge and influence the basis for selecting appropriate models for theories, thus constituting the intellectual ground on the basis of which sociological theories develop their information power....Here, in a third step, social reality is captured in a form which stresses the strength of the observed, the positively existing. That is to say, hypotheses are derived from a set of propositions and subsequently confirmed or disapproved by means of valid data-sentences. The hypotheses, in turn, are themselves also made valid by being integrated into a theoretical infrastructure consisting of model (theory-sentences) and normative perspective (value-sentences). The selective structure, as imposed by the model and the observational instruments, carves out of reality a minimal subset of all possibilities, thus placing the *image* of reality, not reality itself, in a straitjacket.[6]

While Strasser is interested in the normative structure of social theory at its widest level (i.e., a general theory of society), my interest is much narrower—the sociology of knowledge.

The political differences between the critical and technological themes in the sociology of knowledge can be brought out by focusing on the following elements: genesis of knowledge, the type of knowledge analyzed, the role of social science, the role of the social scientist, and the presupposed basic images of man and society.[7] The development of these two themes (critical and technological) in the sociology of knowledge will be utilized to investigate an American sociology of knowledge tradition. Although the following discussion will diverge from the investigation, the two themes will be presented in tabular form at the end of the chapter.

In both the critical and technological themes there is agreement that some existential relationship exists between knowledge and social bases. Furthermore, both themes are in agreement, although for very different reasons, that it is useful to examine these relationships. Both traditions also argue that philosophers have tended to be formalistic and abstract in their examination of the bases of knowledge and that knowledge is socially rooted and is not the product of revealed religion or of divine insight. From this point on, however, there are major political differences between the two. The critical theme will be developed from the works of Marx and of critical theorists such as Lukács, Marcuse, and Habermas. The technological theme will be constructed from the writings of Comte, Durkheim, and Gurvitch. The rest of this chapter will be an attempt to elaborate the critical and technological themes in the sociology of knowledge. Although particular thinkers are referred to, it does not imply that they alone embody these thematic formulations.

Genesis of Knowledge

Marx attacked certain traditional claims of epistemology to absolute truth. In one sense there is no knowing without a knower. The fundamental ground of all knowledge is social. In this sense Marx extends Kant's a priori's[8] to a social level, and he roots them in the process of production. Even though natural scientists may discover laws of nature, these laws constitute only a part of social knowledge. Kolakowski captures the fundamental sense of Marx's theory of cognition that I am striving to elucidate.

Man as a cognitive being is only part of a man as a whole; that that part is constantly involved in a process of progressive autonomization...cannot be understood otherwise than as a function of a continuing dialogue between human needs and their objects. This dialogue, called work, is created by both the human species and the external world, which thus becomes accessible to man only in its humanized form. In this sense we can say that in all the universe man cannot find a well so deep that, leaning over it, he does not discover at bottom his own face.[9]

It is exactly at the moment that man confronts his needs in the form of work that knowledge begins. And because work (the means of production) alters drastically with different periods, knowledge itself is bounded by history. In particular, Marx locates ideas (the dominant ones) in the possession of the ruling classes of every age. Knowledge is power in the fundamental sense of control or exploitation. In Marx's analysis of capitalism, the bourgeoisie was the dominant group, and consequently its ideas were the dominant ideas. These ideas were but the outgrowth of the conditions of bourgeois production and bourgeois property, just as jurisprudence is but the will of the bourgeois class made into a law for all—a will whose essential character and direction are determined by the economic conditions of the existence of their class.[10] Ideas, then, are essentially the abstract, ideal categories of social relations that are rooted in the means of production.[11]

Where the enlightenment thinkers saw the bases of repression in the church, Marx located them in the material base (i.e., processes of production) of the capitalist world. In particular, he noted that the ideology of capitalism was used by the ruling class (bourgeoisie) to deceive and exploit the masses. The economic interests of the bourgeoisie were also the foundation of their religious, political, and legal ideas. Marx proposed no general analytical scheme about the relationships between knowledge and its social base except to indicate that the dominant ideas of any given historical period were always those held by its ruling class. More importantly, Marx exposed the ideology of a particular class at a given stage in its historical development—capitalism. In this sense, he saw a particular historical class as the generating unit of ideology.

Marx's critique of the interests of the bourgeoisie was extended by the critical school to include an analysis of positive scientists. In Marx's age "unmasking" the ideology of equivalence exchange was appropriate, but a present-day critique of society must include an examination of positivistic science. Scientism is the fundamental false consciousness which legitimates the modern era. Positive scientists are the direct outgrowth of the interest of bureaucratic elites which need knowledge of the social order to keep that order running efficiently and properly according to their interests. Both Marx and the later critical theorists see knowledge as being generated by classes or by those groups holding repressive power over others to maintain their own economic and political hegemony.

Herbert Marcuse, for example, extended Marx's economic analysis to include the scientific-technological rationality that now permeates both capitalist and socialist societies. Marcuse's works *One-Dimensional Man* and *Soviet Marxism* argue that a noncritical mode of thinking has come to dominate both capitalist and socialist countries. The Soviet reality seems to be dominated by the transformation from dialectical liberation to a mechanical dialectic which defines freedom as a "recognized necessity." The dialectic had originally been critical and negative in Marx, but under Stalin the dialectic has come to "protect and justify the established regime by eliminating or minimizing all those elements of dialectic which would indicate progress of the socio-historical development beyond this regime." Capitalist societies are in the same bind, since the individual has become subordinated to technological domination. "The people recognize themselves in their commodities; they find their soul in their automobile, hi-fi set, split-level home, kitchen equipment."[12]

Quite unlike Marx, thinkers in the social-technological tradition view knowledge as being generated by the collective sentiments (e.g., Comte, Durkheim) or by cultural emanations of whole cultural types (e.g., Pitirim Sorokin). For Comte and Durkheim, the total social body generates the collective representations which are the outcome of an immense cooperation between past generations and current public opinion. For example, Durkheim's sociology of knowledge clearly placed thinking in a social context. He argued that even the Kantian categories vary with different people and cultures.[13] In Durkheim's words, "There are no gospels which are immortal," and "We know today that not only is the ideal different in different groups, but also that it should vary. The ideal of the Romans was not, and cannot be, ours, and the scale of values varies accordingly." More than that, "the categories of human thought are never fixed in any definite form; they are made, unmade and remade incessantly; they change with places and times."[14]

Durkheim's sociology of knowledge can be seen as a development of positivistic agelicism which was rooted in the work of DeBonald and DeMaistre, and stated the main idea that only society is real and ultimate being. "Since there is only this one real phenomenon, all other phenomena are derivatives, and this conception applied to thought means that all thinking is determined by the group. All categories and thought are drawn forth from the temporal, spatial and morphological intergration of society."[15]

Like Kant, Durkheim was convinced that for us to see at all, concepts were necessary and that thinking by concepts (particularly scientific ones) helped to illuminate the social reality surrounding us. Although Durkheim did not go as far as Marx and Mannheim in formulating the subjective element of knowledge, he was aware of it. He described it in the following way when writing about the individual and Plato's realm of ideas.

Each of us sees them after his own fashion. There are some which escape us completely and remain outside of our circle of vision; there are others of which we perceive certain aspects only. *There are even a great many of which we pervert in holding* [my emphasis], for as they are collective by nature, they cannot become individualized without being retouched, modified, and consequently falsified. Hence comes the great trouble we have in understanding each other, and the fact that we even lie to each other without wishing to: it is because we all use the same words without giving them the same meaning.[16]

For Durkheim, society as a totality is the mind-determining agency. The collective consciousness is the highest form of psychic life possible. It is placed outside and above the individual, from where it crystallizes things into communicable ideas. The collective consciousness also has the power to make logical thought possible and logical thought attempts to rid itself of subjective elements which it retains from its social origins. Since collective representations do contain subjective elements, they must be discovered and then discarded if we are to approach the nature of reality more closely.[17]

In summary, the social-technological tradition focuses on the total society as the generating unit of knowledge. This tradition rejects the idea that knowledge is generated by particular social-historical groups who hold decisive power over others. Knowlege springs only from the complex interaction within society. The social-technologists have a tendency to assume that society is integrated along uniform beliefs or values, while the critical theorist sees just the opposite. This difference of opinion on the origins of knowledge is brought out also in the type of knowledge analyzed.

Type of Knowledge Analyzed

Marx analyzed the mental productions which he thought were repressive, that is, the ideas which acted as instruments of control for the bourgeoisie. His major focus was on the ideology of capitalism. He believed that the then existing political economy only served to hide the true interests of its class. It was not objective science but ideology. All thinking was not false, according to Marx; this conclusion would obviously have undermined his own position. Marx shared with Hegel the rationalist principle that "cognition gives access to universal truths not present in immediate experience."[18] For Marx, truth must be enacted concretely. There must be a movement from abstract conceptions of freedom to freedom in social practice. The class which would lead this movement was the proletariat. Their thinking was not ideological According to Lukács,

This was only possible because for the proletariat the total knowledge of its class situation was vital necessity, a matter of life and death; because its class situation becomes comprehensible only if the whole of society can be understood; and because this understanding is the inescapable precondition of its actions. Thus the unity of theory and practice is only the reverse side of the social and historical position of the proletariat.

Moreover, the proletariat could only attain the correct vision of society under capitalism. Class consciousness was not possible (in terms of complete clarity) in precapitalist epochs. "Structuring of society into castes and estates means that economic elements are *inextricably* joined to political and religious factors." With the development of capitalism, the estates are broken down, and a society divided clearly along class lines becomes possible.[19]

Critical theorists (Habermas, Marcuse) also analyzed what they considered the major ideology of the present world-scientism. Scientism consists of the views that: (1) knowledge is inherently neutral; (2) there is a unitary scientific method; and (3) the standard of certainty and exactness in the physical sciences is the only explanatory model for scientific knowledge. Marx's distinction between the substructure (material forces) and superstructure (ideology) is inadequate for present purposes. Marx's materialism is now reinterpreted as three distinct social systems of action. Substructure is replaced by systems of purposive rational action. Superstructure now refers to the systems of symbolic interaction. And the forms of social consciousness are viewed as the "reflexive recognition of legitimate authority which is internal to the system of self-reflection."[20] These three systems of action are now utilized in examining and criticizing the present state of society.[21] One of the benefits of this new formulation is the illumination that it throws on the interests that are basic to three distinct kinds of science. The so-called strict sciences (nomothetic) assume the interests of certainty and technical control. The historical-interpretive sciences (hemeneutics) are based on the interest of increasing intersubjective understanding. Unlike the first two, critical science assumes the interest of the freeing of men from lawlike patterns of nature and history.[22] The critical school extends Marx's ideas beyond the realm of political or economic thinking. Their idea is that science as practiced in the modern world is the major ideology. But their emphasis is on the same phenomena—those theories or ideas which they take to be ideology or false consciousness.

The social-technological tradition in the sociology of knowledge has tended to examine the psychic totality of a given period or a particular society. It also has tended toward an examination of the commonsense knowledge of the everyday world. Durkheim chose to examine the primitive mind and pointed out that its religious mentality was a reflection of its social organization. This was not to argue that religious thinking was false or repressive, but to indicate the functional unity of religion with social structure. Much like Durkheim, and more contemporary, Georges Gurvitch was concerned with analyzing the correspondence between societal types and mental orientation. He also attempted to indicate the integrative aspects of knowledge and society. Gurvitch argues that there are seven basic types of knowledge: (1) perceptive knowledge; (2) knowledge of the other, the we, the group or classes; (3) commonsense knowledge; (4) technical knowledge; (5) political knowledge; (6) scientific knowledge; (7) philosophical knowledge. Crosscutting these *types* are the five *forms* of knowledge. The forms are expressed dichotomously and are differentially emphasized within each type of knowledge. The forms are: (1) mystical-rational; (2) empirical-conceptual; (3) positive-speculative; (4) symbolic-concrete; (5) collective-individual. I think it is of interest to note that Gurvitch argues that certain *types* of knowledge are less subject to ideological influences, the more distant the *type* is from perceptive knowledge. Gurvitch explains that it will be a long time before a functional analysis can be applied to philosophical knowledge which is inherently exalted, esoteric, remote, and elitist.[23] Gurvitch applies this framework to a variety of groups and finally to global societies and their cognitive systems. He discusses, for example, the knowledge systems of democratic-liberal societies, and of centralized state collectivisms.

According to Gurvitch, the sociology of knowledge must never attack the validity of knowledge. Locating the social bases of knowledge does not invalidate or undermine the rationality of the argument. The sole task of the sociologist of knowledge is to ascertain the presence, the combination, and the effective function of the types and forms of knowledge in society. Gurvitch claims that the sociology of knowledge cannot serve to invalidate false knowledge; it is not a critical enterprise. It cannot be critical for three reasons: (1) it does not claim to take the place of epistemology; (2) knowledge can never be imagined as being free of all social influence; (3) knowledge serves as a layer of social cement and to attack it would undermine societal integration. The most significant role the sociology of knowledge can play is to reveal the inefficiency of knowledge systems ill-suited to the social frameworks in which they are maintained.[24]

Much earlier Auguste Comte had argued that the history of man is basically the history of the development of human thinking. This was rooted in Comte's notions that: (1) the major stages in the history of the race are determined by the dominant way of thinking; (2) the final stage is universal positivism; (3) the chief instrument of human development is the positivists' critique of fetishism and theology.[25]

The major forces dominating the mind prior to the advent of positivism had been, first, the theological and then the metaphysical stage. Comte focused his analysis on the religious mentality not only because of its primacy as a social institution but also because religion combined the necessary ingredients for a social order: intellectual ideas, affect, and practical action. The theological stage was one in which free play was given to spontaneous fictions admitting of no proof. It initiated everything but could establish nothing. The metaphysical stage was characterized by the prevalence of personified abstractions.[26] To Comte this meant the ideas of social contract and natural rights. He identified metaphysics with the rationalism of the enlightenment. Comte was not arguing that the earlier stages were inaccurate in their conceptions, but rather that they were incomplete. The theological stage contributed the development of a special class for intellectual activities, while the theological stage provided the notion of laws or regularities which set the stage for the positive state. The positive stage is the final stage, "based upon an exact view of the real facts of the case."[27]

Within the three stages just mentioned, history can be discussed under two additional notions: social statics and social dynamics. The most interesting point here is that dynamical laws are subject to the realm of social statics. It was a cardinal rule that progress never be regarded as anything but the development of order.[28] Statical laws are by their very nature more general and independent of time and place. The major task of the positive theorist is to ascertain the limit of modifications that a given society is capable of undergoing. "The basic condition of social reform is intellectual reform. It is not by accident of a revolution nor by violence that a society in crisis will be reoganized, but through a synthesis of the sciences and by the creation of positive politics."[29]

Comte viewed past intellectual and social stages as having a crude unity of theory and practice. He indicated that in the fetishistic stage, a single man performed all the necessary activities to bring about a final product. As man has progressed from this state toward the positive state, there has been a gradual separation between theory and practice. For the most part Comte indicated that this gradual separation followed the natural laws of progress, which man is only free to assist, not to alter. Accordingly, theory is a contemplative activity whose major concern is to ascertain the laws of human progress. As such, the positive theorists must not have their minds inundated with the debris of practical affairs. In the final and positive stage, theory and practice are functionally united. Theory dictates practical policy, and practical policy feeds back to the high priests of humanity in a constant interaction.

For Comte objectivity was rooted in each social stage of development. The genesis of knowledge is socially based, but insofar as the evolution of society follows natural laws, it is positivistic in nature. So the development of society was subject to the same natural laws as that of nature. The sociology of knowledge for Comte was not a critical device for radical transformation but rather a way of ascertaining the natural laws of development. For Comte man can only alter slightly the general course of events, and he really has no power to radically transform them.

In summary, the social-technological tradition in the sociology of knowledge tends to stress the analysis of the collective consciousness of societies. Its emphasis is on the total nondialectical view of society. When it does focus on individual perceptions, it is from the point of view that thinking in the modern world is a product of multiple influences both past and present which are incredibly complex. The critical theorist tends to focus on class-bound knowledge. Society is broken into classes, in which one group, through the power that it holds, forces its thinking on the rest of the populace. The critical theorists' analyses tend toward political and economic thought, not religious or collective modes of thinking. In addition, the critical and technological traditions emphasize the importance of the sociology of knowledge, but in distinctly different ways. These dissimilarities can be brought out under the following subheadings: (1) conception and purpose of social science knowledge, and (2) role of social scientists.

The Role of Social Science

The social-technological tradition emphasizes the importance of discovering positive laws. There is a tendency toward positivism that tells us what kinds of contents in our statements about the world deserve the name of knowledge and that supplies us with the norms to make these distinctions.[30] Generally speaking, positivists adhere to the following four norms: (1) phenomenalism, (2) nominalism, (3) denial of value judgments, and (4) belief in the unit of scientific method. Positivism rejects the idea that there is some fundamental reality behind that which appears phenomenally. We can only indicate "that which is actually manifested in experience." It also states that any idea which is formulated in general terms must have real, concrete, individual objects as reference points. We have the right to acknowledge the existence of a thing, they say, only when experience obliges us to do so. Every science is simply a way of ordering quantitative experiences. Moreover, the positivist denies cognitive value to value judgments. Normative statements have no correlates in the world of experience. Therefore, the only cognitive value of normative statements is their technical effectiveness in achieving a desired end (i.e., they can tell us what actions are or are not effective in gaining a desired goal). Finally, the positivist believes in the essential unity of scientific method. There is no a priori reason to believe that the study of man will not someday be subsumed under physics or some other science.[31]

These theorists, then, tend to adhere to a positivist position on the question of knowledge. Comte argued that the evolution of society was subject to the same lawlike behavior as the cosmos. Similarly, Durkheim argued that once the causes of anomie were ascertained, then societal processes (laws) could be reversed and society would be returned to a state of integration. The discovery of laws would indicate what type of political or economic thought was efficient and useful in any given historical period. Interstingly enough, both Comte and Durkheim argued that only sociologists were capable of ascertaining these processes. These men are not likely to argue for radical change through an unmasking process. They are more likely to explain that there is a *cumulative* growth of knowledge leading toward the sociological paradigm. The science of human behavior culminates in sociology. They are expressly against the idea that one class is nearer to the truth than another. The truth can only spring from a total view of society which only positive sociologists possess. Gurvitch, for example, argues that the sociology of knowledge cannot be critical, because this would only create counterattacks from other groups. The outcome would be disintegrative. The most that the sociologist of knowledge can do is to indicate that some social systems would function better with certain mental configurations than with others. When these theorists think in terms of change, it is ameliorative, adjusting, piecemeal, etc. In the final analysis, the sociologist can show that alternative modes of conceptualizing the social world (e.g., religious, philosophical) are inadequate. Only with the discovery of general laws will the fine tuning of the social order by sociologists make any sense.[32]

Critical theorists emphasize many of the opposite elements of the social-technological theme in their analysis of the role of social science. First, reality and/or epistemological statements about it cannot be accepted at face value. We must get behind the phenomenal realm to discover the true economic or political interests. There is no experience, as such, which is not mediated by theoretical or practical interests. Moreover, there are "real" objects which are not manifested in empirical indices. *Beauty,* for example, is an abstract noun embodying cultural meaning which cannot be represented by the adjective attached to that noun *beautiful.* Abstract nouns (e.g., beauty, freedom, liberty, justice) include not only the past and present but also that which is not yet grasped. Marcuse states: "Such universals thus appear as conceptual instruments for understanding the particular conditions of things in the light of their potentialities. They are historical and suprahistorical; they conceptualize the stuff of which the experienced world consists, and they conceptualize it with a view of its possibilities, in the light of their actual limitation, suppression and denial." The noun *society,* for example, is not simply a sum of its individual parts. It indicates not only a description of what has existed or exists now but in addition what a good society could be. This view stresses the *"normative* character of universals" and "may be related to the conception of the universal in Greek philosophy—namely, the notion of the most general as the highest, the first in 'excellence' and therefore the real reality."[33] Furthermore, social science knowledge is not similar to the laws of nature. Man as a reflexive, willing creature can change his historical existence. There are no necessary laws of nature or history. The theory of knowledge is one which cannot be separated from a sociology of knowledge. The scientific dichotomies of subject-object, theoretical-practical, and empirical-evaluative must be eliminated.

The task of the critical sociology of knowledge is to unmask the ideology of the oppressive class with the explicit purpose of transforming the existent society. The intention is to debunk or to destroy the dominant ideology by indicating its false consciousness.

The aim of a critique is not simply to show a theory to be in error, formally or empirically, for the problem is not only the reliability of the theory's assertions. The "truth" of a theory does not boil down to its reliability but also involves the nature of its selective perspective on the world. A critique is concerned with the meaning of this selective understanding, examining it in terms of the social forces that led to the *focalization* of certain perspectives and to the *repression* or rejection of others.[34]

For the sake of brevity and clarity, I will enumerate the elements of a critical theory as espoused by Marcuse: (1) social conditions are constantly in flux—therefore critical theory must be future oriented: a critique of existing conditions includes a future orientation; (2) human thought is an integral part of concrete historical-social reality; (3) there is a critical attitude toward closed philosophical systems; (4) thought acts as a force in change and is conditioned by changes; (5) there is a unity of theory and praxis. In short, critical theory "analyzes society in the light of its used and unused or abused capabilities for improving the human condition."[35]

In *Toward a Rational Society,* Habermas argues, like Marcuse, that scientific-technological legitimation has come to dominate the Western world. This mentality means: (1) separation of "is" and "ought," (2) utilitarian ethics, (3) social theories as control and prediction of a world they have created, (4) practice conceived in terms of technical utilization, (5) man as an object—denied the possibility of self-reflexiveness.[36] In *Knowledge and Human Interests,* Habermas contrasts three distinct approaches to the study of society. "The approach of the empirical-analytic sciences incorporates a *technical* cognitive *interest;* that of the historical-hermeneutic sciences incorporates a *practical* one; and the approach of *critically* oriented sciences incorporates the *emancipatory* cognitive interest.... In relation to this critical orientation, Habermas enumerates five theses which embody the critical theory of society: (1) the achievements of the transcendental subject have their basis in the natural history of the human species; (2) knowledge equally serves as an instrument and transcends mere self-preservation; (3) knowledge-constitutive interests take form in the medium of work, language, and power; (4) in the power of self-reflection, knowledge and interest are one; (5) the unity of knowledge and interest proves itself in a dialectic that takes the historical traces of suppressed dialogue and reconstructs what has been suppressed.[37]

The critical sociology of knowledge roots the idea of critique in the possibility of a much better future. The historical possibility of the next stage is what the critical theorist wants to make known and to bring into existence. Some argue that the role of critical theory is to prepare the way for a radical leap through the necessary organic stages of social development. In Marx's case the leap was to be made by the enlightened proletariat. Later critical theorists have relied on other agents of change to make this radical break. The agent of change may differ, but the pervasive idea remains the same—a critique can lead to immediate, radical change. Furthermore, the purpose of the sociology of knowledge is to bring the irrational, alienated theories into rational consideration. This belief in the law of rationality is expressed by Robert Paul Wolff.

Indeed, there is something like a law of historical development—one of the very few—to the effect that once a matter of major social importance becomes an object of decision, it never reverts to the status of fact of nature or unintended consequence. This might also be called the law of the progress of rationality, for there is a fundamental sense of the term "rational" in which "to be rational" means "to be the author of one's actions, to act rather than to be acted upon." To become *more* rational...means to transform into ends things which previously were not ends. A man becomes more rational just insofar as he brings within the scope of his will some datum of experience which previously confronted him as independent of his will.

Once any feature of the social world is known to be within human control, it is irrevocably an object of decision, so that even failure to act with regard to it becomes a deliberate decision.[38]

The Role of Social Scientists

Critical theorists, like Marx, argued that the sociology of knowledge was the link to revolutionary practice. The role of the intellectual was not only to understand the processes of repression but to aid in their transformation. A critique would make men more fully aware of their potential for changing the world. The critical intellectual's task is to transform "the political process by deepening the mass consciousness and liberating it from its false consciousness. Here the political process and outcome are seen as profoundly affected by the nature of men's consciousness."[39]

When Marx's prediction of the historical failure of capitalism did not come to pass, the later critical theorists looked for other agents of change. Habermas and Marcuse thought that other groups, because of their unique vantage points, could become the leaders of a revolutionary movement. Whatever audience they chose, the message was clear that the critical theorist must not appeal to professional communities alone. They sought larger bodies, such as classes, student groups, or those who represented repressed development.

In relation to concrete historical developments, the critical theorist must keep alive the power of negative thinking. Habermas and Marcuse sought to indicate that instrumental action was not the only interest that guides research practice in the social sciences. Negative thinking was used to attack *Lebensphilosophie* as well as capitalism. The life philosophers (e.g., Nietzsche, Bergson, Kierkegaard) had gone too far in praise of subjectivity. They minimized the importance of action in the historical world and also neglected the material dimension of reality.

The critical social scientist demonstrates how repression works in concrete situations. This may be accomplished through a study of the assumptions of capitalism or the interests of various sciences. The concern is to point out that there are no necessary laws in the movement of history. "In this role the scientist is concerned not only with the means available or to be developed or with devising strategies by which to implement them, but also with the rationality of the goals themselves. He sees his task in formulating alternative policies and his role as essentially that of the 'rational critic.' "[40] Man can become aware of the forces that move him and by so doing can bring them under rational deliberation. The critical theorist acts as an expert on the definition of needs.

The technological sociologist of knowledge believes that the major task of the theorist is to discover general laws or relationships that hold between certain types of knowledge and given social conditions. Once these laws have been ascertained, then those having technical knowledge could solve the existing social problems.

The audience of these theorists is normally other men like himself. The evolution of society was subject to the same laws as the evolution of nature. Therefore one could not critically intervene in these processes, but could alter them only slightly. The priests of society (i.e., sociologists) were the only men capable of ascertaining these laws, therefore they had the main task of guiding society through its convolutions. Durkheim also argued for the value of general laws. Theorists in the technological tradition aim at discovering lawlike behavior. Only with that discovery can knowledge be useful in directing society. The intellectuals' task is to discover the laws of order in society and with others like himself to advise the proper groups (i.e., politicians or other experts) concerning how to handle certain technical problems of control and change. This theorist sees himself as an expert who should be consulted if a society is to run properly. This is a belief in a kind of professional elitism.

Basic Images of Man and Society

Underlying the sociology of knowledge perspectives are differing images of man and society. The conservative theorist postulates that society, as an organic entity, has logical and historical priority over individual human beings. Society is a complex, interdependent phenomenon which is subject to immanent laws of development that cannot be radically transformed. The needs of society cannot be evaluated from the needs of isolated individuals, since the smallest meaningful unit in society is a microcosmic order of that society (i.e., the family). Furthermore, hierarchy (inequality) is necessary to maintain stability in society. Only through hierarchical relationships could human values be transmitted. Authority also is a necessity for social organization. Authority is legitimate and useful when it emerges from the customs and traditions of a people. Society must change to maintain its stability, but only in an organic slow process.

The conservative image of man derives from man's basic subordination to society. Man is viewed as having certain unchangeable needs to which every society responds. By discovering these emotional and impulsive needs, the social order can satisfy them and thereby keep its stability. Men are dependent on the social order for their basic humaneness—not for their alienation. They are subject to the laws of nature and history, and only a few of them (i.e., experts) are qualified to alter these laws. The individual must be protected from his appetites.[41]

The critical theorists on the other hand tend to see society torn into opposing groups in which one has control or power over others. Certain subgroups (e.g., capitalists, positive scientists) represent the interests of the dominant group, which are defending ideological and practical concerns in the everday world. Conflict is inherent in the social world, since certain classes are repressing others. The critical theorist does not believe that the existing order is the best one or that it must remain in a given state. Society in its present form acts as a limiting force on the development of individual potentialities.

For the critical theorist, man is not the same creature throughout history. The human potential for change may be unlimited, and there is no indication that there are necessary laws in human development. In his present state, man is alienated from himself and others. Only by deepening his awareness of the pressures that oppress him can he begin to free himself. The image of man, then, is one in which he is conceived as having a power of will that allows him to transform the given order.

In summary, the critical theorist believes in the perfectibility of man and in the illimitable progress of society through meliorism. There is a denial of the idea that men have a natural proclivity toward violence and sin. Reason, not tradition, is the preferred guide for social welfare. "Order and privilege are condemned; total democracy, as direct as practicable, is the professed radical ideal."[42] Property and the rights associated with it are condemned. Economic reorganization is necessary to create a better society.

On the basis of the preceding discussion, it is now possible to contrast these two sociology of knowledge thought styles in tabular form.[43] These thought styles will not necessarily be represented in their entirety by any one thinker; rather, they should be thought of as prototypes. As such, they will be used as criteria for examining the works of early American social theorists.[44]

Summary

Within a general sociology of knowledge tradition two different political emphases have developed. First, there is a tendency for the sociology of knowledge to assume a critical attitude. The intellectual in the critical tradition sees himself as a critic of the existing order. The goal of the sociology of knowledge is conceived as the unmasking of the hidden interests of various dominant groups within society who hold decisive power over others. This unmasking process should make possible the transformation of the existing order. The social-technological paradigm, on the other hand, aims at establishing regularities between types of thought and general societal conditions. The goal of the sociologist of knowledge is to discover those regularities and to act as a professional advisor to groups interested in maintaining order within society. There is an element of professional elitism in this theoretical tradition. With these different emphases in mind, we will turn to an examination of the period in which the early American social theorists were writing. The stage must be set before the actors may enter.

Table 1   Critical-Emancipatory and Social-Technological Themes in the Sociology of Knowledge

Theme	Critical-Emancipatory	Social-Technological
Genesis of knowledge	Interest groups and classes	Cultural or societal totalities
Type of knowledge analyzed	Ideology a. political-economic b. social philosophies (e.g., idealism, naturalism)	Collective sentiments a. everyday world b. collective mental types and "primitive" thinking
The intellectual and social science		
1. The role of social science	Critical unmasking of repressive forces a. indicate the lack of laws in history b. negative thinking c. change the existing order	Accumulation of knowledge a. establish regularities b. positive thinking c. maintain stability and order
2. The role of social scientists	Rational critic a. deepen public consciousness	Professional advisor a. consult with other experts

	b. analyze concrete repressive conditions in light of "ideal" formulations	b. discover regularities in human behavior
Basic images of man and society	Conflict	Order
	a. society has no priority over the individual	a. society has logical historical and moral priority over the individual
	b. authority, hierarchy, and inequality are not necessary for human development	b. authority, hierarchy, and inequality are necessary for the order and stability of society
	c. radical change is possible	c. slow, "organic" change is possible
	d. man has no basic drives or impulses	d. man has basic drives or impulses which need to be controlled.
	e. man is an imaginative creature capable of tremendous change	e. man is a creature of tradition and not capable of radical transformation

2 / Social Context and Early American Sociology: The Progressive Era

Although we are primarily interested in the writings of six early American sociologists it seems appropriate to indicate some of the social-historical background in which these men founded and established the discipline of sociology. Their relationship to the larger political atmosphere was not an unambiguous one. All of these men were directly concerned with the impact of industrialization on the American way of life. Their concern, however, was not isolated or hegemonic. Many other groups (academicians and others) also were competing in the interpretation of both public and private events. These early sociologists had to fight battles on many intellectual fronts simultaneously if they were to win influence to write authoritatively about the course of affairs of American life. Therefore, some of the major structural transformations of American life will be examined.

Industrialization and the Politics of Business

This period of American history opened with the assassination of President McKinley and ended with the opening of World War I. Between these two events, the rise of the urban masses, industrialization, mass immigration, the emergence of the socialist party, an organizational revolution, and intense, domestic political conflicts took place. It may be difficult for us today to imagine, for example, the impact of industrialism on every aspect of social activity. But the progressive generation did feel this impact.

The American of 1914 could contrast, in his own experience, the old with the new. Looking backward scarcely more than forty or fifty years, he fully recognized that his country had changed rapidly and fundamentally. He had personally experienced the transition from a society relatively untouched by industrialism to one almost transformed by it. Seldom, if ever, in American history had so much been altered within the lifetime of a single man.[1]

During this period, population shift and growth was rapid. In 1860 the estimated population of the U.S. was 31,513,114, but by 1915 it had grown to 100,549,013.[2] A more important consequence of industrialization was the shift from a rural to an urban center of population. Between 1880 and 1910 an estimated eleven million people moved from rural to urban sites.[3] As the country was industrializing, the population shifted to avail itself of new occupational opportunities. Generally speaking, it has been established that industrialized societies tend to experience more rapid social mobility than nonindustrial societies.[4] Colin Clark has argued that the years between 1900 and 1920 were particularly interesting because of the shift from rural occupations to manufacturing and transportation industries. According to the Clark study, three important shifts were noticeable between 1900 and 1920. The primary branch of production—agriculture, forestry, and fishing industries—*declined* 11.6 percent in proportion to the population. The secondary branch of production—manufacturing, mining, and building—*increased* 4.6 percent. And the tertiary branch of production—transportation, communication, and domestic and professional services industries—increased 7.1 percent.[5]

Industrialization was also changing communication systems and the foundations of transportation. In 1900 the total production of oil for all previous decades was 1,000,000,000 barrels; by 1915, however, 2,612,956,000 barrels of oil had been produced. In 1860 it would have been extraordinary for an American furnace to produce 45 tons of steel a day, but by 1904 single furnaces could produce 427 tons a day. This is not to say that the workers had steady employment. In fact, one of the major causes of discontent among the steel mill workers was the irregularity of employment. From 1908 to 1910 the number of men employed in the blast furnaces of the iron and steel industry fluctuated from 18,845 to 46,810.[6] Interestingly enough, this industry was thought at the time to be a source of steady employment in comparison with other industries. Communication also increased greatly because of the rapid urbanization of the country. Daily newspapers increased from 574 in 1870 to 1610 in 1899, and by 1909 there were 2,600. During the same period of time the circulation of newspapers jumped from 3,800,000 to 24,200,000.[7] Telephones increased from 170,000 in 1877 to over 11,716,000 in 1917.[8] This same period witnessed the creation and mass production of the automobile, and by 1908 the Ford Motor Company was grossing six million dollars a year.[9] By this time the railroad had thousands of miles of track crisscrossing the United States, and the industry was so well organized that "by 1900, 95 percent of the nation's railroad mileage lay in six large systems, controlled by the capitalists who financed the consolidations."[10]

As the nation industrialized, the dissatisfaction with the machine age and its ramifications grew. At first, a general interest in the growth of the nation masked the price that was being paid by those toiling in the industries. But by 1900 Frederick Hoffman estimated that 1,664,000 fatal or near-fatal accidents had occurred in industrial labor. [11] With publicity, this accident rate slowed, but between 1900 and 1913 there had been 25,000 fatalities and over 700,000 disability cases requiring at least four-week absences.[12] Despite the improvement, these figures were still ridiculously high. Labor responded to the situation by organizing. In 1899 the American Federation of Labor had a total membership of 28,000; by 1904 the membership had increased to 1,676,000. The proportion of organized workers to organizable workers had jumped from 3.5 percent in 1900 to 7 percent in 1910.[13] Labor used strikes to promote its claim for control over its destiny. While labor organized, business consolidated. In fact, the country experienced a veritable organization revolution. Businesses grew into corporations that amalgamated with other corporations to control the marketplace. Sammuel Hays summarizes this impulse in the following way:

Toward the end of the nineteenth century American economic conditions encouraged a rapid growth in corporate size. Mass markets and mass production had ushered in an era of intense competition. But competition, constantly tending to push production beyond the capacity of markets, gave rise to the uneasiness in the minds of businessmen: by driving prices downward it threatened both immediate profits and long-range industrial stability. Entrepreneurs looked for methods of manipulating market forces to control competition.[14]

The consolidation movement in industry was prevalent to the point that a burst of mergers between 1897 and 1904 tripled the existing number of trusts, so that effective control over sugar, tobacco, steel, and railways had been established. The average citizen was obviously staggered when it was discovered that a man like Andrew Carnegie "earned" $23,000,000 in 1900, while girls at the Triangle Shirtwaist Company were working six days a week for $5.00.[15] Not too many years before Carnegie's fortune was established, Vanderbilt had died, leaving an estimated estate of $104,000,000. When the United States Steel Company combined not only with the Carnegie company but with 70 percent of all the steel concerns in the country, a trust of other trusts was built to the staggering sum of $1,500,000,000.[16] Besides the vast fortunes of business magnates like Vanderbilt, Rockefeller, and Carnegie, smaller fortunes were being amassed. In 1840 there were not twenty millionaires in America; by 1910 there were probably more than twenty in the U.S. Senate.[17] It was estimated that in 1900 the top 2 percent of incomes in the nation held 60 percent of the country's wealth.[18] A natural conflict was building up between the average citizen and trusts for other reasons than their sheer size. Between 1897 and 1913 the cost of living had risen about 35 percent, while real wages in industry had risen but a fraction of one percent.[19] While prices were rising and trusts multiplying, a small but vigorous labor-union movement was developing.[20] The number of strikes and strikers tripled between 1898 and 1902.[21] Although its use was denied by the leaders of labor, violence was an instrument employed against opponents of organized labor. Frank Steunenberg (governor of Idaho, 1896-98), who was instrumental in crippling the Western Federation of Miners, was assassinated by a bomb as he was passing through the gate to his house. The *Los Angeles Times,* which was run by Harrison Otis, a vehement opponent of labor unions, was bombed on October 1, 1910.[22] At least twenty persons were killed, and Otis immediately blamed the union for this action.

One of the key struggles that took place during the Progressive era was the involvement of business in politics. Earlier interpretations of this relationship saw the federal government as a neutral shield between the public and the Morgans, Rockefellers, and Harrimans.[23] But this view has been laid to rest by more penetrating critics, and in the opinion of current historians seems to be that the businessmen held political control over the liberal state. Their involvement in social reform was not motivated by humanitarian reasons. Professor Wiebe paints the follwoing picture of the reform-minded businessman:

By and large, they were youthful; they came from a middle class; they had been standpatters a decade earlier; they considered the new immigrants socially dangerous; they feared organized labor as well as organized capital; and they abhorred the working class.

The only important contribution which businessmen made to the social welfare movement came as a by-product of their zeal for civic improvement. As they scrubbed and polished their cities, some of them did assist in improving local housing and health codes.[24]

As business expanded, it came to hold a number of advantages over other social groups. Their major advantages were the wealth businessmen held, and their extensive organization across the country. It is interesting to note that between 1900 and 1910 over 240 volumes had been published on business management.[25] Business may have inspired many reforms, but it did so out of a desire for control.[26] The uniting of the businessmen and the reformers under political capitalism has been chronicled in Gabriel Kolko's *The Triumph of Conservatism*. Similarly, James Weinstein argues in *The Corporate Ideal in the Liberal State, 1900-1918*, that, "the ideal of a liberal corporate social order was formulated and developed under the aegis and supervision of those who then, as now, enjoyed ideological and political hegemony in the United States: the more sophisticated leaders of America's largest corporations and financial institutions."[27] Businessmen were not only enjoying the political power available but were also replacing ministers and lawyers as men of status. A sample of private institutions indicated that in 1860, 39 percent of the governing board members had been clergymen, but by 1930 clergymen comprised only 7 percent of such members.[28] Although this is a sign that there was an increase in secular learning, it also indicated that religious leaders no longer commanded the same intellectual respect as bankers, lawyers, and businessmen.

The age of reform was also felt in the conventional political parties. After McKinley's assassination in 1901, Theodore Roosevelt, the cowboy conservative, was in office. He was the first of a trio that also included William Howard Taft and Woodrow Wilson and that headed the Progressive movement. In his "square deal" policy for capital and labor, Roosevelt was tending to favor capital. Although he was known as the trustbuster, it was trustbusting of a meager sort. Even after investigations of the Standard Oil Company and the American Tobacco Company had proved that these corporations almost completely controlled their product, the full penalty of the law was never imposed,[29] and after the financial panic of 1907, all Roosevelt's efforts to subject corporations to federal control ceased. Prior to this event his chief objection to using the Sherman Antitrust Act was its lack of discrimination. "It assumed that all combinations were trusts, all monopolies were dangerous and should be suppressed."[30]

Perhaps, the most interesting year during the Progressive era for national politics was 1912. In that year Eugene Debs polled 6 percent of the national vote for the Socialist party, and in the previous year Socialist mayors had been elected in eighteen cities. The 1912 presidential election was a three-cornered race between Taft, Roosevelt, and Wilson. After bitter dissension in the Republican party, Roosevelt emerged as the presidential candidate of a new party, the Progressives.[31] Taft was considered reactionary, and the Republican party was rent by this split between Taft and Roosevelt. Seeing the split, the Democratic party realized that it had a good chance for victory. However, progressive forces at the Democratic National Convention lost the first round when Alton B. Parker was elected as chairman. Parker was considered highly acceptable to the corporations. In spite of this early defeat, Wilson forces held strong even through the early ballots. Finally, on the forty-sixth ballot Wilson was nominated.[32] Although Wilson won the presidency by more than a safe margin, the importance of the 1912 election lay elsewhere. This interpretation is aptly expressed by DeWitt:

The significance of the 1912 campaign is not that the country went democratic; for it did not. Roosevelt and Taft together received 1,316,917 more votes than Wilson. But the country for the first time had gone progressive, because the votes cast for Wilson and Roosevelt exceeded by almost seven millions those cast for Taft. For the first time, the people of the nation recognized that a select minority, and not they, had previously controlled government; and for the first time they voted consciously and deliberately to restore the government, misused and perverted, as it had been, to the control and use of the people.[33]

What makes the Progressive era distinct as a period of rapid social change was an emerging concern for social reform. After the Civil War material achievements had been advancing without any concern for the individual or for natural resources, so that, farmers, immigrants, small businessmen, and land were being abused terribly. The Progressive movement was an attempt "to develop the moral will, the intellectual insight, and the political and administrative agencies to remedy the accumulated evils and negligencies of a period of industrial growth."[34]

A great deal of emphasis was placed on working out tactics for orderly social change. This, of course, involved conscious human energy and effort. To the Progressives, social evils would not remedy themselves but had to be conquered by an aroused citizenry. The Progressive movement was optimistic, in that it had faith that something could be done about the social ills.[35]

All of the early American sociologists were concerned with the impact of industrialization on American life. Most of them thought industrialization could, and would, become a progressive evolutionary force, but they were not unaware of the mixed blessings of industrialism. Likewise, they were keenly interested in the development of corporate enterprises. However, they believed that these phenomena were not inherently evil, but only needed control or regulation. Many of the early sociologists were particularly interested in the Socialist and Labor movements flourishing at that time. In the eyes of the sociologists, only they—and not religious leaders, politicians, labor leaders, or socialists—were capable of seeing society whole. From this presupposition, they deduced the idea that only they could diagnose the problems of modern Industrial America.

The IWW, Socialism, and the Labor Movement

Any examination of labor and socialism during the Progressive era must include a discussion of immigration. Most of the regional and ethnic differences in the country are reflected in the American Federation of Labor, the Industrial Workers of the World (IWW), and the Socialist Party of America. Maldwyn Jones states that "By the early twentieth century the foreign-born formed the mass of the wage-earners in every area where manufacturing or mining was practiced."[36]

Up to the 1880s immigrants had come mainly from northern and western Europe. Between 1860 and 1890, ten million immigrants came from the British Isles, Germany, Scandinavia, Switzerland, and Holland. Between 1890 and 1914, fifteen million immigrants arrived from Austria-Hungary, Italy, Russia, Greece, Rumania, and Turkey. Four states contained one-half the foreign-born population: New York—2,750,000; Massachusetts—1,000,000; Illinois—1,000,000; and Pennsylvania—1,000,000. The Germans were predominantly in the Middle West (Illinois, Wisconsin, Ohio, and Minnesota), with a few in New York, Pennsylvania, and New Jersey. The Norwegians, Swedes, and Danes were located in Minnesota, Illinois, Wisconsin, and the Dakotas. The Finns settled in Michigan, Minnesota, and Massachusetts. Russians and Austria-Hungarians lived in New York, Pennsylvania, and New Jersey.[37] This regional breakdown is necessary for later discussion of the Socialist movement. The early concentrations of immigrants were located in the ports of entry: Boston, New York, Philadelphia, Baltimore, and New Orleans. It was obvious to some social analysts that early immigrants had been trapped economically at their port of entry.[38] The second generation followed the line of least resistance—the railroad—into the interior of the United States: Cleveland, Chicago, Cincinnati, Pittsburgh, and St. Louis.

Some historians have tried to isolate the ethnic and occupational background of the peasant as the primary determinant of his occupation in the United States. There was an apparent tendency toward ethnic concentration in the industries, but it certainly was not a simple function of previous occupational experiences. It was probably based on a combination of the time of arrival of the groups, ethnic rivalry, and cultural differences. For example, few of the Russian and Polish Jews in the clothing trade entered that field because of their previous experience; only about 10 percent had been tailors in Europe. It was not signficant either that the "government industry offered openings for all members of the family."

Unlike Polish and Italian women, Russian Jewish women did not usually remain at work after marriage; and in contrast to the French-Canadians, Russian Jews preferred to see their children at school instead of in the factory. The real attraction of the garment trade to Jewish immigrants was that it opened an avenue to commerce. Earnings in the clothing shops were more closely related to individual effort than in factories, and capital was more readily amassed.

The Italian and Slavic immigrants were predominantly single males and more mobile than the Russian Jews. The Italians and the Slavs were more favorable to railroad and construction work. The Finns worked in iron and copper mining. The Greeks and Syrians were peddlers, and the Bulgarians settled in steel towns. In the final analysis, "the concentration of these and other groups in paticular industries was due also the immigrant's desire to be with his own kind.[39] It should be kept in mind that the immigrants had generally been characterized as radical in their approach to politics. Very few of them actually did participate in radical movements, however, and they were, in general, hostile to reform movements. They viewed government as a necessary evil. Many of the immigrants were Catholic, and were thus committed to a kind of conservatism.[40]

The American Federation of Labor was generally recognized, during its evolution, as one of the foremost labor organizations in the country. It emerged during the late 1870s and finally was established in 1886. Initially the country had a variety of trade unions, usually organized along occupational lines. One of the first serious attempts at a national organization after the depression of the 1870s was the Knights of Labor. Originally it was a secret organization with rituals that were supposed to create solidarity among the workers. In 1886, the Knights of Labor had a strong membership of 700,000. However, most of the members were primarily unskilled workers. While the Knights of Labor were attempting to organize, a number of independent trade unions—cigar makers, typographical union—were calling for a national federation of skilled labor. It was primarily in this conflict between the interests of the skilled and the unskilled that the American Federation of Labor ended its alliance with the Knights of Labor.[41] The American Federation of Labor also encountered some other difficulties. It was fighting dual unions and the simple differences between ethnic groups and their occupational settings.

Inevitably, Gompers and his colleagues on the executive council became involved in jurisdictional disputes between member unions and in disputes about whether unions seeking to join the Federation should be granted charters or should be regarded as "dual-unions"—that is, illegal competitors working on the jurisdiction of unions already chartered. The heterogeneity of the American labor movement—caused, as we have seen by ethnic differences, by variations in the mode of production, by absence of contacts between workers in different sections or regions—led to the growth of competing unions in many trades.[42]

Besides these internal problems, organized labor was confronted with the coalition of government and business interests. At first organized labor had attempted to stay out of national politics, but the attempt to pass a labor injunction bill (1906) turned this perspective around. The labor injunction bill was a judicial order which commanded an individual or union to refrain from striking if the court considered the activity injurious to the property rights of others.[43] For at least a decade before 1906, the AF of L had been lobbying each session of Congress for the passage of an anti-injunction bill. But it must have seemed hopeless when Roosevelt remarked in his message to Congress on December 15, 1905, "There has been a demand for depriving courts of the power to issue injunctions in labor disputes. Such special limitation of the equity powers of our courts would be most unwise."[44]

The important thing to keep in mind is that the AF of L under Gompers stressed skilled labor, little or no political involvement, and the philosophy of pure and simple wages. For the most part, the differences between skilled craftsmen and common laborers in many of the industries was reinforced by ethnic origins. "The northwestern Europeans who had first received a foothold in America still held the better jobs while unskilled Italians and Slavs, like Irish and German peasants before them, had to start at the bottom."[45] In a sense the AF of L never really organized the working class. In 1900 the AF of L only included about 3 percent of the total number of workers in nonfarm occupations, by 1910, only 5 percent.[46] More importantly, these were mostly craft unions composed largely of native skilled workers and were primarily located in the East. Gompers was slow to press for solidarity among all the workingmen. He was quite aware that the wage earners were primarily held together by the feeling that their jobs came out of a common social heritage. Therefore, he believed that national solidarity could be obtained by allowing unions individual autonomy at the local level. The AF of L believed in the philosophy of pure and simple trade unionism. This attitude accepted the existence of capitalism and had for its goals the enlarging of the bargaining powers of the wage earner in the sale of his labor.[47] They scanned long-range goals and argued that they were only interested in immediate goals which could be realized within a few years.[48]

The Industrial Workers of the World (IWW) was of a different nature than the AF of L. The IWW represented the immigrant and migratory workers, the unskilled, unorganized, and unwanted, the poorest and weakest sections of labor.[49] The Wobblies wanted to unite the American working class, with the working class of the rest of the world into one large labor union with an industrial basis and revolutionary aims. The revolution was to be precipitated by a series of strikes, leading to a world strike which would overpower the capitalists. Their philosophy was one of immediacy—but of revolutionary immediacy rather than wage immediacy.

The IWW's membership rarely exceeded 100,000 at any one time. It never attracted more than 5 percent of all trade unionists. The IWW was born in 1905, when union membership had leveled out to about 2,000,000. Organized labor was divided along many lines. The United Mine Workers (UMW) intermittently flirted with the AF or L.

It finally split from the AF of L when the latter would not support the Leadville, Colorado, strike (1896-97). The internal fights of the trade unions, the struggling Socialist Labor party, and the Progressives all contributed to the developmentof the IWW.

The leaders of the IWW, Haywood, Moyer, and St. John, more militant than ever and determined to find a broad industrial basis for dual unionism, were rapidly moving into alliance with Debs of the railway workers, William E. Trautman, editor of the Brewery Workers' newspaper, *Brauer Zeitung,* and Isaac Cowan, American representative of the Amalgamted Society of Engineers of Great Britain which had just been expelled from the A.F. of L. because of jurisdictional disputes with boilermakers, machinists, and pattern makers. With other dissident leaders of the labor and socialist movements, like DeLeon, Ernest Untermann, another syndicalist writer, and Father Thomas J. Hagerty, the maverick Roman Catholic priest, a big, black-bearded, scholarly man, this group provided the industrial spearhead of the IWW.[50]

The Wobblies resented wage slavery. One of the central points of the IWW was the abolition of the wage system. In America, particularly in the West, this had a special significance. In the West memories of the trapper and trader still prevailed and lent support to the notion of economic and social independence. Meanwhile, the West had begun to be governed by private enterprise such as the finance corporation, the mining company, and the lumber trust.

Early in its existence, the IWW was torn with factionalism. The Marxist wing led by De Leon wanted to combine political with industrial working-class agitation. Haywood, on the other hand, was antipolitical and firmly believed in direct action. These internal disputes helped prevent the IWW from becoming firmly established. It had three industrial departments: mining, metal and machinery, and transportation. Except for the UMW, however, there was nothing but a membership which existed on paper.

Although primarily rooted in the west, the IWW came east when it was called upon. It fought in Lawrence, Massachusetts, and in Patterson, New Jersey. But more importantly the IWW was taking on distinct characteristics.

From 1910 onward two distinct factions of the movement began to emerge: the footloose, migratory workers of the lumber camps, mines, and wheat fields of the South and West; and the IWW of the immigrant workers in the great East Coast industries. Each faction became identified with a different policy. The Easterner generally favored greater centralization in the IWW organization and more control of union activities from the center. The Westerner usually believed in less control and more autonomy for local branches.[51]

The IWW appealed most strongly, then, to the weak, diverse, and divided groups in America. The men who supported the IWW rebellion were usually voteless, rootless, and separated from the mainstream of American life.

On the other hand, the Socialist Party of America evolved from the Social Democratic Party and the Socialist Labor party. The SPA, SDP, and SLP formed part of a politcal continuum, with the AF of L to their right and the IWW on their left. The SDP argued that it was hopeless to fight against the giant trusts—that, in fact, they should be maintained, but that the trusts should come under public control. They wanted as well the socialization of all public utilities, particularly gas and electric, railways, and telephones.

"The Social Democrats envisioned a gradual socialization of America through piecemeal nationalization of trusts and municipal ownership of public utilities."[52]

The Social Democrats believed that the working-class struggle had to be fought on the electoral battlefield. The workers, in a word, had to have a political party. By March 1900, the SDP had 4,636 members in 226 branches organized in 32 states. It also had the support of 25 Socialist papers. The interesting thing about the SDP was its affiliation with middle-class reform. It originated in the Middle West from the remnants of the Populist revolt and Progressivism. One of its most distinguished members was Julius Wayland, who created the *Appeal to Reason.* In less than a decade this periodical had a circulation of 260,000 and became the foremost exponent of reform socialism. At the same time, Victor Berger (Milwaukee) had reached similar conclusions about unifying socialism with antimonopoly and good-government reform theories of the middle-class Progressives. Berger reached out for native midwest radicals to support his view. His biggest catch was Eugene Debs (president of the American Railway Union). From the radical left perspective, however, the major problem with the SDP was that it aligned itself too closely with middle-class reform. The SDP had placed a lot of hope on the full coinage of silver, which was defeated, and the failure of the full-silver campaign of 1896 convinced Debs and many others that labor could not depend upon the middle-class and middle-class panaceas. Labor would have to build its own organization.

The SLP was internally split along the lines of the original debates between Marx and Lassalle. The American worker was already enfranchised, so the goal of the American Lassalleans was to use the ballot box for voting Socialist reform measures. The American Marxists, on the other hand, agreed on the need for political votes but thought that it was impossible to develop a strong workers party that could influence elections. With the arrival in the early 1880s of German revolutionaries, the anarchist movement in America swelled and joined the Marxian wing of the SLP. This wing, controlled by Daniel De Leon, abhorred the AF of L and tried to undermine the Knights of Labor's control in New York City. "De Leon believed that the unconditional surrender of capitalism was to be subsumed by organizing workers in a revolutionary, industrial union."[53] There was no hope of converting the Knights of Labor and the American Federation of Labor from their acceptance of the economic system of capitalism.

De Leon had many problems because the other members of the SLP did not share his views. A large part of the SLP was made up of German immigrants who were skilled workers and members of the AF of L. Their effort was one of working from within the organized trade unions. By 1897, there was internal dissension, with De Leon's opponents attempting to replace party leadership with men sympathetic to the American Federation of Labor. The conservative division led by Morris Hillquit believed that political action meant only the attempt to elect Socialists to public office.

It was, then, the anti–De Leon wing of the SLP and the SDP that finally realized their goals were quite similar. With this discovery both sides called for a unity of the two organizations. At its founding in 1901, the SPA was internally diverse, fairly democratic, and open in its structure. The SPA evolved for a number of reasons: "the inheritance of the populist remnants; the existence of a stable labor movement; and above all the emergence of a rising social class whose members felt themselves outside the pecuniary values of business and who found in socialism a justification of their own social position and values. This was the intelligensia."[54] In addition, the spread of factory work, social legislation to guard against industrial hazards, and already existing socialist and labor organizations contributed to the growth of the SPA.

There were three distinct groups in the SPA, and the ideological basis of each group was represented by its leaders. On the right was Victor Berger,[55] the undisputed leader of Milwaukee socialism. He was German-born, a school-teacher, printer, editor, and professional politician. He worked mostly with the German unions in Milwaukee but tried hard to organize the Italians and the Poles in the community as well. He emphasized the need for socialism to be relevant to the American workers' problems and saw likely prospects for the transition of socialism to the United States. He thought that the workers should improve their lot physically, economically, and morally. The development of socialism in the United States would be gradual and would require: (1) the winning of a majority of the population to the Socialist party, and (2) a concentration of industry sufficient to make it ripe for collective production. Berger was an excellent politician and was elected to Congress in 1910. He refused to run a second time because of American involvement in the war.[56]

In the center of many socialist disputes was Morris Hillquit. Hillquit was a Russian immigrant who later became an outstanding labor lawyer. At eighteen, he had joined the SLP, but after continuing arguments with De Leon, he left the SLP and formed the rival Rochester division of the SLP. He often played the role of arbiter between the left and right wings of the party. His moderate temper is illustrated by the following passage. "The Socialist aim in politics is to better the lot of the workers, to curb the power of the capitalist classes, to extend the social and industrial functions of the government and to place the latter more directly in the hands of the people—all with the ultimate object of transforming the present industrial and political system into a social democracy."[57]

On the left was Eugene Debs, who scornfully denounced Gompers theory that the interests of capital and labor were identical. Debs came to socialism via the Woodstock jail, where he had been imprisoned for violating an injunction during the strike of the American Railway Union in 1894. Debs was a native American who had earlier been involved in the populist movement. He was a self-educated socialist for the most part. Perhaps, Eugene Debs was the man who most exemplified the idea of American socialism.

The followers of socialism were primarily distributed along state and local lines. That is, if we look at the vote distribution for socialism, these distinctions become clear. By followers of socialism then, I mean not only the actual party members but those who generally supported the movement. From 1902 to 1912, the SPA grew from 10,000 to 117,984 members. During the same period, Debs polled over 400,000 votes in the 1904 and 1908 attempts at the presidency out of over 13,000,000 and 14,000,000 votes cast. In the 1912 election, he polled over 900,000 votes out of over 14,000,000 votes. On the east coast, particularly in New York City, the socialists were supported by Jewish immigrants in the garment trades. This support was initially from lower Manhattan, where the Jews from eastern Europe had first concentrated. The movement also found allies in Massachusetts, where the state vote in 1900 for Debs was only exceeded by that of New York. The socialists of Pennsylvania (particularly Reading) also supported the Socialist movement. In Pennsylvania state assemblymen were elected to office on the Socialist ticket. Ohio, Indiana, and Michigan had radical Socialists but no political organization. Wisconsin was another stronghold, with a close-knit party organization.

Socialism was heavily supported in Oklahoma. In 1910, there were 5,842 party members, more than in any other state. Missouri, Kansas, Arkansas, and Texas were affiliated with a radical socialism. Their socialist meetings took the form of earlier evangelical and populist gatherings. They were held as tent meetings or in encampments. The Rocky Mountains and the Pacific Northwest, strongly aligned with the IWW, also were amenable to socialism. In 1912 Debs polled over 10 percent of the popular vote in Washington, Idaho, Montana, Nevada, California, and Arizona.[58]

The most important point about the Socialist party is that a great many of its actual members were immigrants. In 1917, 32,894 members out of 80,126 were primarily from the foreign-language federations. By 1919, there were 57,000 foreign-language socialists—53 percent of the party.[59] It should be recalled that these immigrants were coming from southern and eastern Europe and were for the most part unskilled workers. "The truth is simply that the socialist vote was heaviest in working-class districts. Thus most of the small cities and villages in which the socialist party elected candidates were factory towns, railroad maintenance centers, or coal mining camps, while in the large cities they received their heaviest vote in working-class wards."[60]

It can be noted that many of the early American sociologists were concerned with the immigrants. They were so interested in them that some (i.e., Giddings, Ross) formulated analyses on the basis of an element called national or racial minds. In part, their analytic effort was an attempt to judge the value of various immigrant groups for American society. While the immigrants received part of their attention, so did the various workers' movements, but, these sociologists saw little utility in the IWW or the SPA. They seemed to be in favor of labor having some sort of representation as long as existing property rights were not challenged.

The Rise of the University and the Academic Professions

During the Progressive era an academic revolution took place in the United States that was unparalleled in the history of American education. Prior to this academic revolution the colleges had operated under the following set of assumptions: (1) "traditionalism as an educational goal," (2) *"stamping in* as a pedagogical method," (3) "the contumacy of youth as a major expectation."[61] One of the major problems of these early colleges was their financial solvency. For the most part enrollments declined in the period 1826-59. At the same time philanthropic gifts did not keep pace with the rising costs of education. Apparently the colleges turned to their alumni for donations to keep the schools running.[62] However, Metzger notes that there were many forces at work pointing to significant changes in the colleges.

By 1860...The growing emphasis on scholarship, the questioning of old pedagogical assumptions, the enlarging scales of philanthropy, were converting the larger colleges into institutions geared for research. At the same time, as the result of deeper social forces at work, the conserving function of the colleges no longer seemed so large. The unhinging of moral certainties by urban living, the fading out of the evangelical impulse, the depersonalization of human relations in the process of industrial expansion, were destroying that integral vision, that firm and assertive credulity, required of institutions devoted to conservation. Two other forces were to consummate this shift from "conserving" to "searching" in the universities of post war America. The first was to be the powerful impact of Darwinism, which would unlock the creative potentials of American academic science. The second was to be the influence of the German university, whose scholarly lore and academic traditions Americans admired and adopted.[63]

Americans studied in Germany primarily because they believed that "first-rate professional learning in the more specialized scholarly and scientific disciplines was not to be obtained from American colleges, universities, or polytechnical institutes."[64] Between 1820 and 1920 nearly nine thousand Americans studied in Europe. More importantly, their distribution was significant (e.g., in 1895, 30 Americans were at the Sorbonne while 200 were studying in Berlin).[65] In part, these Americans were impressed by "the doctrines of German historians concerning the relation of history to politics in the years immediately following the crisis of the Civil War, where many American students saw in Prussia's rise to national leadership a parallel to the victory of the North in that conflict."[66] These students returned to America, bringing with them such ideas as: (1) universities should be research institutes; (2) graduate students and professors are involved in the same pursuit, knowledge—this meant the regular use of the seminar; (3) academic theory should be used as a tool for legislative reform. The last point is of special significance, since many of the German-trained scholars had been accused in writing of being Marxists and anarchists (e.g., William G. Sumner and Simon Newcomb). In fact, however, the German-trained students tended to be middle class and middle-of-the-road politically.[67]

Prior to 1860, not a single doctorate was given by an American institution. By 1890, however, 164 had been awarded, and a decade later that number had doubled. In the opinion of Jencks and Riesman, the modern American university dates from the 1880s, when Johns Hopkins and Clark functioned primarily as graduate universities. According to them:

The 1890's saw further progress, with the founding of Chicago, the Reform of Columbia, and the tentative acceptance of graduate work as a important activity in the leading state universities. This was also the period when national learned societies and journals were founded and when knowledge was broken up into its present departmental categories (physics, biology, history, philosophy: and so forth), with the department emerging as the basic unit of acadmic administration. Medicine and law also became serious subjects of graduate study at this time, with Johns Hopkins leading the way in medicine and Harvard in law.[68]

This turning point in American higher education was not founded on educational ideals or policies alone (e.g., the ideal of Germanic scholarship). "After 1885 numbers at the major institutions began climbing upward. The increase thereafter was steady; it was to be affected only marginally, for example, by the financial panic of 1893-1896."[69] In addition, philanthropic support, when compared with the preindustrial period, was overwhelming. Prior to the Civil War the single largest gift given to a university was Abott Lawrence's $50,000 contribution to Harvard. This sum seems insignificant when we realize in the final decades of the last century that John Hopkins received a $3,500,000 gift, Stanford was given

$24,000,000, and the University of Chicago was granted
$34,000,000. In addition, foundations were created as a method for
gift giving. The General Education Board founded by John D.
Rockefeller in 1902 had assets of $46,000,000; The Carnegie Cor-
poration founded in 1911 had assets of $151,000,000.[70] In a
word, corporate business permeated the foundations of the modern university. In one study of twenty private and state universities, it was indicated that, in 1860, 48 percent of the members of
the boards of trustees were businessmen, bankers, and lawyers.
By 1900, 64 percent belonged to these same occupational categories. There is no doubt that it was considered an appropriate
activity for the academic fraternity to "cultivate the good will of
donors." It should be noted, however, that it is probable that
professors of social science were generally more hostile to businessmen than were professors of business administration.[71]

The universities during this period also developed two wings of
academic utilitarianism. One wing was led by President Eliot at
Harvard, and the other was modeled after Cornell and, to a smaller
degree, the University of Michigan. Andrew White, president of
Cornell, believed that a university "must be a union of the scientific and the aesthetic with the practical order to produce results
worthy of such an enterprise." White argued for three guiding
ideas: (1) nonsectarianism in religious matters, (2) freedom of
choice among various lines of study, and (3) equality in position
and status among the different courses. More importantly, he was
concerned with the university becoming a "training ground for
politically oriented public service." White particularly criticized
Eliot at Harvard for not extending education toward the real,
practical world.[72]

Eliot's version of academic utilitarianism was somewhat different from White's. White has been described as being utilitarian
without being humanitarian. White had such a thoroughgoing belief in laissez-faire that he came close to opposing full primary education. For the most part, he disliked state universities, labor
unions, and the social gospel. He also was indifferent to poverty.[73]

Cornell's influence spread westward to the University of Wisconsin and the University of Michigan, and the Cornell ideas also
seeped into the far west. More particularly we may note that: "By
1890 a distinctive Midwestern educational spirit was coming into

being. Utility became a rallying cry in a regional rebellion. The East Coast was pictured as standing for books, tradition, and culture, in an undersirable sense. The West, in contrast, meant action, practicality, realism, and progress. College studies, it was held, would reflect the differences of environment."[74] It also can be pointed out that German historicism, which was one of the main sources of sociology, and the conception of the university as a scene of teaching and research were more readily received in the Midwest—at Chicago, Wisconsin, and Michigan.[75] Even with these explicit differences, the university was in general a cautious institution. The universities were interested in maintaining a sober posture of respectability. "Extremely few students, professors, or administrators were recruited from the families of manual laborers."[76] Most of the leaders of the new social science within the university setting, like the leaders of the Social Gospel and the settlement house movements, came from the old-stock Protestant establishment.[77] Moreover, most students were Republican. For example, a study at the University of Wisconsin in 1900—a straw vote—indicated that only two students voted for Debs. This was the year that Debs, the socialist candidate, was rising into national prominence.

Within the confines of the university, professions were emerging and being sustained under its shelter. In particular the universities provided: (1) employment for men who did research and rewards for those who did it well, (2) a supply of professional scholars through the establishment of graduate programs that trained men for the various professions.[78] We may note that:

> The differentiation of high education into three sections—undergraduate college, graduate school and professional school—and the provision for research which was at times only loosely tied to teaching, opened virtually unlimited possibilities for the establishment of new fields. The growth of disciplines, such as the social sciences...was indirectly stimulated by their popularity as undergraduate subjects. Undergraduate demand led to a demand for teachers trained in these subjects, and hence departments, and even in some cases to Ph.D. programmes in these subjects.

Moreover the American experience of departmentalization was unlike anything that had happened in Europe. "In Europe the procedure for university innovation was to convey the idea to the government which then rendered a decision between the conflict-

ing viewpoints based on a more or less public debate of the issue."[79] Unlike the French system, there was no minister of education in America. And unlike the German plan of organization,
there were no sharp lines separating colleges from graduate schools
or technical schools from purely intellectual concerns. The university in America was influenced by public, private, local, and
national consensus. "Our postwar institutions of higher learning
were therefore not merely motley, but mongrel; not only different from each other in size, quality, independence, and sophisti-
cation…but eclectic in their character and purposes."[80]

Summary

It seems clear that America was experiencing an industrial revolution and its concommitant effects in what has been entitled
the Progressive era. The Progressives were concerned with urban
political problems, mass immigration, poverty, and large corporate
structures. However, it seems that many of the reform proposals
made were basically conservative. "Progressivism was a mild and
judicious movement, whose goal was not a sharp change in the
social structure."[81] The ideas of the Progressive tradition were
grounded in the glorification of competition. Most of the Progressives believed in the market economy. They were concerned, however, that the market needed policing, particularly at the state
level.

Political reform at the national level was concerned with the
problem of adjusting the legal-political framework to economic evolution—from laissez-faire capitalism to corporate capitalism. Woodrow Wilson, for example, (progressive that he was), believed, according to Sklar, that "the large corporation and large-
scale industry had replaced the individual entrepreneur and small
producing unit as the central and dominant feature of modern
capitalism."

Usually overlooked in discussions about the great "anti-trust" debates of
the pre-World War I period is that the leading participants were concerned
not so much with the abstract idea of "competition versus monopoly" as
with the role of the corporation in the new industrial order and its relation
to the state. This was as true of Wilson as it was of Roosevelt, Taft, George
W. Perkins, Elbert H. Gary, and Herbert Croly.[82]

For Wilson this relation was rooted in natural law. That is, only institutions which emerged autonomously from man's deliberate, conscious determination were considered good and a product of natural evolutionary growth. Wilson's attitude affirmed the growth of corporate industrial capitalism both at home and abroad as beneficient necessity. Wilson simply wanted to preserve some social space for the little man within the context of the emergence of the larger corporations. "His formula was fair competition and impartial access to credit at home, and expansion of the economic frontier abroad."[83]

Organized labor under the leadership of Samuel Gompers was also politically conservative. It never challenged the order of capitalism. The major value of organizing skilled labor was the pressure that could then be put on large corporations for higher wages and better working conditions. Gompers accepted corporate thinking. And Rodosh argues that Gompers saw society as "composed of various functional economic groups caused by the division of labor."[84] After labor had been defeated in various strikes (e.g., Homestead, Pullman), Gompers argued that the unions could not win in direct collisions with the giant trusts. He accepted the existence of large corporations as inevitable. Gompers, then, sought to organize the worker within the system as an alternative to socialism.

Furthermore, the American university that was emerging in the Progressive era was pragmatic and business oriented.

Central to the growth of American universities was the immensely rapid development of American industry, the settlement of the continent, and the emergence of great fortunes. Industry was dynamic; its growth facilitated, along with the expansion of the nation and acquisition of money, the expansion of science and the acquisition of knowledge. Industry created an almost insatiable demand for technicians, which the older educational system was unable to produce in sufficient numbers.[85]

The new university was community oriented but mainly to the interests of businessmen and technologists. The idea that the life of the mind had an importance of its own was "stifled rather than encouraged."[86] The change in the occupational background of university trustees indicated the growing importance of the business influence in the educational system. The university, also, became bureaucratized. This was not simply an emulative function of large corporations. Part of the impetus toward bureaucratization derived from the professors themselves, who were competing for placement. "Between 1890 and 1900, the number of college and university teachers in the United States increased by fully 90 percent."[87] Even though the academic market place was expanding, the more attractive university positions were close to being exhausted. In this context, those who were already established in the university wanted to protect their position.

It was in this milieu that the first generation of American sociologists—Lester Ward, William Sumner, Albion Small, Franklin Giddings, Edward Ross, and Charles Cooley—brought forth their work. Their writings, are, in part, a response to the problems with which this period of American history confronted them. They attempted to provide analyses and solutions for the problems of industrialization, immigration, and the growing corporations. In addition, they—in their roles as academic sociologists—were involved with the expanding university system. Their own livelihoods meshed with the growth of the universities, which, in turn, was connected with the expansion of the corporate liberal state. These men who were concerned with the whole of society had to fight not only other academics but various social movements as well for their right to speak about public welfare. They had to indicate that, in some way, their perspective was better suited for a modern industrial society. It is this claim that we will seek to understand in the following pages. Our aim is to discover not only the ways in which they analyzed other groups' ideas but the basis for their own claim to cognitive superiority.

3 / William G. Sumner

(1840-1910)

Biography

William Graham Sumner was born in 1840, the son of Thomas and Sarah Graham Sumner.[1] Thomas was a blacksmith mechanic in Lancashire, England, who migrated to America (Paterson, New Jersey). Thomas's father was block cutter and his wife's father was a locksmith and petty farmer. Thomas's early years were not easy, since these were the years following the Napoleonic wars. Prosperity had not come with peace, but instead unemployment and poverty. In addition, manufacturing districts like Lancashire had a large population influx which contributed to poor housing and factory conditions.

In 1836, when he was twenty-eight, Thomas migrated to the United States seeking better working conditions. Arriving in Paterson, New Jersey, Thomas married Sarah Graham, whose family earlier had immigrated from Lancashire. Paterson also had high unemployment, so Thomas looked for work in other states. He traveled through New York, Pennsylvania, and Ohio before deciding to stay in New England. The family finally settled in Hartford, Connecticut, where Thomas worked for the Hartford and New Haven Railroad. Before settling in Connecticut, Thomas and Sarah had two children in addition to William (Joseph Graham--1842; Esther Elizabeth--1843). Sarah died in 1848, when William was eight years old. A few months later, Thomas married Eliza Van Alstein of Liverpool, New York. A son was born to them, but died shortly after birth. Eliza encouraged Thomas to join an association which was formed by the Graham brothers (Thomas

Sumner's ex-wife's brothers). This association invested money in Hartford real estate, and it bought a number of houses for which Thomas Sumner acted as an overseer when the owners were not in residence. Not long after they established themselves there, Eliza died. Again, Thomas soon remarried—one Catherine E. Mix of West Hartford. By her, Thomas had two more children, Henry and Sarah Alice. Thomas's domestic tranquillity was maimed by his own physical disabilities and financial problems. He was blinded in one eye by a piece of steel, and later he was lamed by a fall on the job. His hearing failed. In addition, he suffered financial losses. With what little capital he had acquired, Thomas erected a number of buildings', they initially proved profitable, but later left him destitute. At Thomas's death in 1881, "he was almost as poor as when he came to America."

William Sumner had been raised by his stepmother, Eliza Van Alstein, who was said to have been very strict with affection and money. Due to her economy and the help of a Dr. Beale, however, William was able to enter Yale in the fall of 1859. He had graduated from Hartford High School when he was nineteen. This late graduation was due to the fact that he had worked for two years in a dry-goods store while pursuing his studies. Sumner studied Latin, Greek, mathematics, rhetoric, history, the Constitution, and philosophy at Yale, and he graduated from that school in 1863 with some of the highest honors in a class of 122. He was on his way to Europe when the honors were awarded. This was brought about by a loan from a classmate's brother—Henry Whitney. Prior to graduation he had been drafted by the army, but Sumner had also bought exemption from military service with the aid of Whitney.

Arriving in England Sumner studied French and Hebrew at Geneva. Within four months, on the advice of a classmate, he left for Germany. He studied German, Hebrew, the Old Testament, Egyptology, theology, and Lotze's philosophy for two years at Gottingen. In May of 1866 he returned to England (Oxford) for the express purpose of studying Anglican theology. While studying in England, he received notice that he had been appointed a tutor at Yale.

At Yale he tutored mathematics and Greek. At the same time he was associated with Trinity Episcopal Church in New Haven as a part-time preacher. He also wrote for *The Living Church*, a magazine that encouraged reform of the Episcopal religion and of all Christian religions. He was ordained a priest in 1869 and during the sixties and early seventies, served parishes in New York City and Morristown, New Jersey. In 1870 he was appointed Rector of the Church of the Redeemer in Morristown, where he married Jeannie Whittemore Eliot in 1871. Jeannie was the daughter of a New York merchant who was said to be a direct descendant of John Eliot, the apostle to the Indians.

In 1872, when he was only thirty-two years old, Sumner was called to the Chair of Political and Social Science at Yale. He remained in that position until his death in 1910. During these years at Yale, Sumner was actively engaged in many projects. For twenty years he taught economics to undergraduate students; then his own interests moved toward sociology. He was the first man in the country to use Herbert Spencer's *Study of Sociology* as a text for courses in sociology. He was criticized by many people—including Noah Porter, the president of Yale—for doing this but in the end Sumner won and was allowed to continue using Spencer. Sumner wrote biographies of Robert Morris, Alexander Hamilton, and Andrew Jackson. He also wrote many economic treatises, which were generally considered thorough but not particularly innovative. It was through his political essays and sociological writings, however, that he established his reputation. As a publicist he was against bimetallism, protectionism, imperialism, and popular democracy. One historian of sociology (Luther Bernard) interpreted Sumner's *Folkways* as a response to the fact that the public would not heed his advice.

[Sumner's] disillusionment regarding man's power to change beliefs and practices was probably due very largely to the failure of his own devoted efforts to teach his students and the general public the errors of protection, soft money, popular democracy, imperialism, etc. His strongest effort had gone into the crusade against protectionism, but his own students went home to become protectionists, because their interests were that way. So he developed the theory that pressures (mores and interests), not reason dominate men. This emphasis gets major expression in his *Folkways*, late in life. *Folkways* must be taken as a sort of swan song and his romanticism to his earlier reformist zeal and idealism.[2]

Even though his views were unpopular, Sumner was elected president of the American Sociological Society in 1908 and 1909.

Sumner worked incredibly hard, and after he was forty-five years old he mastered two Scandinavian languages, Dutch, Spanish, Portuguese, Italian, Polish, and Russian. Early in his academic career, he also was involved in local and state politics. In 1873 he was elected alderman of the sixth Ward on the Republican ticket. He was reelected for two more years in 1874. While acting as alderman, he was appointed chairman of the commission on claims and served as a member of the committee on ordinances. In 1874 he was the delegate from his ward to the Republican Representatives Convention, of which he was elected chairman. In the same year he was reported to have written the Republican State Platform. Sumner left local politics in 1876, but in 1882 he became a member of the Connecticut State Board of Education. He continued in that position until his death.

Sumner—like Small, Ross, and Cooley—spent most of his life in an academic atmosphere. Like Max Weber, Sumner argued that he was a citizen as well as a social scientist and that these were fundamentally different roles. It is not clear, however, that he did keep these roles separate in his own writings. It will be of some interest to note Sumner's basic images of man and society, since these conceptions do have a bearing on his analysis of ideas.

Impulsive Man and the Delicate Fabric of Society

According to Sumner, men act from feelings, not thoughts or beliefs. "The feelings are the springs of action."[3] Man in his primitive state began with acts which were attempts to control nature for purposes of survival. The immediate interest of survival stimulated man to social activity. Man was not inherently gregarious. Indeed, Sumner argued that all men have the vices of cupidity, lust, vindictiveness, ambition, and vanity.[4] Only the law sustained by impersonal institutions has held these vices in check. For Sumner, there were four great forces which moved men toward cooperative social activity. They were hunger, vanity, love, and fear of superior powers. Sumner argued that men in a given spatial proximity with similar interests (e.g., fear, hunger) tried to satisfy that interest. These groups noticed each other's efforts and selected the attempt which had proved successful with the least pain or exertion. This activity, then, became customary, a habit (folkway) which was carried on by tradition. This folkway, which was established by selection and approved by experience, was reflected on, and some judgment was made about it. From this reflection a moral opinion about the usefulness of the act for the general welfare of the people was made. If judged favorably, it became a more.[5] Men, then, were guided by impulsive interests and actions, not philosophical systems, moral catechisms, or ideal speculations. "No men have ever emancipated themselves from slavery, poverty, ignorance, vice, or any other ill, by simply resolving to do so. No men so far as I can learn, have ever reached the point of adopting a grand resolution to emancipate themselves from distress, unless they had some new power at their disposal, which raised them to a new plan on which such new adjustment of themselves to their past and their future was possible."[6]

Sumner also rejected any theory of natural rights. Men were born without any endowment of either a physical or metaphysical nature. "A man is born to struggle, work, and endure, as long as he can, by the expenditure of his energies."[7] Man was not a brute simply because he had learned to accumulate capital. Capital advanced society to a higher organization and more complete cooperation in its battle with nature.[8] The folkways aided this process throught the codification of man's experiments with nature. The distinctive characteristic of the folkways was their unconscious formation. "They are like products of natural forces which men unconsciously set in operation, or they are like the instinctive way of animals, which are developed out of experience." The life of man on earth is conditioned mainly by physical existence, the man/land ratio. Life was "surrounded and limited by the equilibrium of the forces of nature, which man can never disturb, and within the bounds of which he must find his chances." Men respond to this condition, as I have indicated earlier, by developing experiments which are successful in their battle with nature. These customs then become even more limiting forces on man's development, yet they also provide the certainty of survival. "Out of the blocks of customs thus evolved and controlled issue all human institutions. Hence the type of society's institutions derives ultimately from the ratio of men to land... Societal life goes back to evolution of its institutions, since they are its adjustments to its life conditions."[9]

Institutions, then, were the major building blocks of society. The original forces of hunger, love (self-perpetuation), fear (religion, ghost-fear), and vanity were the foundations of institutional development. From these interests, a core institutional development occurred: (1) institutions of societal self-maintenance (e.g., industrial organization, property, state—these corresponded with the hunger interest, (2) institutions of self-perpetuation (e.g., marriage, family), (3) institutions of religion (e.g., animism, demonism, ghost-fear), (4) self-gratification practices (e.g., ostentation in dress, social etiquette). However, all of these institutions influence each other reciprocally. Although he analytically divides society up into these categories, Sumner argues that the societal whole is exceedingly complex.

All of these institutions interpenetrate, as do the interests that summoned them into being. Property, for instance, goes back in no small degree to vanity; marriage is not by any means to be connected solely with sex and love; gambling does not find its sole motive in pleasure-seeking; dancing is often religious in nature; and religious practices are not unresponsive altogether to the hunger-interest or to that of sex. Each of these interests produced consequences on the domain of the others which are often, indeed, foreign to its own satisfaction....In no case of evolution is there a possibility of drawing hard and fast distinctions. Categories run into one another across zones of transition and no such zones are clear-cut but all are blurred.[10]

For Sumner, a society was a "group of human beings living in a cooperative effort to win subsistence and perpetuate the species." The main elements for a study of society were man's relationship to land and, consequently, the struggle between men for subsistence.[11] Sumner clearly believed that economic forces were the prime movers of society. According to Charles Page, Sumner criticized both the historians and the socialists for not realizing the importance of this phenomenon.[12] Furthermore, social organization was inherently a complex solution to survival. Society could be appropriately compared to biological organisms. In society, every action has a reaction, and the reaction spreads through the organism "affecting organs and modifying functions."[13] Sumner make this point about the interdependency and extensiveness of social organization to indicate that society has a life of its own. Like Durkheim, Sumner argued that society was not something that could be reduced to a sum of its individual parts. It was a living whole with a life of its own. "Human society, then, by the diversity of its parts, their specialization, the distribution of functions, the mutual service and support of the parts, and their solidarity, is a true system or organization. It has a life different from that of the individual and not simply aggregated or multiplied from the life of individuals. The quality of a combination is not the sum of the qualities of its components." [14]

Moreover, social organization was a product of unconscious evolutionary forces. These forces transcended the range of individual powers and produced characteristic effects of their own. The social order was directly analogous to the physical order. Both were set by the laws of nature. Humans, because of ignorance and self-conceit, only damaged the operation of social laws when they attempted to alter them. For Sumner, the evils of society resulted from statesmen, philosophers, socialists, and ecclesiastics who assumed that they could organize society as they chose. Ultimately, it would "take centuries of scientific study of the facts of nature to eliminate from human society the mischievous institutions and traditions which the said statesmen, philosophers, and ecclesiastics have introduced into it." [15]

The student of society must learn to see society as a whole. He must rid himself of his narrow provincialities—class, nation, race— if he wants to see the truth of organic unity. "He may thus secure an approach to that scientific dispassionateness which has enabled natural scientists to attain their enviable reputation and results." Moreover, the social scientist must realize that he belongs to a privileged class and that "it is the masses who carry the ways and customs, and society moves only as their relatively inert bulk lurches this way or that." [16]

In summary, Sumner clearly argued that man had no natural rights. Man is born to struggle against nature and other men in order to survive (antagonistic cooperation). All people in all historical situations were susceptible to the vices of greed, envy, and hatred. Only the development of societal institutions prevented a war of all against all, and just those institutions which helped the human species were maintained. From the basic drives (hunger, love, fear, vanity), the major institutions developed. The core institution was property. It was through the accumulation of property that people made their biggest advance against nature. Sumner's image of man is clearly conservative in nature. His argument that man has certain vices (e.g., greed, hatred) is not historical but ahistorical. These drives are said to be a part of the natural human condition, and as such not modifiable.

Within the social-technological tradition, Sumner argued that society has logical, historical, and moral priority over the individual. Society had a life of its own and was complex in its operation. We could also be sure that the evolution of society was governed by unconscious sentiments and not by ideals of any sort. He went on to argue that humans cannot fight the forces of nature in society. It was useless to discuss state interference as planned social change.

Furthermore, he stated that inequality was an inherent property of any social system. There was no natural equality between men. Only the fittest survived and attained prominent positions in terms of power or property.

We have to live in the societal organization. It dominates us, and to it we are constrained to make concessions of our liberty of unrestricted action. Its might is greater with higher civilization...It is to be noted that organization is built upon inequality; it produces new inequality from one step to another because some adapt their individual effort to the organization more intelligently than others; it requires a hierarchy of managers which has more and more ranks as the organization becomes wider and more complex; it is aristocratic because it automatically selects the more fit for its positions of greater power; it requires sterner discipline as it becomes larger because it then becomes more impersonal; it gives an imperial postion to those who, selected from all, stand out at last as fit to be commanders-in-chief. To resist these tendencies, which are inherent in organization, is to resist culture, which is an issue out of organization.[17]

The more perfectly liberty was realized, the greater the tendency toward inequality. Human attainments would vary with different degrees of physical, moral, and intellectual forces exerted. Page states that "To Sumner, inequalities of wealth, power, and prestige are essential to societal development. Communities must have classes if they are to advance."[18]

The worst thing that an intellectual could do was to set up some abstract ideal of society and then to try to bring it about. Humans were not moved by thought but by sentiments. They were, in short, creatures of habit. There was no hope of progress in politics except by gradual growth. This growth came from behind, as it were, by the gradual movement of imperceptible stages in the evolution of the folkways and mores.[19] The history of the human race in politics was the same story repeated cyclically. It was the story of persons or classes trying to win possession of state power in order to live luxuriously on the earnings of others. The only distinctive characteristic of modern society were the rise of the middle classes out of medieval cities, the accumulation of wealth, and "the encroachment of wealth, as a social power, on the ground formerly occupied by birth and wealth." The middle class had to fight for its rights and in so doing "established institutions to guarantee personal and property rights against the arbitrary will of kings and nobles."[20]

Sumner's image of man and society does fit our idea of the social-technological theme. He argued that individuals possessed certain innate drives which needed to be controlled by social organization. Moreover, he believed that society had a kind of moral and collective superiority over the individual and that hierarchy and inequality were necessary for social development. It is also clear, however, that it was not society qua society which represented this collectivism. In actuality, Sumner believed that the operations of society were analogous to those of nature and that both obeyed the "laws"—an obvious reference to the laws of evolution. More importantly, it was not society as such that stood above individuals but the "laws," which expressed themselves in societal processes.[21] With this background in mind, we turn to Sumner's analysis of ideas and social structure.

The Structure of the Folkways

Sumner argued that the folkways and mores were the base from which all abstract philosophies of life and ethics emanated. The mores were ways of doing things "which are current in a society to satisfy human needs and desires, together with the faiths, notions, codes, and standards of well living which inhere in those ways, having a genetic connection with them."[23] The mores included a reflexive element, which was codified as the proper way to do something. The folkways were the actual economic adjustments to nature and other men. The folkways evolved prior to the mores and constituted an intermediary causal link in the development of political institutions, industrial prosperity, moral codes, and world philosophy.[23] In Sumner's words:

World philosophy, life policy, rights, and morality are all products of the folkways. They are reflections on, and generalizations from, the experience of pleasure and pain which is won in efforts to carry on the struggle for existence under actual life conditions. The generalizations are very crude and vague in their germinal forms. They are embodied in folklore, and all our philosophy and science have been developed out of them.

When historians or social scientists discussed the zeitgeist of a period, they were giving partial recognition to the importance of the mores. Mores produced philosophical ideas. But philosophy was never original or creative; it was, in fact, secondary and was derived from the mores.[24]

Sumner used a wealth of examples to illustrate the above points, but it would be far beyond the scope or need of our examination to document all of these. Sumner's thinking can be examined judiciously by looking at his analysis of (1) the social stages of foresight, (2) religious, marital, and political mores, and (3) modern mores.

According to Sumner, mankind, like nature, had followed an evolutionary development. This sequence was characterized as follows: (1) collection of food, or nomadic, stage, (2) the hunting stage, which includes the use of tools for killing, (3) the animal-raising stage, and (4) the plant-culture stage. Corresponding with these survival activities, man had developed distinctive mental characteristics. During the collection stage, when nomadic behavior was essential, there was no chance to develop settled and improved adjustments to life. Instruments, capital, or other such agencies to ease the struggle for existence were not part of material well-being. The greater the degree of nomadism of a tribe the less likely its members were to develop culture. They did not develop foresight. Moreover, only "petty coins of speech" were utilized. "They are overwhelmed by a flood of details, in which they cannot discern the ruling idea. The material and sensual constitute their limits."[25] The hunting stage finds men with tools and weapons. This means that a given land area can be worked more intensely. Consequently, when physical improvement of a population occurred, then it was likely that other qualities (e.g., mental powers) would develop in the species.

Since sustenance is surer, there appears an emancipation from the element of chance, which engenders a mood of confidence. Nothing succeeds like success. The weapons and tools are capital and represent insurance against the chances of life. The savage hunter is not seldom a good deal of a man, in his way; he has his qualities of bravery, coolness in facing danger, ingenuity, and he has also his opportunities; for his implements...tend to free his energy from mere animal routine. Not so much time and effort have to be put in on meeting mere existence-needs.... Foresight develops to reach beyond the immediate need; the very fact, indeed, that tools and weapons are made at all indicates the presence of that equality in some strength.[26]

The pastoral stage incorporates the hunting stage and added a new element—the domestication of animals. In this stage the population became denser, and the birthrate increased while the death rate was lowered. The animals acted as a form of capital and protection against ill-fortune. The mental set of these people was one of increasing confidence and foresight. When they migrated, the tools and instruments that were developed were not left behind. Moreover, people at this stage of evolution thought in terms of their chief vocation. For example, about the Akamba tribe of Africa, Sumner and Keller wrote: "Fines are levied in cattle, showing an economy based on beasts as ours on metallic money. Cows are much more valuable than bulls. Unquestionably the animals have some powerful religious qualities; all along occur cases of purification by use of the contents of the stomachs of goats and sheep in which people tread or formally rub their feet."[27] The agricultural stage was the basis of all high cultures. "The agricultural stage represents a distinct advance over anything that went before." Plants were a better teacher of foresight than animals. The agriculturalist developed the qualities of patience and perseverance. He was unlike the hunter and pastoral nomads, who were aggressive and typically warlike. The agriculturalist became industrial in character. "He wants title in perpetuity and has no idea at all of abandoning his holdings and moving on."

He thus automatically develops a degree of foresight clear beyond that of any previous stage; for while the hunter may look ahead a few days or weeks, and the herder a few months or years, the tiller's outlook can hardly cover less than years, and generally extends over decades. This is part of his industrial character set deeply in his mores. The highly sedentary quality of agriculture has its dominant effect in the rapid accumulation and retention, partly through the art of writing, of cultures or civilization.[28]

In addition to his evolutionary analysis of foresight, Sumner also suggested that the customs (mores) of a time and place could make anything right or wrong.[29] In this sense, his framework is much like Durkheim's. There are no social acts which have intrinsic properties of good and evil. The mores decide what acts are taken to be acceptable or unacceptable. Although Sumner did not utilize Durkheim's notion of the "sacred," he did suggest that ghost-fear permeated numerous mundane social activities. In short, ghost-fear interacted with the other basic social forces: hunger, vanity, and sex. Unlike Marx, Sumner did not suggest any specific relations between the substructure of economic conditions (folkways) and the superstructure of religious beliefs and/or ideology (mores), although *Folkways* as a whole directly illustrates the idea of ethical relativity. For example, Sumner shows in the following passage how the mores were used to condone the destruction of religious heretics.

The thirteenth century bred in every heart such a sentiment in regard to heretics that inquisitors had no more misgivings in their proceedings than men would have now if they should attempt to exterminate rattlesnakes. The sixteenth century gave to all such notions about witches that witch persecutors thought they were waging war on enemies of God and man. Of course the inquisitors and witch persecutors constantly developed the notions of heretics and witches. They exaggerated the notions and then gave them back again to the mores, in their expanded form, to inflame the hearts of men with terror and hate and to become, in the next stage, so much more fantastic and ferocious motives.[30]

"The mores, in their origin, were immediately concerned with ghost-fear and religion, because they came down by tradition from ancestors." This traditional element gave them the power of high authority which descended from another world. The ghost-fear element was the original stimulus to duty, and it was typical of the mental set of people for ages. Nobody acted on the basis of abstract religious codes (e.g., the Bible). If they tried to do right they simply conformed to the mores of their epoch. Religions were the creations of fantasy. They descended from the realm of metaphysics, while actual moral behavior evolved from the mores.[31]

It was only when contrasting mores came into contact with each other that reflection on them became possible. There was great difficulty in criticizing them, since we were born in them and were formed by them. "How can we rise above them to pass judgement on them?" The contrast in mores could be seen in relation to the variable status of women.

Some Australian girls consider that their honor requires that they shall be knocked senseless and carried off by men who thereby become their husbands. If they are victims of violence they need not be ashamed. Eskimo girls would be ashamed to go away without crying and lamenting, glad as they are to go. They are shocked to hear that European women publicly consent in church to be wives, and then go with their husbands without pretending to regret it.... Kaffirs also ridicule Christian love marriage. They say that it puts a woman on a level with a cat, the only animal which, amongst them, has no value.... Where polygamy prevails women are ashamed to be wives of men who can afford only one each; under monogamy they think it a disgrace to be wives of men who have other wives.[32]

According to Sumner, "the treatment of marriage amonts to a survey of restrictions laid, in the mores, upon unregulated relations of the sexes." The mores of endogamy and exogamy governed who may marry. The how of marriage also was attendant upon the mores. The important thing was that all forms of wife getting (e.g., capture, abduction, exchange, elopement) were coordinated with general societal status and alter according to it. In particular, even the chastity of the bride was part of the evolution of the mores toward civilized marriage. Premarital chastity preserved vital social forces and, like marriage, "prevented irresponsibility and contributed to orderliness of social relations as respects property, inheritance, kinship-bonds, and legitimacy in general."[33] For Sumner, the marriage institution provided greater efficiency for survival of the species. Given the differentiation of the sexes, the institution of marriage gave advantages to both partners. The form that marriage took (e.g., polygymy, polyandry, monogamy) was greatly dependent on the actual, material living conditions. For example, Sumner distinguished between the mores of polygamy in primitive and in more advanced societies. He argued that in the primitive societies, where women were laborers there was an economic advantage in having a number of women. In industrial societies, it was greed and ostentation that led to polygamy.[34]

Sumner also argued that the mores had their effects on political ideas. "Modern notions of equality are no doubt to be explained

historically as revolts against medieval inequality and status."
These modern ideas of equality could be traced back to the writings of various sects and parties in the Middle Ages. They were counter suggestions "against the existing system which assumed that rights were obtained from sovereigns, from which it resulted that each man had such rights as his ancestors had been able to get."[35] Part of the reason for the predominance of egalitarian ideas in the modern mores was due to the changing material base. The opportunities of wealth, comfort, luxury never before were offered to the whole of a society in any such manner and degree." Material wealth was obvious and immediately available. Classical culture and religious philosophy offered ideals which were no longer held in esteem. "The way was clear for the dominion of materialistic standards and ideals." Since materialism was the dominant ethos, the state and other political institutions rose in importance.

The eighteenth century had bequeathed to the nineteenth a great mass of abstract notions about rights and about the ultimate notions of political philosophy, and in the nineteenth century many of these notions were reduced to actuality in constitutions, laws, and judicial rulings. The masses in all civilized nations were led to believe that their welfare could be obtained by dogmatic propositions if such propositions were enacted into constitutions and laws. This faith has entered into the mores of all civilized men and now rules their discussion of social questions. Rights, justice, liberty, and equality are the watchwords, instead of the church, faith, heaven and hell. The amount of superstition is not much changed, but it now attaches to politics, not to religion.[36]

For example, constitutional democracy in the United States was produced out of the material conditions fostering its existence. "It existed in the sense of social equality long before it was recognized and employed as a guiding principle in institutions and laws." The colonies characteristically lacked industrial organization. All men were farmers first and carried on other occupations incidentally. They all drew their sustenance from the land. When human power was required, they had to cooperate, as in logrolling or barn raising.

[N]ot even the simplest class distinctions, those of employer and employee, were possible here at that time. No man could gain anything by owning more land than he could till; the people who got grants of land made disagreeable experience of the truth of this.... As there could be no landlord, there could be no tenant; no man would hire another's land when he could get land of his own for the labor of reducing it to tillage. Now landlords-tenant-farmers, and laborers are the three groups which form the fundamental framework of a class-divided society; but if they are all merged in a class of peasant-proprietors or yeomen-farmers, there is absolutely no class organization. All are equal, by the facts of the case as nearly as human beings can be equal.[37]

In the final analysis, public opinion had been and still was the major regulative agency of society. Public opinion was a matter of feeling rather than of intellect. In particular, "the course of civilization has been marked by a progressive enlargement of the range of expression accorded to the popular will." The expansion of expression had allowed the formation of peace groups. In this context, interests may come into conflict but could be reconciled without the use of violence. Under modern conditions, the people could no longer appeal to an agreed-upon ruler. Common consent was the new agency, and it played the role that the prince had once held. Moreover, within Sumner's framework, public opinion was the "great engine which controlled the whole of society."[38]

It is clear that Sumner believed that most, if not all, abstract ideas emerged from the folkways and mores of a population. The folkways, it will be recalled, were the practical (habitual) activities of successful adaptation. In part, the differences in folkways were a product of disparate contacts with nature and other men. Folkways, in short, were practical solutions for survival. The mores contained a reflexive component. They were the result of judgments concerning codification of habits of ideas and beliefs that surrounded practical activity. If, upon reflection, a folkway was deemed worthy, it became a part of the mental set of a people. For our part, we want to note that the folkways and mores are products of a whole population—a collectivity, so to speak.[39] Although Sumner was aware of conflict and control by various elite groups, he did not argue that these groups alone create the mores. The elite groups may manipulate the mores for their own advantage, but they do not generate them. In this sense, then, we may argue that Sumner viewed the generation of ideas as the product of the habitual activities of a collectivity. Conflict, it will be recalled, emerged from the social forces universal in the human species. It did not stem from class conflict.[40]

The Power of the Mores

Sumner believed explicitly in the power of the mores to shape and control human life. The mores manifested themselves through the basic social forces of hunger, love, fear, and vanity. One indication of the relative power of these mores is the number of pages devoted to a discussion of them in *The Science of Society.* Hunger (man/land ratio), fear, and self-perpetuation were the most powerful social forces (in descending order), and they furnished the building material of the mores. Because of their power, therefore, the mores were what Sumner chose to analyze. He engaged in systematic critiques of other social theories only when he thought such theories were creating disorder in society. The primacy of the mores, in Sumner's thinking, can be illustrated by the following passage:

In truth, the power of custom over life is one of those matters of fact to which men constantly appeal without reflection or analysis. Custom is by its nature a floating and undefined conception, and is accepted as a sort of pervasive and irreducible feature of life. In its varieties it is highly interesting and can be profusely and edifyingly illustrated, but to deal with it scientifically is difficult. It lends itself to irresponsible speculation just because it is too diffuse, evasive, and resisting to scientific devices for analyzing phenomena.... And yet a science of society, if it is to be penetrating and revealing, must overcome that resistance; for all of society's forms and institutions are found, when reduced to lowest evolutionary terms, in custom. It is the germ of them all. Nothing in the societal realm is more original, underived, and elemental. The study of custom is, for a science of society, what the study of the cell is for biology.[41]

Sumner analyzed many types of mores. They ran the gamut from religious mores to sex customs and the modern practices of obscenity restriction and asceticism. For example, he described the sex mores of the Southern Slavs, which were different from those in the greater part of Russia. The young bride (a Southern Slav) developed an intimate relationship with her attendants. Two of these girls attended her on the wedding day. The bride was a girl given to a man she had never met, and she entered a house where she had to be absolutely submissive to the husband's parents. She could not approach her husband freely or see him during the day. She could converse with his brother, and the elder brother was allowed to become her best friend. These Slavonic marital customs were juxtaposed against alternative ones. One custom which was predominant in Great Russia up until the nineteenth century "was that the father married his son, as a boy, to a marriageable young woman, whom the father then took as his own concubine." When the son grew up he continued the same practices as his father. Constantly reiterating the relativity of the mores, Sumner goes on to indicate that "Amongst all the Slavonic peoples females are a very inferior status and owe formal deference to males. In Bulgaria the wives are from five to ten years older than the husbands, because boys of fourteen begin to make love, but to adult marriageable owmen."[42]

The mores not only told us what to do in the positive sense but also indicated what should not be done if the species was to survive. These constrictions emerged from experience and dogma. Constrictions based on experience were usually connected with food or sex behavior. Those from dogma were generally tied to ghost doctrines. About ghost doctrines and asceticism Sumner writes:

There are also a great many primitive customs for coercing or conciliating superior powers,—either men or spirits—which consist in renunciation, self-torture, obscenity, bloodshedding, filthiness, and the performance of repugnant acts or suicide. These customs all imply that the superior powers are indifferent, or angry and malevolent, or justly displeased, and that the pain of men pleases, or appeases and conciliates, or coerces them or wins their attention. Thus we meet with a fundamental philosophy of life in which it is not the satisfaction of needs, appetites and desires, but the opposite theory which is thought to lead to welfare.

The interesting thing about ascetic policies was that they were never simply the direct product of the folkways. They were reflective and derived from a faith built on experience and judgment. Ascetic policies, therefore, were dogmatic and sustained by faith within a fundamentally pessimistic conviction. Moreover, ascetic acts "can affect interests only by influencing the ghosts or demons who always interfere between efforts and result and make luck."[43]

Asceticism has taken various forms and performed different functions in many societies. In examining the mores, Sumner ad-

heres to a functional analysis of ideas. From the folkways emerge
the mores, and from the mores, an ethos (culture). Werner Stark
suggests that for Sumner, "The whole is held together in that it is
a going concern, a co-operative and integrated life, in a word, a
quasi-organic unity.... Ideas are inseparable aspects of the social
totality, not separable entities."[44] As Sumner points out in his
own inimitable way, Shinto asceticism takes an interesting form in
some of the remote regions of Japan. Every year the community
appoints a man to devote himself to the gods on its behalf. The
orphic ascetic rites in Greece were performed for different reasons:
the faults and errors of this life were not to be eliminated, but
earthly life was itself to be rejected. Eating meat and sex were ta-
boo in these rituals. However, "the rites do not free men from the
touch of the demons."

They purify the soul from the unclean contact with the body and from the
dominion of death. Mysticism is conjoined with this doctrine of purification.
The soul came from God and seeks to return to him. It is released by the rites
and practices from everything on earth, including morals, which are only petty attempts to deal with details, and therefore are of no interest to a soul
which is released.[45]

Ascetic practices also passed into the mores of Christianity. The
best Christians were those who renounced wealth, luxury, pleasure,
and sex. In the Middle Ages the theologians constantly reiterated
the evil of sexual relations. However, asceticism in Europe had
ended by the sixteenth century. Its demise was brought about "by
the ideas and tastes of a period of commerce, wealth, productive
power, materialism, and enjoyment." The modern era, Sumner believed, is characterized by the belief in "rational lines of effort."
Effort is viewed as having a direct relationship to result. "We work
for what we want with courage, hope and faith, and we enjoy the
product as a right."[46]

Sumner believed that besides nature and men, another basic element entered life—that of luck. "The momentousness of chance in
the affairs of societal life is tacitly accepted by everyone, though it
is seldom discerningly recognized." This aleatory element and the
desire of men to control it gave rise to the religious impulse. Luck
was a name for that which was unexplainable in a given stage of
knowledge. The primitive mind was terrified by the aleatory element and had to find a way of coping with it. "By a sort of marve-

lous coincidence the theory was there, right at hand and it was one competent to cover any and all cases. The theory was that of the spirit environment."⁴⁷ Ghost-fear seemed a universal element, although it developed in different ways. Death, to the primitives, was an expected happening, and it was difficult for them to draw a line between life and death. They encouraged the idea that breath indicated the presence or absence of a spirit or soul. Consequently, many of the tribes developed peculiar mortuary practices for the purpose of allowing the spirit to escape from the body. This was particularly true when the corpse was considered a polluting agent.

The Tibetan lama plucks a few hairs from the crown of the corpse in order to give vent to the spirit through an actual but invisible minute perforation of th the skull thus supposed to be made.... The notion prevailed in Scotland and in many parts of England that the soul of the dying flew out of the mouth in the likeness of a bird; hence the doors must be set upon when anyone was dying.... The Jews of South Russia think that dying on an iron bed prolongs the death agony and so provide a wooden one.... When an Australian dies, his hut is pulled down and the materials are often burnt. No one will inhabit a place where a death has occurred. This is not alone from fear of the ghost of the deceased; they say they believe that the wild black who has taken the kidney-fat of the deceased or the spirit who has destroyed him, will wander about the site of the old encampment.⁴⁸

Behind the evolution of the institutions of industry and religion lay another stimulating force—self-gratification. The human species has not always struggled solely for existence. "There has nearly always been some leisure that could be spent in doing what men wanted to do instead of only what they must do." However, the important point about self-gratification was that no institutions comparable to property or religion had developed around it. Self-gratification took many forms (e.g., tobacco, liquor, games) and seems largely limited by one consideration—the time element. Even though many of the pursuits of self-gratification appear to be of no consequence for social evolution, there is one element that has played an important role. Vanity as a form of behavior sought "self-distinction, exaltation of personality, recognized superiority of various sorts, admiration, and applause." According to Sumner, vanity in the form of ambition is one of the most powerful driving forces in men. More importantly, vanity performs a number of useful functions for both the individual and his class or society.

Among other things, vanity has led to higher standards of living, foresight, and thrift. "Vanity stimulates the individual to produce variations for selection to work upon; and group vanity in the form of ethnocentrism is one of the main factors promoting that conflict and competition without which there can be no selection resulting in the survival of the fitter."[49]

It is interesting to note that although Sumner's *Folkways* exudes an ethical or functional relativism, he does not hold that view consistently. His analysis of the political mores is a prime example of this contradiction. Sumner's political view of socialism or ideal democracy was based on what he considered to be the way society actually worked rather than on how it should have worked. Sumner had no time for metaphysical ideals or absolutes, particularly in the realm of politics. He criticized socialism for not understanding that "rights do not pertain to *results,* but only to *chances.*" Rights "pertain to the conditions of the struggle for existence, not to any of the results of it; to the pursuit of happiness, not to the possession of happiness." No one of us has a necessary right to property, since that may mean somebody else is under an obligation to provide us with property. Each only "has a right to acquire property if he can."[50] Socialism as well as sentimental ethics failed to understand the phenomenon of modern industrial organization, which controls our social activity, determines our conceptions of good and evil, and "reforms the oldest and toughest customs, like marriage and property."[51] One of the reasons for constant reform agitation was the heritage of eighteenth-century dogmas which proffered liberty, equality, and happiness as natural rights. "Every human being, on this theory, comes into the world with an outfit and a patrimony of metaphysical, if not of physical goods."

We may be very sure that all these theories of world beautification can produce nothing but disillusion and disappointment for those who put faith in them, and disintegration for society in which they are current. The human race never received any gratuitous outfit of any kind whatever; no heaven myth ever was more silly and empty than such a notion; talk about the "boon of nature," and the banquet of life" and the "free gift of land" is more idle than fairy tales.[52]

Sumner particularly resented speculation when applied to politics. He thought that ideals played an important role in the development of an individual, but their use in any other manner was futile and tended to create chaos. Sumner criticized the German *Sozialpolitik* tradition, among others, for being too speculative. It was only in the dreams of men that new political institutions were built (e.g., Utopias). Utopian political thinking could never be tested, since each scheme started with the postulate that the political order must and could be made over again. This was patently impossible. It was commonly assumed that American political institutions were made by our fathers, but that was not the case. "The truth is that the fathers devised some expedients in governmental machinery, all of which have failed of the objects they aimed at or have been distorted to others."[53] In the final analysis, then:

The economic development of human society must go on its own way and work out its results, and the human race must make the best of them. The race, however, does not make mistakes, and so long as, in all parts, it obeys the dictates of its interests, it will push on a true evolution which cannot but serve to enhance the prosperity of the race as a whole. It is only when nations allow their action to be dictated by speculations about the future of civilization and humanity that they may wreck the natural development.[54]

In particular, Sumner criticized the then predominant mores of American democracy. He argued that: (1) the time during which American democracy had been tried was too short to warrant any judgments; (2) American democracy was a consequence of industrialization and prosperity, not the cause of it; (3) American democracy lived on the capital inherited from aristocracy and industrialism; there was no pure democracy.[55] Moreover, the so-called public will of democracy was particularly inept. The public could not keep its attention on more than one question at a time, especially in the case of the uneducated man. On the other hand, "the educated man can embrace a large number, but his doubts are more numerous as to them all." For Sumner, the theory and practice of elections also failed because of its incorrect assumptions concerning human behavior: (1) voters did not have their opinions already formed on election day; (2) they would not deliver their opinions without fear or favor on election day; (3) they might not vote with a view to the public welfare; (4) the mechanism of the ballot box was not an adequate mechanism for expressing the public will.[56]

In summary, Sumner argued that there were certain common errors in political thinking. The first was an error of poltical judgment in which men thought the world could be made over a priori. The second error was the reliance on great principles. Political discussion stood on assumptions rather than on "things as they are and human nature as it is." The final error was one of political philosophy. There was no best government. It was only a relative term which has meaning for particular groups at specific times. Furthermore, political philosophers had expected too much to happen through radical change.

Experience shows that the hope of steady improvement by change is delusion. All human arrangements involve their measure of evil; we are forever striking balances of advantage and disadvantage in our social and political arrangements. If by a change we gain more advantage on one side, we lose some on another; if we get rid of one evil we incur another. The true gains are won by slow and difficult steps; they consist only in better adjustments of man to his circumstances. They are never permanent because changes in men and their circumstances are continually taking place; the adjustments must be continually re-established and the task is continually renewed.[57]

In summary, Sumner tended to analyze the mores of different cultures at various times. As he viewed it, the mores were functionally integrated with a given culture and were therefore part and parcel of it. At first glance it would seem that he was a cultural relativist who evaluated "ideas" in terms of their fitness with a culture. It is also the case, however, that Sumner criticized some of the social and political theories of his time. He did show an interest in criticizing certain utopian and socialistic schemes. In this sense, then, Sumner does not fit the social-technological theme perfectly. He did criticize, but the grounds from which he examined the modern political mores were not radical in nature. He did not view competing ideologies in terms of class conflict. For him, the question of elites in society was inconsequential, as I will try to show in the next section. Sociology was not to be the vanguard of a revolutionary movement.

Ascetic Sociology: The Safety of the Past

In part, Sumner's critique of enlightenment politics and democracy rested on the notion that no adequate knowledge of social processes was available, so intervention could lead to pernicious effects. Science, in its most general form (i.e., natural and social science), was the "investigation of facts by sound methods, and deduction of inferences by sound processes." Science, in a sense, was organized common sense. It aimed to learn what some phenomenon was and how it had become that way. "The further it goes the more it enlightens us as to consequences which must ensue if acts are executed by which things and men are brought into the relations which science has elucidated." Science, in particular, must be open to reexamination and further testing. "Consequently the modes and habits of thought developed by the study of science are very different from those developed by the study of religion."[58] Sumner did distinguish between the natural sciences and the social sciences. But he claimed that their interests are the same—the discovery of natural laws. "Sociology is the science of life in society."

It investigates the forces which come into action wherever a human society exists. It studies the structure and functions of the organs of human society, and its aim is to find out the laws in subordination to which human society takes its various forms and social institutions grow and change. It must, without doubt, come into collision with all other theories of right living which are founded on authority, tradition, arbitrary invention, or poetic imagination.[59]

This science of society was not nominalist in orientation. Like Durkheim, Sumner argued that the motives of men were, in part, inconsequential. Sociology studies what men have actually done, not what they imagined they had done. Social science, if it wanted to be successful, would have to follow the lead of natural science. In particular, "no one should undertake to study the evolution and life of human society without having first acquired for himself at least a layman's knowledge of Darwinian evolution."[60] On the other hand, social science should maintain a great distance from philosophy and metaphysics. "The aim of science can never be the proposal of *a priori* views or even the verification of them." Sumner, in the following passage, expresses his amusement at the nonsense of metaphysics and his own proclivity to identify common sense with science.

Much muddlement is due to metaphysical blurring of terms. It is contended that there is no "law" or "natural law" in society. This is because of the old metaphysical conception of law as an independent power in nature, whereas it is only a formula in human words to state and hold fast observed sequences and relations. Everyone knows what "I see a man" means, unless he has been led to fuddle his mind by asking himself: "What do you mean by I? What do you mean by see, and man, and a?" From the standpoint of science such queries are chatter, and the bedevilled worker plagued by the buzzing of it, might be excused for lashing out with the savage: "This makes our heads swim! Better to think of nothing and be at peace. Enough of this!"[61]

Social science, for Sumner, had some problems with which the natural sciences were not affected. Social phenomena were inherently more complex than natural processes, and the social world always had to be interpreted. Interpretation, in turn, was subject to numerous biases. Tradition, prejudice, fashion, habit, and other such obstacles continually interfere with the social science interpreter. In addition, it is very difficult for sociologists to rely on social experiments. Social experiments would require that some individuals would have to sacrifice their time and energy to be used as subjects, and Sumner was clearly against this. For him this meant that sociology requires a special method and that "probably no science requires such peculiar skill and sagacity in the observer and interpreter of the phenomena which are to be studied."[62] It also can be noted that the facts of social science were "more complex, shifting, and elusive" than natural phenomena. The relations in society are qualitative phenomena and cannot be expressed in simple mathematical equations. In addition to the problems of interpretation and complexity, the social sciences had to deal with an element of caprice in human affairs. "Historical causes, such as the vanity of kings, the ambition of prelates, the whims of democracies, the rivalries of statesmen, the love of women, are "accidental", inasmuch as they are not consecutive or predictable." While the prime forces of social life—hunger, love, vanity, and ghost-fear—can be conceived of as positive and definite and "perhaps even mathematical to some degree, their complexity defies analysis if that is attempted by quantitative methods."[63]

The major problem with sociology and policy formation was that no social laws had been established except in broad outline. "It must be confessed that sociology is yet in a tentative and inchoate state." And "it will be a long time before the science of society arrives at any possibility of application remotely comparable with that of the laboratory sciences." Sumner argued that, given this state of the discipline, the social scientist should be ethically neutral. And, likewise, he should stay away from policy formation.

"The thing to do is to abstain from empirical undertakings and to let the problems solve themselves under liberty." Moreover,

The essential fact of the matter, especially as respects contemporary evidence, is that what is most needed in any scientific study of society is the austerity of distance and detachment; for no man of us is capable of so insulating himself from the social currents that flow about him as not to have his immediate judgment concerning contemporary things deflected this way and that. We are all creatures of circumstance, the displays made by those who lay claim to the power of self-detachment from environment form an edifying commentary upon that truth. But judgment clears rapidly as we pass into spheres of observation which the subjective element can less readily enter. One of these spheres is the study of peoples remote in place, time, or culture. This means the study of the earlier historical and the primitve or non-historical peoples.[64]

When dealing with the past, the social scientist was less likely to pass judgment on present mores. And it certainly was not his task to evaluate such phenomena. The aim of social science was to "investigate the nature and recorded evolution of society rather than to advise forthwith as to its manipulation." Social technicians were under the illusion that they could obtain objective data to proceed in their reform schemata. But we actually had "no calculus for the variable elements which enter into social problems and no analysis which can unravel their complications."[65] Moreover, those who would make social policy always left out one important consideration—"the forgotten man." He is the man who was never taken into consideration, and yet bore the burden of decreased liberty, increased taxation, and a loss of independence. The forgotten man was described by Sumner in the following manner.

As soon as A observes something which seems to him to be wrong, from which X is suffering, A talks it over with B, and A and B then propose to get a law passed to remedy the evil and help X. Their law always proposes to determine what C shall do for X. As for A and B, who get a law to make themselves do for X what they are willing to do for him, we have nothing to say except that they might better have done it without any law, but what I want to do is to look up C. I want to show you what manner of man he is. I call him the forgotten man.

The forgotten man was the victim of social reformers and speculators. He was a simple laborer who earned his living by productive work. He worked under contractual arrangements and asked for no favors.[66] He was, in fact, the mainstay of a country's capital.

Impersonal Sociologists

There was no doubt that Sumner believed in the power of the mores to govern the life of society. The mores were the product of the totality of a society's resources, both material and intellectual. But he did analyze the role of small elites in the progress of societal evolution. In the realm of science, it was a doctrine of "first moral and sociological importance that truth, wisdom, and righteousness come only by painstaking study and striving." These things were so difficult that only a few attained them, and these few carried society, as they always had done. Ironically, even these elite groups ultimately have very little impact on the evolution of society.[67] All groups in society were caught in the vortex of the folkways and mores. Since the laws of society, which had absolute control over us, could not be revised, the inevitable consequence was to accept our situation and to learn to live happily with it.[68] "In the ordinary course of life it is best and is necessary that for most of us, and for all of us most of the time, these current rules of action which are traditional and accepted in our society should be accepted and obeyed."[69]

For Sumner, there was virtually no possibility of changing the world. Every one of us was swept up in the stream of social life. It swallowed philosophical systems, experiments, the errors and fallacies of men, without an afterthought. The only things that could divert this stream were the great discoveries and inventions, "the new reactions inside the social organism, and the changes in the earth itself on account of changes in the cosmical forces.... These causes will make of it [the world] just what, in fidelity to them, it ought to be. The men will be carried along with it and be made by it. The utmost they can do by their cleverness will be to note and record their course as they are carried along, which is what we do now, and is that which leads us to the vain fancy that we can make or guide the movement. That is why it is the greatest folly of which a man can be capable, to sit down with a slate and pencil to plan out a new social world."[70] For example, the effect of the improvement in material technology during the eighteenth century was the production of a social and economic order (i.e., industrialism) "which is automatic in the mode of its activity; which is delicate and refined in its susceptibility to the influence of interferences." This economic order was so vast and delicate that we could neither comprehend it nor master its details enough to control it. For Sumner,

Under such circumstances the conservative position in social discussion is the only sound position. We do not need to resist all change or discussion— that is not conservatism. We may, however, be sure that the only possible good for society must come of evolution not of revolution. We have a right to condemn, and to refuse our attention to flippant and ignorant criticisms or propositions of reform; we can rule out at once all plans to reconstruct society, on anybody's system, from the bottom up.[71]

For all of his discussion of past societies and ethical neutrality, Sumner still believed that modern society was superior. Its superiority lay in the contractual arrangements between men. "A society based on contract is a society of free and independent men, who form ties without favor or obligation, and cooperate without cringing or intrigue," and therefore, they are "given the utmost room and chance for individual development, and for all the self-reliance and dignity of a free man." Employers and employees made contracts based on their own self-interests, which furthered the progress of the universal law of supply and demand.[72] The liberty of labor was not a final solution; indeed, it sharpened the intensity of competition in life.[73] But competition drew out the highest achievements of man. "It makes the advantages of capital, education, talent, skills and training tell to the utmost. It draws out the social scale upwards and downwards to great extremes and produces aristocratic social organizations in spite of all dogmas of equality." For Sumner, the modern self as we understand it first obtained liberty through property. The serf's entitlement to personal property (i.e., his right to appropriate and use certain things exclusively for himself) and the state's support of that right was the beginning of civil liberty. This social movement produced "the great middle class of modern times; and the elements in it have been property, science, and liberty."[74]

Sumner also argued that the modern monogamous marriage was the best possible arrangement between men and women. Monogamy stimulates the vigor and intelligence of the race. "The family education of children is the institution by which the race as a whole advances most rapidly, from generation to generation, in the struggle with nature.... The value and importance of the family sentiments, from a social point of view, cannot be exaggerated. They impose self-control and prudence in their most important social bearings, and tend more than any other forces to hold the individual up to the virtues which make the sound man and the valuable member of society."[74]

In the final analysis, Sumner adhered to the contemporary mores of industrial capitalism on a world scale. He argued for the values of property, responsibility, and liberty. To him these terms meant the law of supply and demand without state interference. They coincided with his faith in industrial organization and capital. He was against American imperialism in Spain, Mexico, and the Philippines. Moreover, he argued for the rights of the plutocrat. If a man was willing to risk capital—which was inherently property—then he was entitled to any profits obtained. Sumner also had no faith in ameliorative plans for social reform. The fittest would survive and the rest must perish. This is the law of both nature and society. Science was useful in society insofar as it seeped into the attitudes of the educational system. Science repudiated the dogmas of socialism, metaphysics, and philosophical ethics. But the main role of science was simply understanding the past more adequately. Sumner contended that there was every justification for a science of society which would be "purely scientific; so austerely unmindful of contemporary problems as deliberately to seek distance and detachment from them."[76] The main function of science was the investigation of truth, and in that activity it was colorless and impersonal. If science was to aid us at all, that help must come through other means than social reform. Sumner argued that in the long run: "Social improvement is not to be won by direct effort. It is secondary, and results from physical or economic improvements. That is why schemes of social amelioration always have an arbitrary, sentimental, and arfiticial character, while true social advance must be a product and a growth."[77]

Sumner's conception of sociology does not fit the social-technological theme perfectly. He does view the task of sociology as the formulation of laws or lawlike generalizations. However, he indicates that we are not yet in the possession of such laws. In addition, he suggests that there are many sources of bias which must be controlled if an objective sociology is to be achieved. Because part of this lack of knowledge, he argues that sociologists should be neutral in regard to policy formation—dictum which he himself did not heed. Moreover, in Sumner's formulation, sociologists ought to study the past. Only the past can give us the detachment required for doing an objective study of society.

Summary

Sumner, of course, does not fit closely our schema for a social-technological sociology of knowledge position—although his conception of man and society could be closely equated with it. He argued that men were dependent on the social order to control their impulsive nature. Man had no natural rights and was a greedy, self-serving, and vain creature. Man always had been in this state, and only impersonal social institutions held these vices in check.

Society, for Sumner, had ethical, logical, and epistemological priority over the individual. Without society, men would not have survived. Progressive social organization had liberated man from the whimsical forces of nature. Moreover, society was a reality sui generis, having a life and development apart from the indiviudals who made it up. Society was a complex of institutions which evolved from the basic forces: hunger, sex, fear, and vanity. With the advent of industrial organization, society had become even more complex and delicate in its operation. The interpenetration of societal parts was so subtle that the malfunction of one section adversely affected the whole. Society tended toward equilibrium and it should be maintained in that state.

Somewhat like the social-technological tradition, Sumner tended to view knowledge as being generated by the societal totality in the form of the folkways and mores. Metaphysics, philosophy, ethics, and the recipe knowledge of everyday life were generated from the predominant customs. These customs evolved from the need to control nature and other men. They had proved their worth by enabling the human species to survive. The knowledge that Sumner analyzed was not considered ideological in nature. It did not express, for the most part, the domination of some men over other men. The mores were simple reflexive judgments reached about some habitual activity as to its usefulness in the maintenance of societal order. In particular, he wrote primarily about the mores of past societies. When he did analyze the present mores, it was from the point of view that men should not tamper with the delicate social mechanism.

Sumner thought social science should follow the lead of natural science. Laws of society should be formulated, even though this may take a long time. He also argued that social science meets with certain difficulties that are not manifested in the natural world. On the one hand, there is a problem of the incredible complexity of social phenomena; on the other hand, there is the problem of luck or caprice in human affairs. Given these difficulties, social scientists must work hard to formulate laws about social behavior. The purpose of social science was to aid in the development of these laws. Once the laws were discovered, men would know what they could justifiably interfere with in the social process.

The primary role of the social scientist was not criticism, since he had no place to stand from which to launch a critique, but a deeper understanding of the laws of societal evolution. In this activitiy, the social scientist belonged to a small group whose primary task was the accumulation of knowledge. His secondary purpose was to transmit this knowledge to the next generation through educational institutions. In this way the scientific attitude would eventually permeate the popular mores. Sumner, then, had faith in the development of a science of society. More particularly, he hoped that social science would affirm the values of monogamous marriage, property, and labor. Although society evolves of its own accord, the social scientist could aid in this development by dispersing the value of scientific knowledge to the future leaders of the country, who would receive this knowledge through educational institutions.

Although Sumner is not clearly committed to sociology in the short run as Comte and Durkheim were, he does believe in its efficacy over the long run. Science was simply an advanced form of the mores which could initiate people into the harsh realities of life. To some extent, Sumner might be classified as a pessimistic social-technologist rather than an optimistic one. He clearly manifests conservative tendencies, but it is not a traditional European conservatism. Moreover, there are a number of elements in Sumner's writings which do not fit our analytic framework. First, like Marx, he does emphasize the importance of material or economic conditions in shaping the ideas of men. He does not suggest, however, that class location was the basis of false consciousness or distorted thinking. For Sumner, social scientists had multiple sources of cognitive error. Sumner went on to suggest that sociologists should not espouse any kind of reform because of these biases. In this sense, then, he does not fit our notion that social-technologists should aid in the intervention of social processes. The irony of this position, however, is brought out in Sumner's own pronouncements about the existing state of affairs. He was ideologically inclined toward a kind of social Darwinism, which was itself a value-laden position.

4 / *Lester F. Ward*

(1841 - 1913)

Biography

Lester Ward was born in Joliet, Illinois, the tenth and last child of Justus and Silence Ward.[1] Justus Ward (1788-1857) was an itinerant mechanic and jack-of-all trades who had fought in the War of 1812. According to Luther Bernard, Justus was interested in the frontier industries of lumbering, canal building, and road making. The Ward family migrated continuously westward during Lester's early years. By the time Lester was seventeen, his father had died, and he and his brothers had to make their own way. We catch a glimpse of his early years in a letter he wrote to Mrs. Emily Cape: "I was hampered in youth by poverty and adversity, by the necessity of earning a living, by being born in a backward region, and having to find my way to a more enlightened one."[2]

Ward received no educational training abroad. At the age of twenty, Lester enrolled in the Susquehanna Collegiate Institute, a preparatory school, at Towanda, Pennsylvania. Although he was preparing himself for college, Ward responded to Lincoln's call for additional troops. He enlisted as a private in August 1862, and five days prior to leaving, married his childhood sweetheart, Elizabeth Vought. While Sumner was studying at Geneva, Göttingen, and Oxford, Ward served for twenty-seven months in the Union Army, and he received three wounds at Chancellorsville.[3]

Poor and depressed after the war, Ward petitioned for a clerkship in the Treasury Department. This was the beginning of nearly forty years in government service. He began his college studies at the age of twenty-six. In 1870 he acquired a B.A. from Columbian (now George Washington) University. The year 1871 brought a Bachelor of Laws degree. In 1872, he was awarded an M.A. degree, he was admitted to the bar, and he received a diploma in medicine.

While in the service of the government, Ward changed occupations quite frequently. Moreover, he seemed to master every position. Chugerman has chronicled Ward's government service in the following manner:

Original researches in botany and geology earned him repeated promotions until he became the outstanding figure in the Smithsonian Institute, in the Biological Society of Washington, and in other national scientific bodies. He was made librarian of the Bureau of Immigration and finally became chief of the Division of Navigation and Immigration. He became distinguished for botanical research both in living and fossil forms, and was given the title of Honorary Curator of Botany and Paleobotany in the National Museum in Washington. In 1881 he was appointed geologist in the United States Geological Survey, and two years later, chief palentologist.[4]

In 1906, after nearly forty years of government service, Ward went to Brown University. The Sorbonne and other great universities had offered him the same opportunity, but he had turned them down. Ward seemed to enjoy his stay at Brown University, although it was a short one. In the spring of 1913 he died at the age of seventy-two. Ward's accomplishments were many. He was a botanist, paleobotanist, and geologist in addition to being a social scientist. He mastered the standard European languages (i.e., German, French, Italian, Spanish) as well as Greek, Latin, Hebrew, and Sanskrit. It is also claimed that he could work with the Russian, Chinese, and Japanese languages. In addition to his books in sociology, he had written over 8,000 pages of articles, book reviews, and assorted polemics. Although Ward did not have an academic post until late in his life, he was involved with a major institution—the government. The pay was not outstanding, but at least permanent employment was secured. Ward was elected the first president of the American Sociological Society and served in that post for two years; he also acted as president of the International Institute of Sociology.

Ward's work is often contrasted with Sumner's. Ward was very critical of the existing order and, in particular, of religious domination. From March of 1870 until August of 1871, he edited and published the *Iconoclast*. He was anxious to free others from ecclesiastical exploitation. In addition, he was a vehement critic of social Darwinism as espoused by William Sumner. Although Ward also adhered to an evolutionary model of society, he believed there was a corresponding "development of the ability to rationally control the environment." In short, evolution "can be brought about not only through the unconscious forces of nature, but also through conscious and deliberate control by man."[5] Social evolution was thought to be essentially telic rather than genetic. Ward saw governmental planning as inevitable, but felt it should be guided by an intelligent social science.[6] He was a thoroughgoing reformist who clearly believed in conscious intervention in social processes.[7] In the next sections, we will try to determine if Ward's sociology of knowledge is more social-technological or critical in orientation.

The Pursuit of Happiness: Individual and Societal

In the preface to the second edition of *Dynamic Sociology,* Ward indicated that the first six chapters of that work were inadequate from a psychological perspective. A major part of Ward's intellectual effort indicated that the social forces were primarily individual and originated in the feelings. "The motive of all action is feeling. All great movements in history are preceded and accompanied by strong feelings...Throughout all times past, the mass of mankind has been carried along by the power of sentiment."[8] The desires and wants of men were the basic forces of any society.[9] These forces were specifically named and broken down into two categories; essential and nonessential. The essential forces were gustatory, protective, sexual, and parental-consanguineal affections. The nonessential forces were aesthetic, emotional, and intellectual.[10]

Ward's utilitarian assumptions about man inform the corpus of his works. Ward not only argues that these social forces existed and governed the action of the social world but that there was a scientific grounding for this argument. "The fundamental law of human nature, and therefore of political economy, is that all men will, under all circumstances, seek their greatest gain. All the alleged exceptions of this rule are apparent only." Underlying the desire of egoistic gain was the desire to be happy. This desire "is the fundamental stimulus which underlies all social movements." Ward contends that physiologically the human organism was so constituted that it would perform no action except from the desire for happiness.[11]

Ward was well aware that these desires for happiness were not satisfied. Indeed, he attributed many contemporary problems to the lack of fulfillment of basic human desires. It is interesting to note that Ward's social forces are generic to the human species for all times and places. He believed this generalization had been known but never systematically elaborated. Moreover, these forces had a physiological basis. At one point Ward argued that the great primordial half of the mind was affective, and it embraced all the affections. One characteristic of feeling was that of seeking an end. "That is to say, it is appetitive, and this is popularly recognized by the word *appetite*...Appetition is a motive and impels to action. It is this that constitutes it as a force. It is the sensor side of the motor fact, and the force is proportional to the intensity of the feeling."[12]   Feeling constituted the ground of existence for relatively plastic organisms. It was only by their ability to distinguish pleasure from pain that organisms had survived.[13] The evolution of what Ward called the subjective side of mind was its increasing ability not only to distinguish pleasure from pain but to create new forms of pleasure. The organism created new ways of acquiring pleasure from the environment. Since Ward made the distinction between the subjective side of mind (i.e., the physiological basis) and the objective side of it (i.e., the social forces), it is worthwhile to examine the latter side. The objective side of mind was concerned with the continuity and the perpetuation of the species and not simply with individual gratification of desire.

The nonessential forces (i.e., moral, aesthetic, intellectual), which Ward referred to as sociogenetic, "are wants seeking satisfactions through efforts, and are thus social motives or motors inspiring activities which either create social structures" or modify already existing structures. "They [sociogenetic forces] reside in the individual but become social through interaction, cooperation, and cumulative effects. They are all primarily physical or physiological, even those classed as spiritual, for the organism is the only source from which they can emanate. They all have, therefore, their physical seat in the human body..."[14] Again, we note that the sociogenetic forces were physiologically based. They operated only indirectly for the continuity and perpetuation of the species. Sex, for example, was an act of pleasure which only indirectly guaranteed the perpetuation of the species. The social forces or actions had three essential effects: to satisfy desire; to preserve or continue life; and to modify the surroundings. These forces, then, constituted the dynamics of social action. They were the basis from which civilization had developed. Moreover, the continued evolution of society was predicated on the incomplete satisfaction of these desires. There was no potential end point. All human organisms constantly exploited their environment, and consequently the demands of organisms were in excess of the environment's ability to supply. In brief, "gratification is never equal to desire. There is a permanent residuum ever striving after more complete satisfaction."[15]

Ward, to this point, does not unequivocally fit our schema for the social-technological tradition in the sociology of knowledge. His basic image of man fits our framework only in part. Rather than arguing that man is a creature of tradition, Ward suggests that there are basic social "forces" which reside in every individual—indeed, are physiologically rooted there. Moreover, these forces are the causes of institutional developments in society. "Accordingly, for Ward, any attempt to understand the fabric of society was to proceed from a prior understanding of the motive forces in man."[16] However, his image of society and of man's sociality remains to be discussed.

Man, for Ward, had not evolved from a gregarious state. As he viewed it, humans were made up of many antisocial qualities. "The social instinct must have had to battle long and hard against the momentary selfish desires of individuals." It won simply because "the desire of each to protect himself by sustaining the community gradually came to exceed the desire to gratify immediate personal wants which were incompatible with the existence of society."[17] These antisocial qualities (sentiments such as avarice, love of fame, anger) were not evil, but when uncontrolled they harmed other members of society. Society itself was a product of the forces that emananted from individuals. Ward utilized a biological analogy in describing the nature of society. "Society is simply a compound organism whose acts exhibit the resultant of all the indivicual forces which its members exert. These acts, whether individual or collective, obey fixed laws. Objectively viewed, society is a natural object, presenting a variety of complicated movements produced by a particular class of natural forces."[18]

The evolution of society had progressed through four stages. The initial, or autarchic, stage was one in which man was far removed from a social state. The second period originated when an accumulation of individuals occurred in certain localities (constrained aggregate). In this stage there were no morals or virtues, only selfish passions. Elements of government marked the third level, where leadership positions and marriages were somewhat regulated. In this third stage, "Government, so necessary for the prevention of internal war, became the cause of external war, yet the latter was undoubtedly the lesser of two evils, and will itself disappear, in turn, when all governments shall be consolidated into one. This event, if realized, will form the *fourth* stage of social progress."[19] The progress of society depended on the gradual development of institutions which regulated and satisfied the desires of men. All institutions which had developed (e.g., government, marriage, slavery) satisfied some social demand. Therefore, institutions, according to Ward, were neither good nor bad, only socially necessary.[20]

According to Ward, the work which any mechanism performed (i.e., physical, organic, or social) was its function; whatever the mechanism was intended to do was also its function. Unfortunately, Ward did not indicate how intentions were determined. He did argue that at the level of social structure, various institutions performed a variety of functions—particular work that they (institutions) were created to perform. Society itself only existed for a particular purpose—its function. Government and the state existed to curb antisocial impulses. Religion and the church functioned to protect members from the spirits of the nonmaterial realm. "Every ethnic custom before it passes into a mere 'survival' has a purpose or function and performs it. Marriage and the family have the supreme function of continuing the race. And so on, to the end of the list."[21] The institutions which had evolved were the product of the laws of natural selection or adaptation. Under this law, only those institutions were preserved which proved advantageous to the species.[22]

The protection of society by government operated with the notion that men under government would not be injured as badly by each other as they would be without government. However, "governments always institute themselves, they never wait to be instituted. They always emanate from the few seeking power, never from the many seeking protection." Ward did not believe that the current governments were dominated by any single class. The state was not just the outgrowth of a hegemonic class. Indeed, he argued that modern "governments have become so extremely sensitive to the social will that a single adverse vote will overthrow a cabinet, and...appeals are every year taken to the suffrage of the people." Although the state had not yet lived up to its potential promise, it probably was the most important institution in modern society, according to Ward.[23]

Society, however, had not evolved through the power of the state alone. Initially, it developed through conquest, struggle, caste, and inequality. "All social processes that can be called economic have their origin in exploitation." Slavery was the original stimulus to work. The only way captors could benefit from wars was to exploit the potential labor power of the captured.[24] Slaves were the first form of metasocial property. The major value of property was the incentive it furnished for accumulation. "Without accumulation property would have very little socializing influence."[25] In another context, Ward indicated "The recognition of permanent property gave to man an object to pursue, an incentive to industry beyond the mere present demands of his nature. It substituted a future for present enjoyment."[26]

As permanent property evolved, initial inequalities were perpetuated. Inequality was not something particularly reprehensible to Ward. As far as he was concerned, the agents of civilization had always been a small number of geniuses. If the elites were eliminated from every country, worldwide intellectual stagnation would have occurred. Even in a democracy the control of society was in the hands of the intelligent few.[27] Modern societies did have classes. The differences between classes was not economic, however, but was determined by the amount of knowledge and information they controlled. There was an "unequal distribution of the extant knowledge of the world."[28] The lower class was unintelligent and full of ignorance. It was intellectually inferior, not because of its economic position, but because it lacked information.

Modern societies also were characterized by open hostility between laborers and capitalists. Ironically, their dependence upon each other was absolute. Exchange was carried on by redundant third parties, who undeservedly received the greatest share of the wealth. [29] This created a huge waste of manpower. It was only through the power of the state that society was run efficiently and for the benefit of the greatest number. Increased education about the laws of social forces would precipitate correct legislation for handling the divisiveness of then modern society.

In summary of this section, Ward argued that men had certain emotional traits and a great deal of egoism which kept them from becoming purely social creatures. The social forces had their roots in the organism and were universal. The evolution of society stemmed from these social forces. Institutions developed from them and acted as a restraining force. The major problem of modern society was that it had not taken into consideration the tremendous potential telic powers of man. With his telic powers man could reorganize society along more efficient lines. Once the laws that govern society were discovered, these laws could be put into operation for the whole of society.

It can be noted here that Ward shares with Sumner the belief that there are certain universal traits in the human species. The major characteristic of both Ward and Sumner's analyses was their focus on the insatiability of human desire. Humans desired to maximize their utilities. No matter how they differed in other regards, both their views emphasize man as a consumer of utilities. Here, of course, I do not only refer to the consumption of material goods but also to the consumption of social status, power, etc. This opinion parallels, if it is not a reflection of, the development of capitalist society. Capitalism requires "an abandonment of authoritative or customary allocation of work and reward to individuals, and its replacement by freedom of the individual to use his energy, skill, and material resources, through contractual engagements, in the way that seems to him best calculated to bring him the greatest return." The market system presupposed that men will act as maximizers of utilities.[30]

Even though Ward and Sumner shared certain basic beliefs about the nature of man, however, they also diverged on some important issues. Where Sumner thought that man was controlled by the laws of nature and society and had very little chance of controlling these laws, Ward was much more optimistic. Ward not only believed that intervention was possible but that it was desirable, which is not a belief that Sumner held. Sumner's policy was 'hands-off' the social forces, but Ward claimed that this attitude was anachronistic. Interestingly enough, the divergence in their beliefs can be traced, in part, to their opposing conceptions of man and nature. Where Sumner saw hundreds of years of painful, gradual evolution, Ward discussed the inefficiency and wastefulness of nature because of its unconscious processes. For Sumner, man was a part of nature which had become conscious—although not very consscious. Ward, on the other hand, believed that the telic powers of man made a qualitative difference within nature—an evolutionary leap, so to speak. Man was, to some degree, part of nature, but also something separate from it and superior to it.

With these differences noted, attention will be devoted to how Ward examined the relationship between ideas and social structure and also to his arguments for the cognitive superiority of sociology.

The Web of Social Conditions

Ward did not argue that ideas ruled the world. He made a distinction between world ideas and the ideas of various elite groups. No idea had any effect unless it was possessed by the whole society. To better understand Ward's position on the genesis of ideas, we will examine his critique of the economic and ideological interpretations of history. From his point of view, these two positions were not irreconcilable. But, interestingly enough, he felt that only world ideas which had become beliefs could act as idea forces. In this sense, various religions were viewed as having persuasive effects. But "beliefs rest on interest." And interest was nothing but feeling. World views then grew out of feelings. These feelings were the hallmark of individual and group salvation. The belief, or idea, as an intellectual substance was not a force. The force lay in desire or feeling. According to Ward,

What we are dealing with, therefore, is those ideas, opinions, or beliefs which have been created by the economic conditions of existence, using the term "economic" in its widest sense, and which, being regarded as essential to the safety or existence of the group or of society, are entertained by all its members without any attempt to inquire into their objective truth. They become social forces by embodying the feelings that created them.... The true order of the phenomena is that the conditions arouse the feelings and the feelings create the ideas or beliefs. These last are the final form into which the whole is crystallized in the human mind, constituting the thought of the age and people in which they prevail, and in harmony with which all activity takes place.[31]

The development of the mind had gone through a long process of evolution.[32] Ward indicated this by contrasting primitive with modern thinking, religious with scientific ideas, with contrasts also between Eastern and Western thought. Mind was objectively "modified, conditioned, and, as it were, charged with all the influences of the surrounding and impinging world."[33]

No matter how primitive the social state, foresight had to be exercised. The habit of making provisions for the future had arisen. In particular, the pastoral state stimulated reverie and observation. "Many of the most beautiful products of the human imagination, as well as the most valuable facts of science, have emanated from shepherds as they have idly watched their flocks."[34] When men began to tame wild animals and enlisted the service of these animals in various ways, a new set of faculties had emerged. Like Sumner, Ward argued that: "A larger degree of foresight was required. The successful efforts very early made to improve the breeds of animals required considerable reflection, although a large part of the progress made was doubtless due to accident."[35]

Ward also believed that the moral codes of all peoples and nations, "with the whole mass of rules, precepts, and customs that attend it, constitutes a derivative and factitious institution, growing primarily out of the blood bond." Although morality in its primitive state was coordinated with religion and law, this did not mean that primitive morality was altruistic. The same parental instinct that exists in animals was the basis of attachment by kinship in the human species. Later in evolution, as kinship attachments formed into groups, "the attachment became coextensive with the group, but did not extend to other groups." Even later, when "primitive hordes combined to form clans" there was always attachment, but primarily through a "blood bond, and the sole basis of adhesion was that of real or fictitious kinship."[36] Morality, however, did not develop from blood bonds alone.

Religion played a great part in the evolution of thought. Religion had a long genesis, which started with anthropomorphism. The "only being the primitive man knows to possess the power of spontaneous activity is himself, and he naturally imputes to every other change the same power." Much like Comte, Ward went on to suggest that in the next stage the intelligence or will of man are ascribed to spiritual beings—this is the reign of polytheism. After some time, the numerous spirits are reduced to one, and monotheism holds sway. During the reign of monotheism, speculation is encouraged and matter is broken up into discrete categories. At this stage ontology and metaphysics dominate human thought: "The faith in such entities is not reverential, and the bolder spirits soon question them and dare to institute investigation. The result is always the same; and the true order of nature is brought to light."[37]

Furthermore, "opinions are the results of circumstances, and are to be regarded as among the modes of existence which follow fixed and definite antecedents, and depend wholly upon them." Nobody changed their opinion simply because they desired to do so. It also was not possible for a person to change another person's opinion. The true origin of opinion was in sensation. The mind was made up of an objective and a subjective component. The latter was conscious experience or feeling. The concomitant of this side of the mind was desire, emotion, and will. The other side of sensation was perception. It cognized "the object itself, its qualities and character." When there were a number of sensations which appeared alike, we induced that the same quality produced them. This was what perception was about.

Perceptions form the basis of mental judgments, and these constitute ideas and opinions. Hence the primary cause of every opinion is the experience of the senses. That experience consists of the circumstances by which the individual is surrounded, and which are incessantly appealing to his senses, giving him new perceptions.... Circumstances are therefore as much the cause of opinion as they are of mountains, rivers, or storms, and the opinions obey laws as definite and necessary as those which such physical objects obey.[38]

The source of most of our opinions emerged from language. "It is on the wings of sound and through the medium of speech that come the first ideas of everyone's existence." Thousands of such thoughts and ideas were poured in, until the mind was crammed. The mind was so constituted that it would accept everything without discriminating between truth or falsity. If nothing contradictory was said about an opinion or idea, it would be accepted. "But the mind seldom makes an effort of its own to see whether there exists any such offset, either intrinsic or extrinsic."[39]

Ideas and opinions also were influenced by subjective phenomena (e.g., physical health, nerves and senses, sex, nationality). Ward did not mean to argue here that some men were incapable of handling ideas, but only that the above-mentioned phenomena may have created in them a certain incapacity for handling ideas. One of the greatest blocks to mankind's intellectual development had been the struggle for existence. As long as man was compelled to work from morning until evening just for subsistence, there was no time "to read, study, and investigate, whereby alone his mind can be awakened." As an example, Ward compared the European with the Shilook in the following manner. The European had the written history of his race and other races for thousands of years. He had intercourse with the worlds of science, art, and literature. He lived in a world surrounded by libraries, newspapers, and magazines. "The Shilook, on the contrary, is confined to the savage wilds of interior Africa. His language is barely capable of expressing the coarsest desires; literature is unknown, as is all symbolic communication. His history is confined to his tribe, and is a mere tradition, enlarging and evaporating into a myth as it recedes into the past. He has no art, not even that of furnishing clothing for his body...."[40]

From another angle, Ward argued that there were differences between men's and women's thinking. In the main, women did not possess the abstract reasoning powers that men had acquired.[41] Applying Lamarckian biology, Ward reasoned that women's brains were smaller than men's because they had not been used. The brain could only develop by use. "The causal faculty of woman has had no exercise, therefore it has not developed." Thinking then is dependent, in part, on the social circumstances. As Ward viewed it, "where the only objects with which women come in contact are those of the kitchen, the nursery, the drawing-room, and the wardrobe, how shall she be expected to have broad ideas of life, the world, and the universe?" Only by broadening the base of women's education could their ideas be changed.[42] It is circumstances which created the size of the brain and influence its ability to handle abstract discussions. We have come full circle now with Ward's thinking about the evolution of ideas, as I will try to indicate in the next three paragraphs.

Following an evolutionary naturalist line, Ward argued that the foundations of knowledge are in the individual (i.e., without the ability to hear symbols, ideas could not have been communicated). The individual organism's ability to perceive similarities developed judgment. Judgment about some phenomena was the beginning of intellect (e.g., an evaluation of some object's utility or nonutility). With language, the capability of naming similar things (nouns) and the power of intercommunication enhanced the survival capabilities of various groups. This survival was not stimulated only by the battle against nature. We can imagine that intercommunication was greatly facilitated by the ability to destroy an enemy, thus reinforcing the value of communication.

The development of religion and its concomitant world views aided the survival of the race. According to Ward, the great religions all had a rational component. They indicated how men should relate to the world and to each other. The only serious problem with religion was that it sought causes in a transcendental sphere. Causes, however, are intramundance. They belong to the natural world. Laws ruled not only the stars but the behavior of men.

As man's ability to communicate developed through oral language, written symbols, the alphabet, printing press, etc., his ideas about himself did not keep pace. Only with the emergence of science did we acquire a proper foundation for the understanding and explanation of both the natural and the social world. Ideas were mediated by the individual organism's contact with his surroundings. The greater the contact (in quantity and quality) the greater would be his or her intellectual development. This development would be passed genetically to the next generation. Hopefully, the next generation would also strive to make social conditions more favorable to the acquirement and dissemination of scientific knowledge.

Ward did not argue that a set of particular ideas was generated by class interests. And he used the term *circumstances* so broadly that the only safe way of understanding it is to equate the term with both the biological-psychological and the social climate.

The Biological and Cultural Basis of World Views

Ward scrutinized all knowledge from the perspective of contemporary science. He analyzed religious systems, primitive thinking, national minds, etc., from his conception of the ideal of science. Therefore, an understanding of Ward's critique of other ideas presupposes some familiarity with his view of science.

Applying a Kantian distinction, Ward argued that nothing in concrete science could be verified a priori. "The practical truths of the universe are established *a posteriori*—by massing the evidence." Truth could be verified in one of two ways: (1) by the senses; (2) through reason. In addition, truth must be verified intersubjectively. Verification by more than one person was necessary.[43] "A true science is a field of phenomena occurring in regular order as the effects of natural or efficient causes, such that a knowledge of the causes renders it possible to predict the effects. The causes are always natural forces that obey Newtonian laws of motion. The order in which the phenomena occur constitutes the laws that govern the science."[44] The invariability of nature's law constituted the ground from which all action, ideas, and art were evaluated. Laws were derived inductively from sense experience, because sense experience was the supplier of all knowledge. If man could gain knowledge of the laws that govern human society, then he would be in a position to alter that society. Ward believed that much of this knowledge was already available. Man must gain control of not only natural forces but societal forces. There was no doubt that society could be run more effectively and efficiently through social telesis.

From this position Ward measured the utility of other modes of thought. Two world views with which he was preoccupied were optimism and pessimism. Optimism had as its root idea that man was a favorite of nature. "Writers of a teleological bias are continually advancing what they regard as proofs of intelligent design and benevolent provision in behalf of sentient beings, especially man."[45] Optimism went against the hard facts of existence. Man was not given any special status in nature. His development had been the product of evolution which was neither good nor bad, but only necessary. Optimism led to individual and collective stagnation. We should not reason optimistically, because it would stifle our connection with the natural world. Unless we correctly understood this connection, man was capable of the most horrid acts in the name of higher humanity. Optimism emerged from the feelings, while pessimism "is exclusively a product of reason and resides in the intellect." Pessimism saw the facts and strangled every dream. Pessimism, however, was also false. First, many hopes were realized. Second, anticipating good in the future was beneficial for present actions. Pessimism stifled action and was the governing force of resignation. There was, however, a correct relationship between man and the universe which was not a belief, but a recognition of truth. According to Ward, nature was not friendly or hostile to man. Nature qua nature had no moral attributes. The attribution of moral qualities to nature was anthropomorphism and a form of specious reasoning. Nature simply was the domain of rigid laws. Since man is a product of nature, he also is mutatis mutandis a product of the laws. However, "just because nature is a domain of rigid laws, and just because man can comprehend that law, his destiny is in his own hands. Any law that he can comprehend he can control."[46] The philosophy that stood against pessimism was not optimism but *meliorism.* Meliorism was "scientific utilitarianism inspired by faith in the law of causation and the efficacy of well-directed action."[47]

The present world was governed by a multitude of errors which scientific thinking could set straight. Error was not something confined to the masses of people. Many great men also had held incorrect beliefs. Aristotle thought the brain was bloodless and without sensation. "Kant, while forced to admit determinism in history and in society at large, taught free will to the individual." Error consisted in a "false interpretation of phenomena due to insufficient knowledge." Some errors were self-mutilation, superstition, asceticism, zoolatry, witchcraft, and persecution. These errors belonged to man's primitive stage. Primitive man falsely interpreted natural phenomena. "Thus shadows and reflections were found to be due to the nature of light and the laws of radiation after the science of optics had been founded; echoes were explained on the now familiar principles of acoustics; dreams, delirium, insanity, epilepsy, trance, and even death are explainable on natural principles contained in the sciences of psychology, physiology, pathology, and psychiatry..."[48]

Ward also examined other cultures for their progress, or lack of it, toward scientific reasoning. For example, the Asiatics were said to be extremely imaginative. This "consists not only in a great facility for creating unreal and fantastic mental images, but in actually receiving the same as true and possible." In the East, only societies which were deprived of a proper understanding of nature could develop a quietistic philosophy (denial of the will). The irony is that if denial of the will was in practice believed, it would terminate the development of any race. It only was because of the failure to enforce such a belief system that the Orient has survived. Moreover, the ease with which European "nations can seize, hold, and govern India, Cochin China, and parts of China, attests the superior social efficiency of optimistic over pessimistic races."[49] Eastern religion and Western religion were pessimistic and optimistic respectively. Both were ignorant of the laws of nature. The Eastern peoples sought to escape the evils of life in Nirvana, which was a negative state. Christians and Mohammedans cherished the doctrine of immortality. This doctrine was a hopeful one, and positive in what it promised. "With their belief in an ultimate righteous retribution they were able to bear their temporal ills with fortitude and to enjoy whatever good this world had in store for them."[50]

Western civilization still had to fight the effect of religious explanation. Religious explanation was supernatural (transcendental), while scientific explanation was natural. The mark of intellectual progress was the movement from the former to the latter. "The weapons of religion have been coercion and exhortation; those of science have been skill and strategy." In the initial groping of the human mind, each of these two explanations sought domination over the other. One tried to show that phenomena were governed by invariable laws. The other was more interested in occult phenomena, which supposedly were produced by the voluntary action of spiritual beings. The superstructure built upon the former explanation was science and inventive art, and on the latter the religious edifice.

The "conflict", however, arose from the simple and necessary circumstance that, with the advancement of intelligence brought about through the operation of the first method, the deeper and more obscure phenomena already claimed by religion were one after another recognized as coming within the domination of fixed laws and claimed also by science. Religion had nothing to gain and everything to lose; and it has, in fact, been constantly losing from the first, and must continue to lose to the last. It has thus been a true 'warfare of science', science having all along been on the offensive.[51]

Ward also criticized political philosophy in its laissez-faire and socialistic forms, but before examining these criticisms, I want to suggest that he scrutinized national and sex-typed minds as well. The feminine mind, according to Ward, was always on the defensive. Since she must protect the future of the race, she had developed a conservative mental inclination. Women would never take any risks. The female mind possessed caution as a part of its constitution. "This mental constitution of the female mind manifests itself in all the affairs of life. Its central characteristic is extreme *conservatism*. All innovation is looked upon as likely to be attended with danger. Life is possible under existing conditions, and although it may scarcely be worth its cost it is better than to risk a change." Although women participated in many reform movements, it was done from self-interest. Unlike men, she never participated in anything that was held to be good in itself. She simply favored those reforms which would make for personal safety. "Women's reforms are simply crusades against real or supposed evils that threaten the safety of themselves and their children."[52] Like Giddings and Ross, Ward examined national minds. For example, in discussing Comte, Ward parenthetically began a discussion of the French mind at its best. The French mind was not light and trivial; Lamarck, for example, broke open the way to a new biology. Political economy originated with the physiocrats. Comte laid the foundation for a scientific ethics, and no other fiction writer has approached Victor Hugo in moral power. "The French mind penetrates to the very heart of every problem it attacks and is not deterred by practical obstacles. It has thus been the great organizer of human thought, leaving the details and frictional hinderances to the German and English schools. France has furnished the warp of science and philosophy, other nations their woof."[53]

Ward also contrasted various political philosophies with his idea of meliorism. Socialism desired to bring about reform in human institutions rather abruptly. It was hard to reform social structures, on account of their stability. The point was that socialism was, strictly speaking, politics—an art possibly, not a science. Anarchism and socialism were political programs. "They are not scientific theories of principles and do not belong to social science." Applied sociology, on the other hand was a science, not an art. Applied sociology could only promote certain general principles "as guides to social and political action. However, even in this aspect, it had to be extremely cautious. The principles of action would be, by their very nature, abstract generalizations. Applied science can have only the most general bearing on current events and the popular or burning questions of the hour."[54] While socialism recognized the problem of unequal distribution of wealth, its solution was not the correct one. Individualism, on the other hand, did not know how to diagnose the contemporary ills of modern society. Their argument of noninterference was rooted in observations of nature which were incorrect. Nature was not very efficient and made a great many errors. The most inefficient ways to run an economy was to let it run itself.[55] We will return to some of Ward's criticisms of individualism and socialism in the final section of this chapter.

In summary, Ward analyzed what he imagined to be major civilizational ideas. These ideas could be classified as cosmological, biological, anthropological, sociological.[56] From the perspective of modern science, many countries, religions, philosophers, and masses of people held the wrong beliefs. Modern science indicated what everyone should believe. Ward did not argue that these beliefs were the false consciousness of a particular class of people under capitalism. Like Comte, Ward viewed the evolution of ideas as cumulatively progressive. This did not mean that progress was linear, with no setbacks. For Ward, the possibilities of class revolution based on the fetishism of commodities was a slim, if not nonexistent, possibility. The correct road to social reform was through scientific education toward a sociocracy. This theme will be developed in the next section.

Sociology: In Between Socialism and Utilitarianism

"Science," according to Ward, "may be defined as an *explanation* of the phenomena of the universe as presented to the senses."

The mark of real science was its pure and applied stages. The goal of pure science was prediction. The object of applied science was application.

> That science [Sociology] should also be studied first for the sake of information relating to the laws of human association and cooperative action, and finally for the purpose of determining in what ways and to what extent social phenomena may, with a knowledge of their laws, be modified and directed toward social ideals.... The supreme purpose is the betterment of society. The knowledge is the important thing. The action will then take care of itself.[57]

Science relied on the facts of sense experience. The facts inductively led toward general laws. General regularities were synthesized into a body of laws. The goal of sociology was to reach a stage where the laws could be mathematically formulated.

All phenomena followed invariable laws whose "manifestations are numerous and manifold." Knowledge was scientific when the uniform principle was discovered which explained all the manifestations. "This principle is the law," and "Every true science must be a domain of force;...each science must preside over some one of these various forces, and...any field of knowledge which has not been brought under the operation of some natural force is not yet a science in the proper sense of that word. The mere accumulation of facts does not constitute a science, but a successful classification of the facts recognizes the law underlying them and is, in so far, scientific." Ward believed that sociology was a science, because it had discovered the major forces that ruled society (mentioned in the first section of this chapter). Remember, the important point here was that the major social force underlying all social action was feeling. Feeling was the mainspring of human action. Only insofar as this point was understood could applied sociology perform its task. "It is the regularity of the laws of human action that furnishes the hope of sociology."[58]

Sociology existed for the express purpose of eliminating suffering: "The real object of science is to benefit man." In particular, the discovery of social laws would enable man to control the laws and forces which sociology explained and bring them into harmony with man's desires. According to Ward, nature was extremely inefficient. Nature was a bad example to follow, and not only in political economy. The level of adaptation that nature provided was so inefficient that for everyone of a given species that survived, from ten to ten million were destroyed. Man through his telic powers could increase not only the survival rate but satisfaction of the pleasure principle as well. Indeed, that was the aim of sociology. We know that the human organism is constituted so that it will perform no action except from the desire for happiness. However, it also is the case that many actions miss their mark because of inadequate correspondence between the organism and its environment. The purpose of dynamic sociology, then, is to establish "the laws of correspondence, if possible, to devise means whereby a larger proportion of those actions may succeed in securing the object at which they aim."[59]

Artificial social control (meliorism) for the masses had nothing to do with ethics. The a priori deduction of what men ought to do did not conform to good science. Happiness, for men, was contentment, freedom from pain, and the appropriate means of satisfying desire.[60] The study of ethics would not tell us how to acquire happiness. Men should be taught to act in their own best interests. The only thing that made an action right or wrong was the kind of effect it had for the greatest good in general. "The proper way to induce men to desist from unjust action is to make it for their own interest to do so, and teach them in an unmistakable manner that it is so." If we wanted to prevent certain actions, we had to show the performer that more pain and less pleasure would be the consequences of his actions. Utilitarian philosophy, when consistently held, rejects all moral philosophies and the idea of moral responsibility. It simply argues that the circumstances which surround human actions are the causes of such actions. If a so-called wrong has been done, "there must have been a cause in the nature of things." If the actions of men are to be changed, then circumstances must be altered. Since all causes "consist of real and tangible circumstances, they can in most cases be reproduced or prevented in future according as they produce beneficial or injurious results."[61]

All the prevailing theories of human rights were incorrect. They were ideal conceptions which never had been or could be realized. All things were ruled by force. In the human realm, social forces were the rulers. Natural selection had guided man and developed his intellect, but now it was time for him to take control of his own development. Science taught humans that all actions emerged from the side of feeling. The social agitator who wanted to make things better was an idealist or an artist. He did not understand the forces that moved society.[62] The scientific control of social forces was called sociocracy. Sociocracy was distinct from the prevailing philosophies of both socialism and individualism. In a long passage worth quoting in full, Ward wrote:

1. Individualism has created artificial inequalities.

2. Socialism seeks to create artificial equalities.

3. Sociocracy recognizes natural inequalities and aims to abolish artificial inequalities.

4. Individualism confers benefits on those only who have the ability to obtain them, by superior power, cunning, intelligence, or the accident of position.

5. Socialism would confer the same benefits on all alike, and aims to secure the equality of fruition.

6. Sociocracy would confer benefits in strict proportion to merit, but insists upon *equality of opportunity* as the only means of determining the degree of merit.

A cycle is thus completed. Sociocracy is a return to nature from which society has departed. Individiualism was the original and natural method recognizing natural inequalities and apportioning benefits according to natural ability. Individual telesis has completely abolished this method. Socialism recognizes this, and would remedy it by an equally wide departure from the natural. Collective telesis can alone remove the artificial barriers raised by individual telesis and place society once more in the free current of natural law.[63]

Sociologists: Practical Planners

The sociologist was not a reformer, according to Ward. The sociologist did not advocate a particular course of social action. He could point out "what the effect of a certain course of action would be as deduced from the fundamental principles of science, and to state what he conceives the tendencies to be as judged from the history of development." The sociologist must act as an expert in social affairs. He demanded that "every question capable of definitive settlement be put out of the public arena." Conflict about anything that everybody knows must cease. "A true sociologist will scarcely have an opinion on a current question."[64] For Ward, the true scientist would have no particular interest in current social events. Where others read newspapers and other popular literature, the scientist concerns himself with "pronounced, abstruse and incomprehensible" works. Current events are only important insofar as they provide evidence for the laws of social phenomena. The scientist ostensibly has no declared principles, and when consulted for an opinion he will only give one based on the evidence that is available. This scientist does not confuse what the social world is with what it ought to be. Moreover, the results of scientific investigation are given to the world freely. This type of man stands above the mundane confusions of the everyday world. His knowledge of the social forces prevented him from being stampeded with the uneducated masses. A "small class of advanced minds simply look on and smile at the mad surge of bitter polemic that engrosses the great mass." It was this class of men that had contributed greatly to the progress of the species. In particular, the mechanical inventors, scientific discoverers, and philosophic thinkers were singled out for special recognition.[65]

Since science must be the brain and legislative force of society, scientists should aid in formulating scientific legislation. Specifically,

Legislation will consist in a series of exhaustive experiments on the part of scientific sociologists and sociological inventors working on the problems of social physics from the practical point of view. It will undertake to solve not only questions of general interest to the state,—the maintenance of revenues without compulsion and without friction and peaceful conduct of all the operations of a nation,—but questions of social improvement, the amelioration of the condition of all the people...in short, the organization of human happiness.[66]

Sociocracy would lead to the view that party politics were children's games. Once we rid ourselves of "this puerile gaming spirit and have attention drawn to the real interests of society then it will be seen that upon nearly all important questions all parties and all citizens are agreed." It did not matter what party or government was in office. They all had to deal with the direction and control of social forces. The same principles that individuals applied to natural forces should also be applied to the social realm. The social forces did conform to Newtonian laws.[67]

Since the most fundamental social force was the desire for happiness, all legislation had to be drawn with this interest in mind. The sociologist could inform the politician of the true forces in society. In particular, according to Ward, a number of specific proposals could be made. The first considerations for reform were (1) increasing productivity; (2) providing the means available to raise a family; (3) freedom from fear; (4) increasing possibilities for education; (5) mobility.[68] The first element, however, of a truly progressive system was scientific education.[69] Since democratic countries were supposed to be representative, the only way "to increase their intellectual status" is "by increasing that of constituencies."[70] Every individual should be put in possession of all abstract generalized knowledge. The dispensing of scientific information was absolutely necessary for progress. "The equalization of opportunity means the equalization of intelligence, and not until this is attained is there any virtue or any hope in schemes for the equalization of the material resources of society."[71]

The inequality that exists in society was due to the inequality of intelligence or the unequal distribution of already existing knowledge.[72] The social scientist could help alleviate this condition in a number of ways. He could discover the fundamental laws that governed society. He could show that it was opportunity and social conditions that created social inequality. And finally, he could show broadly what reforms were possible and desirable. He may do all this from an ethically neutral standpoint. Finally, as an expert, he could consult with governmental agencies and indicate what needed to be done.

Again, it can be noted that certain elements of Ward's thinking do not fit our paradigm of the social-technological tradition. There is very little doubt that he wanted to establish the existence of social laws. Indeed, he suggested that such laws already existed. In addition, he believed that the role of the social scientist was to act as an expert in public affairs, and that ultimately conventional politics would be eliminated by a "science of politics." Again like Sumner, however, Ward does not conform to that tradition in one important aspect. Ward was not simply a "positive" thinker. He was a critic of the existing order, although, like Sumner, his criticism was not from a Marxian-like perspective. Unlike Sumner, Ward argued that present inequalities were due to deficiencies in knowledge distribution. Therefore, a change in the material-economic conditions would not alleviate contemporary problems.

Summary

Ward's writings, in part, represent the socio-technological paradigm in the sociology of knowledge. Ward argued that all human action came from the side of the mind of feeling. The desire for happiness was rooted in the human organism. This desire had manifested itself in a number of institutions and was endemic to the human condition. Many contemporary problems were the result of misunderstanding the basic social forces. In Ward's analysis, inequality and hierarchy were the result of unequal knowledge, not simply a function of economic distribution.

For Ward, society existed to satisfy the desires of men. Men depended on the social order to guide and control their feelings. Society had an autonomous order of its own. It followed the laws of psychic evolution. Radical change was not desirable, since it would upset many traditional institutions. Only when the laws of social science were correctly understood could the correct legislative policies be instituted.

In the social-technological tradition, Ward indicated that past social theorists had not correctly understood the laws of society. The individualist and socialist positions were both incorrect. The social bases of knowledge were not located in homogeneous class-bound interests. The influences were multiple, although the major influence had been religious. Religion had been not only an agent of social control but the major intellectual force for interpreting both man and nature.

Ward stressed the importance of analyzing world views. These views were mainly generated by religious agencies. He also criticized the errors of common/sense thinking. In Ward's view all modes of thought had to be analyzed from the perspective of science as he understood it. Ward's polemics were mainly directed against traditional religion. From the scientific view these theories were simply a priori nonsense or ad hoc rationalizations with no empirical support. In addition, both socialism and invidiualism misunderstood the true nature of the social forces.

Although Ward made a distinction between psychic and physical phenomena, the former were also amenable to scientific study. Psychic phenomena could be explained through general laws. Indeed, only in the formulation of general laws did man have a chance for future happiness. The social scientists could help mankind by: (1) formulating general laws; and (2) acting as advisors to proper governmental authorities. The intellectuals could act in a general advisory capacity. They could not propose specific solutions, but could only indicate in general outline what the possible outcomes of a specific policy might be.

A scientific sociology applied to politics would eliminate the need for archaic party politics. If massive scientific education for the masses were instituted, the United States could come closer to its espoused democratic values. Scientific sociology would indicate how it was possible to legislate for the general happiness of humankind.

Further, we may note that Ward was in partial disagreement with Sumner. For Ward, social science was for some practical purpose; it was not just an academic exercise. He firmly believed that sociology could help bring about human happiness. Ward did not pay attention to the material-economic conditions, because he believed the solution to social problems was in the cultural sphere. If, and only if, people were educated in scientific reasoning, a better world could be brought about. It was not capitalism as such that Ward criticized, but *certain* belief systems that were attached to it. Where Sumner argued that material conditions determined the existing state of ideas, Ward stated the reverse. According to Page, Ward "was convinced that ideas are potent forces in social change, and that if proper ideologies can be diffused, the solution for economic and political problems will follow automatically."[73]

5 / *Franklin H. Giddings*

(1855 - 1931)

Biography

Franklin Henry Giddings was born in Sherman, Connecticut.[1] Giddings, like Small, emerged from a thoroughly New England and religious background. Both sides of his family were New England Puritans of the strictest type. His parents, Edward Jonathan and Rebecca Jane Fuller Giddings, were descendants of George Giddings, who had emigrated from St. Albans, England, in 1635 and had settled in Massachusetts. Franklin Giddings' father (1832-94) was a prominent congregational clergyman of Massachusetts and the author of *American Christian Rulers.* Furthermore, he was a "Congregational minister of evangelical and orthodox tendencies who threw around his children a strict Puritan atmosphere."[2] Many long and tedious hours were devoted to religious rituals in the Giddings household.

The young Giddings apparently did not care for religious instruction and found other outlets for his energy. He spent a lot of time with his two grandfathers. On the one side he was taught surveying and mechanical drawing and received instruction in the rudiments of farm work and management. From his other grandfather he learned the art of tanning and spent much of his time puttering around the workshop. Franklin apparently enjoyed outdoor sports, and on occasion he would get up at 4 A.M. to skate before school started. While he spent time on his grandfathers' farms, he also was plodding his way through high school. And, Giddings did not find much of value in his high school education. A local teacher, Henry

H. Scott, did introduce the young Giddings to the writings of Spencer, Huxley, and Darwin, however.

By the time Giddings entered Union College (1873), he already was acquainted with the writings of the above men as well as those of John Tyndall. When he entered college in Schenectady, New York, he was prepared to study civil engineering. Once again, however, he did not find any inspiring leadership and left after two years of study. He became associate editor of the *Winston Conn. Herald* in 1875 and taught school in Massachusetts and Connecticut. In 1877 he received his A.B. degree from Union College. This would be the last formal academic degree he would receive, although he was awarded other, honorary degrees (i.e., Ph.D. and Litt.D. from Union; LL.D. from the Universities of North Carolina and from Iowa and Columbia Universities). From 1878 to 1885 he was editor of the *Berkshire Courier* (Great Barrington, Mass.) *New Milford Conn. Gazette* and a literary critic for the *Springfield (Mass.) Union.* During these years he was associated for the most part with the *Springfield Republican* and the *Springfield Union* newspapers. In 1885 Giddings worked with the Massachusetts Bureau of Labor Statistics under the directorship of Carroll D. Wright.[3] During this time Giddings also wrote articles for both academic and non-academic periodicals (e.g., *Political Science Quarterly* and the *Massachusetts Bureau of Labor Statistics.*)

These articles attracted the attention of men in the university world. Consequently, when Woodrow Wilson (associate Professor of history and political science) went to Wesleyan University from Bryn Mawr in 1888, Giddings was invited to Bryn Mawr as a lecturer on politics. At Bryn Mawr he was promoted rapidly, and by 1892, he was a full professor. During his stay at Bryn Mawr, Giddings taught courses in development of political institutions, political economy, methods and principles of charity and correction, and methods and principles of administration. In 1890, he began offering a graduate seminar on modern theories of sociology. During his last two years at Bryn Mawr (1892-94) Giddings also gave lectures on Friday afternoons at Columbia University. These lectures were given in the absence of Professor Mayo-Smith, who was on leave. Eventually, Giddings was appointed to the first full professorship of sociology at Columbia University in 1894. The separate chair of sociology at Columbia was established, in part, through the liberality of University President Seth Low, who liked Mayo-Smith's plan for uniting theory with social reform.

Thereafter not only was historical and theoretical instruction in social science greatly extended but a statistical laboratory was established and "field work" was undertaken in cooperation with philanthropic institutions of the City of New York.

Moreover Professor Giddings on coming from Bryn Mawr found that one of the expectations connected with the chair of Sociology was that the occupant should serve on the Council of the University Settlement and the Charity Organization Society. For many years, therefore, after coming to Columbia, Professor Giddings was one of the directing minds guiding the policies of these institutions.[4]

For the rest of his life Giddings remained at Columbia University. In 1906 he was appointed to the special chair of Carpentier Professor of Sociology and the History of Civilization. He reached emeritus status in 1928. During his academic years Giddings was also involved in many other activities. For more than twenty years he was a member of the editorial staff of the *New York Independent* newspaper. He served as a trustee of his alma mater and of the Albany Medical College. He was one of the founders of the American Academy of Political and Social Science and for three years edited the publications of the American Economic Association. He served as a fellow of the American Statistical Association and the American Association for the Advancement of Science. He produced more than fifty Ph.D. graduates and was president of the Institut Internationale de Sociologie. In addition, he served as president of the American Sociological Society for two years (1910-11). Giddings's importance and his intellectual distinction from Ward and Sumner is developed in the following passage by Luther Bernard:

Since the cessation of the labors of Ward and Sumner, Giddings has been the acknowledged protagonist of Sociology in America. As the third President of the American Sociological Society, he followed these two men in that office but he can hardly be called a follower of them in any other respect. Certainly in the working out of his sociological theories, though undoubtedly affected somewhat by perusal of their writings just as he was by wide reading in the works of other contemporaries in almost every field of knowledge, Giddings has shown very little evidence of direct influence by these two men—except possibly their ideas tended to arouse critical reactions.... Giddings, like Spencer, has always realized the fact that society as well as the individual is a product of evolution, subject to the vicissitudes of an inexorable objective process within the limits of which, however, psychic phenomena function but cannot play a final determinative part.[5]

Giddings also was concerned with the relationship between ideas and social structure, and his analysis of this relationship does differ from those of Sumner and Ward. For the most part, however, his writings fit our conception of the social-technological tradition in the sociology of knowledge.

The Emotional Basis of Man and Society

Giddings argued that man's nature was essentially social. Man was neither a Hobbesian nor a Rousseau-like creature. Every man carried within himself both conservative and progressive tendencies.[6] The element that came to predominate in individuals depended upon the demands of society at a particular time. If there was a fundamental drive which moved a race, nation, or individual, it was not something superrational but was instead subrational or protorational. "It is deeper and more elemental than reason. It is the will to *carry on* sustained by faith in the possibilities of life." He argued that physical appetites or drives were controlled, modified, and brought to higher levels of rational social organization. Humans did have primary desires, such as the sexual impulse, but these instincts were controlled and modified by the social situation.[7] However, "all the conscious activities of mankind spring from certain internal motives, such as passions, appetites, desires of various kinds, and ideas." There were four fundamental motives: appreciation, utilization, characterization, and socialization. Appreciation was founded on the simple pleasures of sensation (i.e., the sensory organs), and utilization was a form of appetite. "The craving for food is the primary cause of most of the first efforts put forth by any living creature." These same efforts later appeared in the search for shelter, clothing, and articles of convenience or adornment. Characterization was the desire of the entire self for total integration. "It is a desire for completeness and expansion of life, a protest against any incompleteness, failure, discouragement, lack of resolution, or breadth of view." The motive of socialization initially emerged from "the pleasureableness of acquaintance companionship, and sympathy." Later, coooperation was found to serve useful social ends.[8]

On one level Giddings argued that it was difficult to know all the peculiarities of human behavior. Emotions throughout the history of man had played a large part in social development. Some of these emotions were fear, dread, anger, and hatred of evil and of obnoxious persons, envy, and jealousy. For a society to operate effectively, these emotions had to be brought under control. For example, Giddings wrote: "What is it that we have to control: fear, anger, hate, envy, jealousy, obsession of superiority, obsession of inferiority? I could offer a much longer list, but I picked these out because they are, from the standpoint of the student of society, the impulses, the emotions, that absolutely must be brought under control if society is to maintain its integrity and do its work properly."[9]

Giddings held that, in the final analysis, men were susceptible to such emotions, but that the primary fact of human nature was its malleability and sociability. Human nature, in essence, only developed through the use of language and social cooperation, and "its primary factor is a consciousness of kind that is more profound, more inclusive, more discriminating, more varied in its coloring, than any consciousness of kind that is found among the lower animals." The secondary factor of human nature is its "volume of desire," which is modifiable beyond that of any other species.[10] Consciousness of kind was "that pleasurable state of mind which included organic sympathy, the perception of resemblance, conscious or reflective sympathy, affection, and the desire for recognition." In self-consciousness, four processes were active: (1) each individual makes his neighbor's feeling or judgment an object of thought, (2) in the same instant the individual makes his own thought an object, (3) he judges that both are identical, (4) he then acts in total consciousness that others have come to like conclusions and will act in similar ways.[11] Consciousness of kind was the basis for the evolution of society.

Giddings distinguished four evolutionary stages: (1) zoogenic, (2) anthropogenic, (3) ethnogenic, and (4) demogenic.[12] Zoogenic society was composed of both large and small aggregations. It was not completely separable from animal life. Its main characteristic was sociality or working together instinctually. Anthropogenic association created the conventional use of signs in communication and ceremonies. It was in this stage that the evolution of speech made possible human nature, "whose chief characteristics are the developed consciousness of kind, intellectual curiosity, and expensive desire." The ethnogenic stage had highly evolved forms of habits, usages, and property. Its social composition was made up of clans, hordes, families (e.g., metronymic or patronymic), or tribes. Demogenic association was the final stage, in which "there was an evolution of institutionality and ideality." This civil society also had three further stages of development, which were organized in exactly the reverse order of anthropogenic association. These stages were: (1) establishment of political unity, military organization, and security; (2) development of legal organizations, organized criticism, personal freedom, development and diffusion of a social constitution; (3) economic and ethical regulations (e.g., popular education, realizing the life possibilities of the masses).[13] These stages of social development represented different emotional and intellectual attitudes. The lower the stage of evolution, the more its members were susceptible to emotional forces.

As a creature of superstition, of ignorance, and of fear, man is almost wholly a creature of emotion; rational deliberation plays but a little part in his conduct. Consequently, populations in which there is no systematic communication, no continual exchange of knowledge, and no discussion of principles, are subject to impulsive social action. They seldom exhibit a calm and firm restraint of passion. They know little of that deliberatively planned conduct which is theproduct of rational like-mindedness.[14]

Modern society also was influenced by emotional forces. But the main difference was that demogenic societies, to a certain degree, shaped their own destinies. They had "guided their progress by the light of ideals that reason has created, through critical reflection upon the revelations of experience, and by a comparative study of the relative value of human desires, as tested by experiment."[15] The important point, for Giddings, was that his theory of the consciousness of kind refuted contract, imitative, and sympathy theories of the origin of society. Giddings considered his own theory as a developed form of instinct theory which dated back to Aristotle. This idea had a number of elements: (1) it was assumed that the basic forms of social relationships were discovered in the very beginnings of mental phenomena; (2) mental activity was a response of sensitive matter to some stimuli; (3) any stimulus could be felt by many organisms at the same or different times; (4) organisms responded in like or unlike ways, with differing degrees of intensity or persistence. For Giddings, consciousness of kind (like response to the same stimulus) constituted the origin of all cooperative behavior, while in unlike response, "we have the beginning of all those processes of individuation, of differentiation."[16]

According to Giddings, society in its modern form was extremely complex. Its very existence depended upon like-mindedness, like interests, like feelings, and similar judgments about the way things should operate. Society was a product of both unconscious developments and conscious planning.[17] In its development society tended toward increasing differentiation with increasing homogeneity. Giddings wrote about society in the following manner:

We conceive of society as any plural number of sentient creatures more or less continuously subjected to common stimuli, to differing stimuli, and to interstimulation, and responding thereto in like behavior, concerted activity, and becoming therefore, with developing intelligence, coherent through a dominating consciousness of kind, while always sufficiently conscious of difference to insure a measure of individual liberty.[18]

In addition to the complexity of society, there was the reality of hierarchical relationships. No society had existed without certain inequalities. This was due, in part, to the fact that men were born with constitutional or genetic differences. Individuals are not born with equal vitality and strength. However, Giddings also claimed that individuals were not born with the same "mental and moral endowment." These differences, both physical and intellectual, are the foundation of stratification and differentiation in society.[19] These constitutional differences, in short, were the basis of class formations in society. Economic and political classes were secondary to the real class divisions, which were vitality classes, personality classes, and social classes. These classes were found in all social communities, large or small, and throughout all times. The vitality class had three divisions: high, medium, and low. The high vitality class had high birthrates and low death rates. And it had acquired "a high degree of bodily vigor and mental power." This class corresponded mainly with the better farmers. It also included, in smaller proportions, the individuals "living in towns and cities, and engaged in business or professional life, or employed as mechanics or even as laborers." The second vitality class roughly paralleled the business and professional people of large cities. These men usually worked with their heads and not their bodies. The third vitality class was equated with "the ignorant and uncleanly part of the slum population of the cities, and to the equally ignorant and uncleanly, shiftless, and thriftless part of the rural population."[20]

There were also three personality classes: (1) geniuses and men and women of talent, (2) individuals of normal intellectual and moral power, and (3) the defective. The first personality class was essentially small and harbored only men with inventive power. This class included mechanical inventors, businessmen, statesmen, and professional men "who have the gift of originality and can devise new and better ways of doing those things in which they are interested." The second class included the bulk of the population who were mainly imitative. They were not socially defective and basically had good judgment. They didn't have foolish fantasies and "they can appreciate the enormous advantage of being directly guided in the practical affairs of life by the advice of the men of talent and genius." The third personality class contained those who were defective in mind or body. These men were the insane, imbeciles, suicidals, inebriates, and the deaf and dumb. This class relied on the other two personality classes to keep it going.[21]

The social classes were four in number: the social, nonsocial, psuedosocial, and antisocial. The social social class was characterized by men with a highly developed social nature. They were sympathetic, friendly, and primarily interested in improving social relations. They improved the happiness of mankind by defending and preserving "the great social institutions of the family and the state." This class inspired the rest of the population with its unselfish leadership and loyalty. They were a "true natural aristocracy." The nonsocial class was composed of congenital and habitual paupers, who were the degenerates of society. They feign the qualities of the social class but "pose as victims of misfortune." The antisocial class was peopled with "instinctive and habitual criminals in whom the consciousness of kind is approaching extinction, and who detest society and all its ways."[22] They had no social virtues and lived by open agression.

For Giddings, these social classes represented the natural divisions in society which were based on individual constitutional differences. These differences led to permanent conflicts in society, since "individuals and combinations of individuals will always be as unequal in power as they are unlike in aptitude and purposes." These differences, then, had to be controlled through societal organization. Giddings explained:

All kinds of drives, which are made up of a combination of drives of individuals, and certain interests and controls of all kinds are developed in society. There is no such thing as a society without a great many controls and people that are impatient with all controls are impatient with the very fact of society. You cannot have society without control and you cannot have society without inequalities of ability because control developed out of these inequalities, and in society there is always some kind of rule.[23]

Social and political control evolved when it had become necessary to devise a plan of organization broad and elastic enough to "include men of more than one cult and of more than one kinship, or, as often happened, of personal allegiance to more than one chieftain." In particular, political organizations were created to harmonize various interests. "The primary purpose of the state is to perfect social integration. To this end it maintains armies and carries on diplomacy to protect the nation against agression or to enlarge its territory and population; and it maintains tribunals and police to enforce peace within its own borders. The first business of legislatures, courts, and executives is to combine, defend, and harmonize social groups, classes, individuals, and interests."[24]

Giddings, like Sumner and Ward, attributed certain characteristics to individual organisms. Although Giddings's classification system is different, the point remains the same—individuals were born with certain emotional characteristics that had to be brought under control (fear, anger, hate, envy, etc.). Giddings, however, did indicate that the plasticity of the human species was greater than that of any other species. In this sense, his image of man clearly deviates from Ward and Sumner and from the social-technological tradition. He also indicated that from an evolutionary perspective, modern societies were superior to those of the past. They provided, among other things, greater individual freedom.

Giddings also clearly indicated that society had logical and empirical priority over the individual. Interestingly enough, he further argued that hierarchy and inequality were necessary for order in society. His argument was based on the constitutional differences between people. He provided no empirical support for this argument but rather relied on every man's commonsense appreciation of it. Likewise, he evaluated the superiority of modern capitalist societies on the basis of science (i.e., rational likemindedness). It was from this perspective that Giddings's evaluation of other ideas than those of "science" emerged. It is to these ideas that the discussion will now turn.

Consciousness of Kind as Genesis

Giddings argued that the consciousness of kind was the originator of all social development including knowledge. Consciousness of kind, however, had evolved slowly, through man's interaction with nature and other human beings. The original stimuli presented to man has been threefold: (1) other humans, (2) the events of nature, and (3) the concrete objects of nature. Collectively considered, these stimuli may be termed the "environment." More interestingly, Giddings went on to argue that the human environment is determined by the physical one.[25] He further argued that in the early stages of human development climate had a decisive effect on mental growth. "The Southern peoples of the northern hemisphere are more excitable and impulsive, in both individual and social activity, than are the people of colder northern climates." Moreover,

Rapid alterations of heat and cold, and especially swift transitions from winter to summer, and from summer to winter, combined with a dull monotony of surface, as on the steppes of Russia or the vast plains of America, strongly predispose a population to moody emotionalism. An equable climate, combined with a varied and interesting topography, as in ancient Greece and in modern England, predisposes a population to intellectual activity and to a control of emotionalism by thought.

In lands where earthquakes, famines, and pestilences are most frequent, the habitual state of fear represses a cool critical intellectual activity, and stimulates imagination and emotion. These are the states of mind that most powerfully contribute to sympathetic like-mindedness and impulsive social action.[26]

In short, consciousness of kind, broadly speaking, organized all questions of social choice, social volition, or social policy. All motives were centered on this principle. The collective experience of a given tribe, race, or nation forced men to accept what they could not understand and to obey what they did not believe personally. "His thoughts are only partly his own; they are also the thoughts of others. His actions are guided by the will of others." Social cooperation itself depended on this realization of similarity. From an evolutionary perspective, Giddings argued, consciousness of kind had its root in a "like response to the same stimulus."[27]

The evolution of societal consciousness depended on the perception of different stimuli. It was through the interaction of total mental cultures and changing environmental conditions that differences became apparent. When this happened the mechanical solidarity of groups became more differentiated and consciousness moved to a so-called higher plateau. In the initial states of man's evolution, therefore, it was in the interaction between man and nature—or alien groups—that perceptual differentiation emerged. For Giddings, then, the greater the nervous disturbance (i.e., alien element), within certain limits, the more distinct was consciousness. "Evolution begins in a primary conflict the effect of which is integration, and completes itself in a secondary conflict, the effect of which is differentiation."[28]

Giddings argued that there were four stages in the development of reason. These stages were (1) guess or conjecture, (2) reasoning by analogy, (3) deductive, speculative, or dogmatic reasoning (4) induction.[29] The stages corresponded with the development of civilization toward a more rational organization. The first stage belonged to the primitive mind. Giddings, much like Sumner, argued that the "savage mind" is conjectural and confuses luck with industry or work. The primitive may not carry out an efficient project (from our perspective) because he may believe that luck is against a particular plan or procedure. When this happens "his economic activity in these directions is instantly inhibited." The second stage also was characteristic of the savage mind (e.g., Aleuts and the Galelaresse of Halmahera). "The mind begins to form conclusions by assuming that essential resemblance, or identity, goes with superficial likeness." Correlative with analogy is the use of magic. Magical reasoning had two fundamental principles: (1) like produces like, (2) things which had been in contact with each other, even though they no longer exist, continue to act on each other. Magic, in essence, gave plan and direction to the entire economy. Giddings used the following example to illustrate the interpenetration of magical thinking and economics. "A Black-foot Indian who has set a trap for eagles will not eat rosebuds, because, if he did, when an eagle alighted near the trap the rose-buds in the hunter's stomach would make the bird itch and, in-stead of swallowing the bait, the eagle would merely sit and scratch itself." The third state was characteristic of the Babyloni-ans, Egyptians, Greeks, Romans, and some later Western peoples. This reasoning had acquired logic. "Granted certain premises, the deductive thinker can with a high degree of certainty arrive at necessary conclusions." In this stage, man "begins to people the unseen realms of the sky, of the sea and of the underworld of earth with personalities of supernatural power; he begins to create the immortal gods." Additionally, man ascribed the distribution of good and evil to these beings. "His whole welfare he conceives is determined by their attitude toward him as an individual, or, to the yet greater extent, by their attitude toward the community to which he belongs."[30]

All three of these stages of thinking belonged to what Giddings terms a cermonial economy. Among other things, such an econo-my presupposed: (1) the relationship of a group or groups of peo-ple to the natural environment, (2) gregarious relations among individuals, (3) division of labor. More importantly, however, these three stages characteristically bestowed more importance on the performance of a rite than on labor. More time and wealth was bestowed upon sacrifice rather than upon the accumulation of capital reserves. The luck economy was coincident with anthro-pogenic association. Magic economy was equated with the first half of ethnogenic association, and sacrifical economy with the latter half of that period. "Only with demogenic or civic associa-tion does ceremonial economy in all its forms slowly begin to give place to the business economy of the modern man." The fourth stage, which was characteristic of demogenic association, used in-ductive reasoning. "Systematic induction begins with observing the resemblances of things that are unlike, and, on the basis of re-semblances of differences, sorting things into classes." Only when the human mind had become critically judgmentally aware of premises could cause and effect in nature be observed. Then man understood that his economic prosperity depended upon industry, invention, and efficient organization of men. This state, Giddings wrote, presupposed a complex social development.

Such a change in man's habits of reasoning probably could not have occured apart from the commingling of Kinsmen and strangers, of native born and foreign born, which engendered...a people in distinction from...a wide kindred. Demogenic association brought about comparisons of traditions, and of experiences, in the course of which long accepted beliefs were for the first time questioned. From such shock dogmatism could not wholly recover. New catagories of things and of thoughts were inductively formed.

Reacting upon one another and together reacting upon traditional culture, demogenic association and inductive thinking converted an ethnic society into a civil social order, and created civilization. Successive steps of the process can be made out. The consorting of ethnically heterogeneous elements assimilates practices; incidental discussion correlates ideas. Consorting and discussion assimilate standards of living, and thereby standardize consumption, a standardize consumption and a verified knowledge that accumulates and permeates, further assimilate. Survivals of the luck, the magic, and the sacrificial economies are resistant to attrition, but they lose prestige.[31]

Giddings argued that different forms of cooperation had various effects on the development of the "everyday mentality" of groups. To better illustrate Giddings's concern with the effects of social organization on commonsense thinking, I will confine my discussion to two areas; the modern democratic world of public opinion and Giddings's characterization of American mental types. Throughout his writing Giddings' interest was in the effect of the "total" social organization on men's actions, beliefs, and ideas. [32]

As society evolved from anthropogenic association to ethnogenic and finally demogenic association, its inner relations became increasingly complex. This evolution was neither unilinear nor unequivocal for all social groups. Indeed, Giddings explained that some groups were not capable of adapting to changing circumstances. [33] In the overall emergence of demogenic association, its distinguishing characteristic was its complex rationality. This was contrasted with imitative, impulsive, and primitive thought. Only critical, comprehensive thinking could check impulsive social action. However, this style of critical thinking must also have to become a habit of mind. And, it can only become a habit of mind when it is employed in practical activity. This, in turn, could only happen when the practical activities of life themselves have become complex.[34] We note then that modern rational thinking depended on complex societal organization for its existence. That behind all power in a republic lay public opinion. "All authoritatively declared law must be held to be law until it is repeated, but as a phenomenon of the social mind it is doubtful whether any rule that public opinion will not enforce is really law." Public opinion itself could only exist under certain social-political conditions, as Giddings explained:

Public opinion, therefore, can exist only where men are in continual communication, and where they are free to express their real minds, without fear or restraint. Whenever men are forbidden by governmental or other authority to assemble, to hold meetings, to speak or write freely, or whenever they stand in fear of losing social position, or employment, or property, if they freely speak their minds, there is no true public opinion; there is only a mass of traditional beliefs or outbursts of popular feeling.[35]

The higher forms of cooperation depended not only on like-mindedness but on "good faith" as well. Although there were laws for the collection of debts and the regulation of contracts, "a majority of business transactions are really based upon good faith and good repute and nothing more." Essentially, the existence of public opinion depended on: (1) dense population, (2) rights of different classes, (3) liberal constitutional government, (4) general education, and (5) sympathy between classes.[36]

Giddings postulated a general rule for the evolution of society. He argued that the character of pluralistic reactions was determined by the strength of the stimulation and by the similarity or dissimilarity of the reacting mechanisms to the stimuli. Simple pluralistic behavior was complicated and was developed by interstimulation and response. "Each individual of a group or assemblage is a complex of stimuli to his fellows, and each responds to fellow stimulation."[37] This general principle of interstimulation can be illustrated by looking at his analysis of democratic-liberal values and their effect on other institutions.

Democratic ideas had their social base in the improvement of the material conditions of life, the redistribution of population, and great social struggles (e.g., those of race, nation, and class). As a result of Columbus's voyages, there was a population redistribution. The migration of colonists "relieved economic pressure in other lands and gave opportunities to those who had the courage...to try out possibilities in new situations." The development of new inventions (e.g., steam power, transportation, electricity) created a new powerful class in society which threatened the aristocracy. The manufacturing classes' dependence on labor led to an increase in the power of the wage earning classes. The effect of all this, according to Giddings, was universal suffrage. More particularly, Giddings wrote about the genesis of the policy of equality.

As the policy of unification when pressed too far creates reactions against itself, so also does a regime of unlimited liberty. It creates conditions of great and increasing inequality. The energetic and the enterprising, unrestrained in their activity, acquire control of the machinery of government, of the administration of law, and of economic opportunities...Having through liberty obtained power, they proceed by all possible means to monopolize liberty itself, taking care to maintain those legal forms of freedom that protect property...and that encourage competition among wage-earning laborers, while more than willing to restrict competition among themselves. An increasing density of population intensifies the struggle for existence. Class differentiation is hastened, and presently social cohesion is threatened through the exploitation of the weak by the strong. From the exploited comes the demand for wider opportunity and a larger share in material prosperity. It is perceived by the intelligent that if a disruption of the community through a revolt of the discontented, or a general revolution, is to be prevented, some limitation of the liberty of the strong to curtail the liberties of the weak must be imposed, and that practically this means a certain limitation of liberty by equality. It is under these circumstances that the idea of equality arises, and that its influence over the multitude creates the democratic movement, as that term is understood in modern times.[38]

While liberalism had certain positive benefits, it also influenced other ideas and had disintegrating tendencies. In the past (i.e., in the later part of ethnogenic association), marriage was not governed by individual preferences. "Religious, economic, and social considerations were of great weight." The major purpose of marital union was to perpetuate a family, a patrimony, and a religious faith. In modern times, however, liberalism which substituted contract for custom introduced the notion of romantic love. Romantic love is primarily thought of as a means to individual

pleasure. The consequence of this development is that the traditional duties of the family—estate transmission and integrity—
disappear. For Giddings, the "religious-proprietary family thus
becomes the romantic family, which is a much less stable institution."[39]

In sum, Giddings's viewed the genesis of ideas as a product of
"consciousness of kind," and this, in turn, was generated by inter-
human association and contact with nature. At some points, Giddings's writings display a certain tendency toward geographical
determinism not unlike that of Montesquieu. However, he also
suggested that ideas were produced by "total" patterns of interaction. Unlike Sumner, Giddings did not emphasize the "material"
conditions of life as being primary determinants; unlike Ward, he
did not write that "ideas" determined material conditions. Giddings's view fell halfway between Ward's and Sumner's. Ideas
were produced by the interstimulation of humans and nature.
Similarly, ideas rebounded back to change the existing social structure. However, Giddings did share with Sumner and Ward a macro-
evolutionary perspective.

Collective Thinking

It has already been shown that Giddings analyzed various mentalities from an evolutionary perspective. His concern with the
evolution of thought was based, not on an ideological critique,
but rather on an analysis of the cummulative progress of thought
toward real knowledge or science. In this sense, then, Giddings
analyzed past theories. For the most part his critique was that
past theorists had failed to see society as a whole. Past scientific
theories of society were extremely fragmentary. Some theorists
had emphasized the political, economic, or ecclesiastical aspects of
society. However, "no one attempted to describe association and
social organization in their completeness; no one tried to comprehend the concrete, vital whole."[40]

Platonic and social contract theorists had assumed that men observed the utility of association and then consciously tried to perfect the social organization. "The social bond, therefore, is reason." Machiavelli and other writers on sovereignty discovered the
power of impression functioning in a strong personality, while

Durkheim maintained that society created the mind. All these theories were wrong, because they did not go to the elementary social facts. Giddings wrote:

It is demonstrable, however, that neither imitation nor impression is the most elementary social fact. It long ago became unnecessary to argue that reason is not. When an audience springs to its feet at the cry of fire, its initial action is not imitation. Example and imitation enter as complicating factors the instant that movement toward the door begins...The initial action is merely a pluralistic response (i.e., a reaction by more than one individual) to a common stimulation. In terms of like or of unlike, of prompt or of slow, of persistent or of intermittent response, all the phenomena of natural grouping and of collective behavior can be stated and interpreted. Intermental action is interstimulation and response. Like-response, complicated by intermental action, may become competition or may become concerted volition. It may become solidarity. Unlike-response differentiates and individualizes; it may disintegrate.[41]

The mistake of most ethical theories since the Protestant Reformation had been to focus on the isolated individual. They attempted to work from the individual to society. This focus was an accurate response to the suppression of the individual under the church. But so far as ethical systems "have assumed the individual as an independent starting-point of social and moral phenomena, they have been radically untrue." Within the individualistic tradition it may be noted that both Hobbes and Locke were wrong. Hobbes assumed that the state of nature was always desperate, and Locke made the opposite mistake of "assuming that it always is a condition of mutual toleration and spontaneous cooperation." Similarly, socialists and staunch individualists were wrong about the development of the social organism. The former argued that the state could perform all the functions of private agencies, while the other believed that society could achieve its goals without authoritative government. Both are right in principle, but wrong in fact. They are wrong, because knowledge of the social laws leads us to believe that their is a tendency toward *equilibrium*. Both state and social organizations have *self-limiting* mechanisms which altered with changing needs and conditions. The distinguishing quality of modern social science was "a minute and relatively precise knowledge of those slow but certain processes of biological and social change by which the transformation of brutality into humanity is effected."[42] Modern science, in contradistinction to past science, assumed the continuity of all phenomena. Both the physical and the biological world beat with the impulse of past generations. "There can be no theory, then, of anything, or group of things, of any change, or series of changes, which is not a coordinate part of universal theory."[43] Moreover, every science must appeal to sense perception for developing its explanations. Giddings also attempted to depict the "mentality" of given groups, nations, races, etc. He made a serious attempt to analyze the mental groups he believed existed in America. In particular, he was concerned with various immigrant groups. Both of these elements in his writings will be brought out in the next few pages.

According to Giddings, children and savages had similar mentalities. They look at inanimate objects as personal. "Beliefs about their supposed habits and powers constitute a large part of the culture." Although savages and children were alike, men and women were different in their thinking. He further argued that even political thinking varies with the different stages of evolution. For example, he wrote:

The less developed a community is, and the cruder its thinking, the more likely it is to emphasize the importance of that resemblance which is, or is supposed to be, correlated with the degree of kinship. The savage bases his whole system of social organization upon distinctions of real or of nominal blood relationship. The mentally more advanced barbarian begins to have conceptions of aristocratic distinctions based on descent, and these notions become important in the earlier stages of civilization. Gradually, however, the notion of kinship yields to conceptions of mental and moral resemblances, irrespective of the blood bond, and the preferred mode of resemblance may be oligarchical in type or democratic; expressed in either case, in culture, in economy, in law, or in politics.[44]

Primitive man had ideas, and he did consciously contemplate his situation; "he perceived relations which the lower animals have never discriminated, and his imagination runs riot in explanatory activity." However, it never occurred to him that his own well-being was within his own control. There is a tendency for the primitive to see the world as made up of ghosts or spirits. These supernatural creatures are endowed with mysterious powers of good and evil. The primitive believes that economic well-being is determined by his relation to these powers. During the period of ethnogenic association, distinct religious ideas became correlated with ancestor worship. This came about by the dominance of the male in the family. When the male became the authority, he was so regarded in life and death.

While the household may continue to regard natural objects and forces and miscellaneous spirits with superstitious feelings, they entertain for the soul of the departed founder of the house the stronger feeling of veneration. They think of the ancestral spirit as their protector in the land of shades. To the ancestral spirit, therefore, they pay their principal devotions. Thus without entirely displacing other religious observances, ancestor-worship necessarily becomes the dominant faith.[45]

Giddings also tried to characterize the mental life of modern man. In general, the modern mentality was typified by: (1) differentiated ability as an incident of production, but also a remarkable uniformity of mind and habit in respect to consumption, (2) the scientific view of nature—live by knowledge, not belief. Belief was distinguished from knowledge in that it did not require evidence. "People can believe things with the most absolute conviction in their minds without having any evidence to go on whatever." Knowledge was based on evidence and facts and was of such a nature that it was constantly checked and questioned.[46] "The chief culture conflict today is obviously the world-wide struggle between scientific secularism on the one hand, and, on the other hand, the various cults of supernaturalism, obscurantism, and dogmatism." Science, ultimately will win, because it has practical interests on its side. One does not have to understand science to see its practical benefits. Science has helped to safeguard the crops, to control epidemics, and to cut economic costs.[47]

More particularly, Giddings was fond of comparing national mental types. In his opinion England was the most advanced nation in the development of rational public opinion. Giddings argued that France emphasized the ideals of equality, while England valued liberty. These differences in mental operations were described in the following manner.

Thoroughly protestant and practical, England cares for the concrete achievements of the present. Men, as she regards them, may or may not be equal in their metaphysical being or in their potentialities: for practical purposes of everyday business and everyday politics they are unequal in extreme degree;

and it is practical common-sense to let the best of them achieve their best without too many hampering restrictions. France is still to a great degree Catholic in sentiment, if not in confession, and is still mystical in feeling, if not in profession. To her it matters little that individual liberty is imperfect, as long as men who feel a strong sense of social solidarity may meet on the same plane and cherish the same visions...The Frenchman does not insist that men are equal in talents or in virtue. What he chiefly demands is external equality—of conditions, of opportunity, of benefits from society, from education, and cultural institutions—in short, equality of treatment. Consequently, his thought is largely centered upon the functions of government and its provision for each and all of its subjects.[48]

Giddings further argued that America combined the English ideal of liberty with the French ideal of equality. The problem was that America could not perform such a simple synthesis, since it also was made up of Gauls, Celts, Germans, etc. In an attempt to grasp the American mentality, Giddings developed one of the first provisional classifications of mental types. In his analytic framework, he divided the normal population into the following psychological groups: MEI, MIE, EMI, EIM, IME, IEM. Of these arrangements, MEI and EMI are found only among animals, babies, and defectives.[49] The other four types are explained in the following passage.

In some individuals a forceful character, an agressive disposition, intellect of low-grade, and strong emotion are combined with a prompt and persistent motor activity. This type we call the *Ideo-Motor*. In other individuals a convival character, an instigative disposition, an imaginative intellect, prone to reason from analogy, a weak but persistent and usually good-natured emotion, are combined with motor reactions that are usually intermittent and of less promptness than in the ideo-motor type. This type we shall call the *Ideo-Emotional*. In an individual of a third sort, an austere character and a domineering disposition are combined with dogmatism of belief, strong emotion, and intermittent activity. This type may be named the *Dogmatic-Emotional*. In a fourth kind of individual all the emotional and motor processes are dominated by a critical intellect, and even his disposition and character are intellectually controlled. This type we may call the *critically-intellectual*.[50] (My emphasis.)

These four types and their usual characteristics are schematically illustrated in Table 2. Giddings divided the American population by nationalities into various mental types. In the overall classification the United States had the following divisions: ideo -motor,

2.9 percent; ideo-motor to ideo-emotional, 8.1 percent; ideo-emotional, 29.2 percent; ideo-emotional to dogmatic-emotional, 33.5 percent; dogmatic-emotional, 19.3 percent; dogmatic-emotional to critical intellectual, 6.3 percent; critical-intellectual, 1.6 percent. The American people, then, were primarily ideo-emotional to dogmatic-emotional.[51]

More particularly, we may note the way in which Giddings identified certain nationalities with particular mental types. Of the native-born parents, only those from the New England states, Pennsylvania, New York, and New Jersey had critical-intellectual capacities. Those from the South Atlantic and South Central states were primarily ideo-emotional. Of the foreign-born whites and native-born whites of foreign parents, only the Scotch, English, and French had any critical faculties. The Scandinavians, Russians, and Germans are primarily ideo-emotional to dogmatic-emotional. The Latins, Negroes, Irish, and Italians are mainly ideo-emotional.

Giddings used the indices of politics, law and order, occupations and literature to ascribe these mentalities to various groups. Giddings did not set up any rigid criteria for determining these types and his subjective preferences come to the forefront in the following passage.

The literature produced by New England native whites has been from the earliest time chiefly dogmatic and polemical, secondarily critical, and only in a third degree imaginative and emotional, since even the poetry and other *belles lettres* products of New England have always had a strong dash of the critical and moralizing element.... On the other hand the literature proceeding from authors of Irish nationality is chiefly imaginative and emotional, secondarily polemical, and only in a very slight degree critical and scientific.[52]

Giddings did tend to analyze the collective sentiments or mental types of various groups. His analysis suggests that from an evolutionary perspective, different styles or stages of thinking can be characterized. The collective sentiments of various groups are, in part, the product of a total way of life. The causal factors are multiple in number, and they range from geography to religious factors. Giddings, then, did analyze the type of knowledge which we take to be associated primarily with the social-technological position. In addition, he did criticize other political and economic theories. However, the crucial issue for him was not criticism but the development of sociology as a science. The development of so-

Table 2 Composition of Mental Type (Normal Population)

Type of mind	MIE (ideo-motor)	EIM (ideo-emotional)	IEM (dogmatic-emotional)	IME (critical-intellectual)
promptness of reaction, continuity of activity	prompt persistent	prompt intermit-tent	slow, inter-mittent	slow, persistent
kind of movement	largely instinc-tive, involun-tary	semi-invol-untary, imitative, sympathetic	largely voluntary (belief)	largely voluntary (judgment)
degree of emotion, tem-perment, formation of belief or judgment	strong, choleric, subject-ively determined, habit, conjecture, autosug-gestion	sanguine, objectively determined by mood, emotion	melancholic, subjectively determined by mood, emotion	phlegmatic, objectively determined by evidence
mode of reasoning	conjec-tural	imagina-tive (analogi-cal)	deductive, speculative, critical of logic but not premises	inductive, critical of logic and premises

ciology would help to separate politics from science. It is to this latter issue that we now turn.

Sociology: The Reduction of "Intentions" to Physical Laws

Giddings argued that the social sciences, like the physical sciences, were amenable to quantitative exploration. There was nothing inherent in the social process to inhibit such investigation. One of the current tendencies was to loaf and generalize. "We need men not afraid to work; who will get busy with the adding machine and the logarithms, and give us *exact studies,* such as we get from the psychological laboratories. *Sociology can be made an exact, quantitative science,* if we can get *industrious* men interested in it."[53] The only peculiarity about the social sciences was its concern with psychical phenomena as well as physical influences. The former was due to the evolution of human consciousness and its subsequent influence on natural processes and the social order. That is, man at a certain point added a new dimension to nature—his psychical awareness of the world and the attempt to master it. Giddings argued that past social theorists had not examined this dual nature very thoroughly. Interestingly enough, he argued that psychical laws were subservient to universal cosmic laws. In essence, this meant that social evolution was a product of physical laws which determined "the aggregation, the growth, the movements, and arrangements of population; they determine the amount, the kinds, and the combinations of social activities." Within these physical processes mental activities asserted themselves in the form of social policies or ideals. "Society is not a purely mechanical product of physical evolution. To a great extent it is an intended product of psychological evolution." However, the institutions, laws and policies that culminate in social relations are not determined by conscious social choices. In the main, they are shaped by the process of survival. And, survival is "conditioned by cosmic law over which man has no control."[54]

Science determined what these cosmic laws were through the process of inductive reasoning. To the scientific mind the universe was an orderly arrangement. Furthermore, induction was the systematic observation and recording of resemblances and differences in the world. According to Giddings, inductions were based on class, fact, generalizations, scientific law, and conditional statements. Class contained facts which resembled each other on one point. Facts were observations of discrete phenomena which were in close agreement. A generalization was a relation between an unvarying class of facts and some other facts not in that class. A scientific law was based on the constant relation between a fact of variation and some other fact of variation. Conditions were the necessary antecedents for some given facts to exist.[55] There were actually three processes involved in inductive scientific reasoning. "Strictly speaking, all true induction *is* guessing; it is a swift intuitive glance at a mass of facts to see if they *mean* anything; while exact scientific demonstration is a complex process of *deducing* conclusions from the induction and then testing the deduced conclusions by the observation of more facts."[56] Scientific explanation, then, was "description in conceptual terms carried to the limits within which verification by perception is possible, and that conceputal description verifiable and verified by perception, is explanation." The main object of science was to extend description until it includes "all knowable facts of matter, life, mind, and society, and places each fact in its proper place in the complete system." In its pursuit of truth, science was interest free. Science does not measure truth by its utility. It can only compare observations and generalizations with other evidence that is available. Science can create pleasure, and in the long run it may do so. In the short run, however, it may contribute only pain. "With either result the scientific man as such has no concern."[57]

Sociology, as a science, had the particular task of learning how social relations evolved and how they reacted on the development of the individual personality. Sociology had three main quests: (1) the discovery of the conditions that determined the aggregations of people and the types of social intercourse promulgated; (2) discovery of laws that governed social choices (law of subjective processes); (3) discovery of laws that governed natural selection and the survival of choices (law of objective processes). In a word, sociology was a science "that tries to conceive of society in its unity, and attempts to explain it in terms of cosmic cause and law." To accomplish this, it must work out a subjective interpretation of psychical laws and an objective assessment of physical laws. "These two interpretations must be consistent, each with the other, and must be correlated."

For not only does sociology insist upon a recognition of the unity that underlies all the various phases of society that are investigated by special social sciences, it insists also that one fundamental logic underlies the objective or physical, and the subjective or volitional explanations of social phenomena.... In systematic sociology only do we find a distinct recognition of both social volition and physical evolution and a conscious grappling with the problem of their scientific reconciliation.[58]

Sociology, for Giddings, eventually was to aid in the practical development of man. "Sociology was the science of the production and distribution of adequacy, *of* man and *in* man." Sociology tells us how, "as far as it is possible, we can *become* what we desire to *be*."[59] Adequacy had to do with health, endurance, reproductiveness, intelligence, self-control, etc. "The practical manifestations of adequacy were: individual initiative, individual responsibility, and an individual participation that is efficient and helpful in collective endeavor." More specifically,

Sociology enables us, in a measure, to govern the conditions on which social stability and social progress depend. It enables us to appreciate the profound distinction between impulsive and rational social change, and to discover the dangers that lurk in the practice of attaching the sanctions of religion to irrationality. In addition to all these services, sociology enables us to attempt a rational and constructive criticism of our social values, and to combine them in a realizable social ideal. It extends its scientific description of society into the past, and projects it into the future. Its forecast is no impossible Utopia. It assumes that if the work of description is accurately done in the present, the sociologist of the future will have no occasion to substitute for it a wholly new system of facts; but will merely complete the system already begun. In a word, the supreme practical value of sociology is that, like every other science, it completes in thought, for the daily guidance of mankind, a system of facts, which, as yet, are only partly given.[60]

Sociology, when taught in the universities, also served other purposes. First, sociology taught that consciousness of kind was the basic fact of all social existence. This fact stressed the importance of loyalty, group solidarity (i.e., the ability to meet the enemy together), and the value of industrialization for the civilized world. Second, it attempted to emancipate the human mind from fear of natural or social phenomena. Third, it taught the value of social control and, in particular, rational self-control. Fourth, it tried to obstruct unchecked beliefs. And, finally, sociology inculcated the value of public opinion. That is, the progress of a republican government depended on rational public opinion.[61]

Sociologists: The Elite Class

To better understand the role of intellectual in Giddings's thought, we must first turn to the role of elites in society. Giddings, as I already indicated, argued for the necessity of hierarchical relationships in society. In short, he believed that some men were more capable than others. In the first place, he argued that no community could survive without a true elite. Whether this elite was hereditary or emerged by improved educational opportunities was of little concern to him.[62]

The true elite class was that group of people who rank highest in the generic social classes: vitality, personality, and social. This group was small, yet without it society could not survive. This preeminent social class performed various services. It set the standards for mankind, and it also did the original thinking for society. "Most great truths have been discovered by great men," and their application to human well-being, in every sphere of practical activity, "has been made by men of only a lesser degree of intellectual power."[63] Finally, the elite class contributed most of the superior forms of beauty and happiness to mankind. Interestingly enough, Giddings reserved the supreme position for those who could organize men, not nature. This supreme psychic class (the organizers of men) then did the directive work of society, in politics, business, the professions, science, and art. For without it, the efficiency of the social organization could not be maintained.[64] The role of the sociologist, then, was to discover the laws of social reaction, make them known in the universities, and help direct the activities of social organization through the discovery of scientific truth.

But, what, exactly, is it that sociologists have discovered which will lead to a better society? For Giddings, progress lay in a "continuous harmonizing of a continually appearing unlikeness of feeling, thought, and purpose in the community with a vast central mass of already established agreements."[65] More specifically this meant the values of science, industrial democracy, and the nation state. The value of science for rational cooperation was expressed in the following manner.

Disciplined cooperation established security; systematic communication diffuses knowledge and stimulates critical inquiry. Knowledge and investigation give command over natural forces. Those nations in which social organization is highly developed, are emancipated from superstition and fear; they are able to rise superior to emotion and impulse; they believe in scientific investigation; they have habits of calm and discplined action.[66]

The modern division of labor also was valued because it gave a definite aim to life. It habituated men to a discipline and thoroughness which culminated in rational thinking. "At the same time it releases men from their tasks to enjoy more hours of leisure than they could otherwise command." Moreover, "the struggle to rise in the world is the means by which the strongest and many of the best human traits are produced." To fail in this struggle is to fail in life. Therefore, the men who were unemployed were always the relatively inefficient—the ones who failed to adapt.[67]

The development of the nation-state also was important. Men could not ignore national loyalty in the interest of international-ism, because men had not yet "found a way to coordinate and cor-relate and integrate the economic, the religious, the scientific, the fraternal, and all the good-will interests of mankind without ex-cluding any nation or any race."[68] The nation would remain the working organization of mankind until man could reintegrate along other lines. The nation-state was not a negative phenomenon in Giddings's eyes. The creation of the territorial state did not im-ply that ethnic unity had to be obliterated. In fact, the modern state only subordinated ethnic unity to a higher ideal. Insofar as the state maintains unity within its boundaries, it strives to cre-ate a new ethnic unity which blends with other elements. Simply stated, "the consciousness of kind has broadened."[69] Giddings concluded from his study of aggression and nonresistance that "within the more enlightened nations, habits of non-aggression and non-resistance largely dominate the affairs of private life." However, unless the whole course of history was wrong, there would be no cessation of war. The nations that would prevail, ac-cording to Giddings, were those that depended on ethnic diversity internally and yet were united by a common standard of conduct, loyalty, and liberty. Nations that are highly centralized politically, that stamp out local liberty, suppress individual initiative, and es-tablish socialism, "will end in degeneration." "Only when the de-mocratic empire has compassed the uttermost parts of the world will there be that perfect understanding among men which is ne-cessary for the growth of moral kinship. Only in the spiritual bro-therhood of that secular republic, created by blood and iron not less than by thought and love, will the kingdom of heaven be es-tablished on earth."[70]

Like Sumner and Ward, Giddings argued that the purpose of so-ciology was the discovery of facts and the creation of general laws. Again, however, his view on the role of sociology was halfway between Ward's and Sumner's. Where Sumner suggested that sociologists should not intervene in the social process and Ward argued that they should, Giddings drew a distinction between a sociology of the long run and of the short run. He argued that in the short run, sociology was not necessarily concerned with practical utility. He also stated, however, that in the long run sociology probably would have certain practical benefits. Moreover, in addition to discovering the regularities of human behavior, he believed that sociologists should help harmonize various interest groups. The ultimate goal was an expansion of like-mindedness, and not an overthrow or revolution of the existing order. He was committed to a modified laissez-faire position—in between Ward's and Sumner's positions.

Summary

Notwithstanding the qualifications already mentioned, Giddings, like the other academic sociologists, primarily espoused a social-technological sociology of knowledge position. Although he argued that man was basically a social being, Giddings believed that his drives or impulses had to be controlled. Like other control theorists, he wrote that men get their basic identity and meaning from participation in the ongoing social system. Men were not limited and oppressed by a given social order but gained their sustenance from it.

Society, for Giddings, was a complex mixture of physical and psychical elements. It inherently had to be hierarchical and inegalitarian in its structure for two reasons: (1) the inequalities of class and status were reflections of the genetic and biological inequalities of men; (2) social order depended on hierarchy (i.e., control by elites) for efficient operation. He also held the view that society, through the aid of natural evolution and human intentions, was moving towards a highly differentiated but rational order. The main point was that modern society, although exhibiting a high division of labor, was based on similar *consumptive interests* and a general consciousness of kind. It was organically *solidaire* in its values.

Giddings further argued that knowledge was not generated or dominated by particular interest groups. It emerged out of the societal totality. Social cooperation was the basis of all thinking, whether it was abstract thought or the folkways of everyday life. Moreover, in the past, knowledge had been generated by emotional concerns and not by an impersonal search for the truth. Giddings, from an evolutionary perspective, wrote that the different stages of thought (i.e., magic analogy, induction, deduction) had been correlated with different stages of total social organization (i.e., zoogenic, anthropogenic, ethnogenic, demogenic).

For the most part Giddings did not engage in an ideological critique of past social theories. For example, in his writings there is no attempt at a radical unmasking of the hidden interests of other social theories. Giddings argued that the major fallacy of past social theorists was their failure to see the concrete, vital, social whole. Modern sociological theory realized the connectedness of all phenomena both social and nonsocial. From this point of view Giddings analyzed the mental configurations of total social groups. He tried to grasp the essential thinking of primitive men, as well as the French, English, and American mentality. He also scrutinized the modern mind in general. In this latter attempt he devised a schema of psychological types which he thought was representative of various ethnic groups within the American community.

In the social-technological tradition, Giddings argued for a positivistic conception of knowledge. Although social interaction was complicated by the addition of psychic behavior, there was no reason to believe that psychic laws could not also be assimilated under more general cosmic laws. The investigation of man would yield general laws if the proper scientific method were utilized—induction. The role of sociology was the discovery of general laws, particularly that law which went to the foundation of all social interaction—consciousness of kind. Based on the knowledge of general laws, the social scientist was to assess what was possible in a given society. Moreover, he should act as a professional advisor. His talents should be used in modern educational institutions and in conjunction with other professional groups (i.e., elites and leaders) within society. In particular, the social scientist should preach the values of hard work, monogamy, nation-state, science, and industrial democracy.

6 / *Albion W. Small*

(1854 - 1926)

Biography

Albion Small was born in Buckfield, Maine in 1854, the oldest son of Reverend Albion Keith Parris Small, D.D., a Baptist minister.[1] The Smalls had been in Maine for nearly three hundred years; they originally had settled in the southwestern county of York in 1632. They owned at one time (by title from the Indians) all the northern part of that county. His mother, Thankful Lincoln Woodbury Small, was said to be a descendant of Samuel Lincoln of Hingham, Massachusetts, the earliest American ancestor of Abraham Lincoln. Albion Small never verified this, but he was overtly interested in his lineage.

Albion Small's father had a distinguished career, which enabled him to give his gifted son a good education. Originally A. K. P. Small was the minister of the Baptist church in Buckfield, Maine. The village was estimated to have 225 people. There, the older Small served for seven years and developed a reputation as an outstanding preacher. In 1858 he was called to one of the important churches in Bangor, Maine, where he performed his duties for ten years. After these years in Bangor, Reverend Small became pastor of the Free Baptist Church in Portland, Maine—the largest city in Maine at that time—when the younger Albion was fourteen. Finally in 1874, the elder Albion was called to the First Baptist Church of Fall River, Massachusetts, one of the largest and most influential churches in that state.

Albion received the benefits of his father's rise in status and economic well-being. During his high-school years, the younger Albion worked on his uncle's farm. After high school, he went to Colby College in Waterville, Maine (which later became Colby University), pursuing, like his father, a course of divinity training. There were approximately 150 students at Colby. Albion soon outstripped the rest intellectually and politically. He was the leader of his class and an outstanding figure in the student body, even though there were only nine students in his graduating class.

Upon finishing his course of study at Colby at the age of twenty-two, Albion immediately entered the Newton Theological Institution in Massachusetts. He graduated from that institution in 1879. Because of his father's improved increased economic situation Small was able to continue his studies in Germany with his father's blessing. One of Small's biographers notes that: "Evidently the teaching at .the seminary did not greatly impress him and I have heard him say that he was ready to abandon the idea of the ministry at the end of his course there. But the opportunity to go to Germany to broaden his outlook in both theology and the humanistic studies kept burning the lambent flame in his devotions."[2]

Albion studied at the Universities of Berlin and Leipzig between 1879 and 1881. While at Leipzig and Berlin he took courses in history and national economy and came somewhat under the influence of the German historical method. He also met and married Valeria von Massow, who was the daughter of a German general. In the same year that he married (1881), he was offered a position at Colby College. Cutting his studies short, Small returned to the States.

At Colby, Small taught history and political science. After seven years as an outstanding teacher, he took a sabbatical leave and continued his studies at Johns Hopkins. There he read history, political science, and was taught welfare economics by Richard Ely. "In fulfillment of his duties as Fellow he taught a course in American Constitutional History."[3] His requirements for the doctorate were satisfied with a thesis on the Continental Congress.

Upon his return to Colby, Small was appointed its president at the age of thirty-five (1889). It is interesting to note that when Small returned, he replaced Noah Porter's course on moral philosophy with a course entitled "Sociology." Only one year later Small was reputed to have had a conversation with President Harper (University of Chicago) about sociology, and in 1892, Small was elected Head Professor of Social Science at the University of

Chicago. Apparently, Small's notion of sociology and Harper's disagreed somewhat. Luther Bernard wrote: "[Small's] contact with sociology grew in the three years he taught the subject at Colby and the breach with history widened. Brought to Chicago in 1892 to head the new department of sociology and anthropology, he was already too far beyond the theological viewpoint to meet the needs of the divinity students, always prominent in the thoughts of President Harper. Consequently Charles Richmond Henderson was invited to the university in 1893 to teach practical ecclesiastical sociology."[4] Small's administrative tasks were enormous at Chicago. Not long after his appointment to the Department of Sociology he became Dean of the College of Liberal Arts. In addition, he was appointed Dean of the Graduate School of Arts and Literature in 1904. In 1895 he founded the *American Journal of Sociology* and maintained active editorship for thirty years. He helped form the American Sociological Society in 1905 and was president of that organization in 1912 and 1913. He also worked in international sociology and was president of the Institut Internationale de Sociologie in 1922.

In addition to his professional and administrative interests, Small was an active participant in church activities. While at Chicago, Small served as a trustee and deacon for the Hyde Park Baptist Church for more than thirty years. We also may note that Small took time to lecture various Christian organizations on the subject of sociology. However, Small's real interest was clearly in social science, and this was exemplified by the fact that he left most of his estate ($25,000) to the University of Chicago for the support of social science publications.

In summary, we may note that Small came from a background of financial and status security. Small spent his entire life attached to the university in one form or another. He was not particularly enamored of the socialist movement or any other radical organizations. His occupational experience was one in which he was well anchored in the dominant institutions of his time. He also was firmly committed to the development of a scientific sociology.

Idealism, Organicism, and Interests

Small believed that the fundamental subject matter with which all social sciences (particularly sociology) were concerned was the "social process as a whole." By this he meant, I believe, a certain kind of idealistic organic schema. The world outside of us was not partitioned in its fundamental nature. Rather, the divisions existed in our head. Reality is one, and any divisions we create are a product of our own thinking. "The aim of sciences is to comprehend these apparent diversities as members of the unity of which they are aspects."[5]

The bases on which these classifications were made were not arbitrary but reflected traditions, customs, and scientific concerns. In a sense, the world which confronted the scientists was inexhaustible in principle. Not only were there many divisions, but one part *could not* be established as more primary than another. Small wrote about this in the following manner.

Classification is an arrangement of abstractions around selected centers of interest. No single classification can ever visualize the social reality, because the reality presents as many aspects as there are subjective centers of attention. The object cut up into abstractions has to be represented by combination of all the classifications which our alternative centers of interest incite us to make. These alternative classifications cannot be put together in any hierarchical order, if faithfulness to reality is to be maintained. To visualize the social reality, it is necessary to learn how to think these classifications as they shoot through and through each other in objective facts, forming the most complicated plexus ever observed.[6]

This idealistic/organic assertion was carried into Small's actual analysis of society with certain reservations. Small believed that the organismic analogy had a certain value which had been misused by past social theorists. He argued that the organismic analogy held four key ideas: (1) the organism was alive, (2) it was not homogeneous, but was composed of distinguishable parts, (3) these discrete parts were capable of cooperating with each other, (4) the complete life of the whole was realized only in the cooperation of the parts.[7] Small further argued that sociology had for its object of study "the varieties of groups in which individuals are associated, with the organizations, relations, functions and tendencies of these various associations."[8]

Like Giddings, Small argued that the social body exhibited an orderly development which was both psychical and physical in nature. In particular, the social organism was really only the objective manifestation of thoughts, beliefs, and technical activity. The common fund of ideas represents "the accumulated experience of many generations," which appears in the actions of individuals and groups. For Small, this heritage not only influences the structure and function of society but also constitutes the "super-organic" and "super-psychological" side of society.[9] Moreover, the social order was maintained by man's teleological behavior and his function within that order. Society was made up of men in associations, who conditioned each other. "Each man diminishes the amount of available space in the world; he increases the demand for food; he augments the potential supply of labor," and he multiplied the complexity of desires that had to be coordinated for the accommodation of human action. Small's criticism of the static organic analogy rested on two ideas: (1) men acted purposefully, and (2) actions were processes, not stable structures; therefore, associations had to be examined according to their functions.[10]

If society was an organic unity that had parts with various changing functions, then Small's question had to be: "Are there invariable elements in that social order?" Small had to answer this question because of the premises with which he started. If social reality was complex, organic, and constantly changing and if we all saw various parts of it, then it would seem to follow that there was no possibility for representing it as it was. Yet this was Small's explicit purpose. Like many of his generation, Small answered this question by postulating certain basic human interests which had not changed through the course of history. He wrote: "The entire range of time and space occupied by human beings is a continuum filled with unbroken persistence of human interests toward satisfaction. Every occurrence of human life is a function of all the social forces engaged in this ceaseless effort to express themselves. To explain society, we must be able to state every type of occurrence that takes place in human reactions in the individuals that are factors in the occurrence."[11]

According to Small, there were six basic interests from which all human actions evolved: (1) health, (2) wealth, (3) sociability, (4) knowledge, (5) beauty, and (6) rightness. Each such interest was "an unsatisfied capacity, corresponding to an unrealized condition, and it is predisposition to such rearrangement as would tend to realize the indicated position."[12] These six interests were represented in the subjective desires of given individuals, and the objective conditions of human satisfaction were based on these interests. The interests were combined in individuals in different amounts, and they contended with each other in our personality. Moreover, the career of an individual is persistently the struggle against the interests of other individuals. All social action, then, was the movement and countermovement of persons impelled by the particular assortment of interests which was located in each. "Society is what it is at any time as the resultant of all the efforts of all the personal units to reach its own peculiar sort of satisfaction."[13]

Society then was a working out of the various interests that were struggling with each other. The task of sociology was to formulate the various permutations of these forces and their meaning for present society. Although he used the organismic analogy, Small did not believe that society was a harmonious whole. In fact, he argued that conflict within a given society led toward more advanced forms of legitimate organization (e.g., the state), which synthesized past conflicts of interests. "The human process is at best not a Quaker meeting. The struggle of interest with interest... has not yet reached the stage in which turning the other cheek is a frequent occurrence. The only people who are generally understood or respected today are those who think they have rights and accordingly fight for them."[14]

For Small, the main movement of history was an evolution of an ascending scale of wants in people's minds (today called relative deprivation). The struggle tended toward a pecuniary evaluation of the relative worth of men and wealth. "Civil Society...tends to become endeavor after coordination, adaptation, perfection, explanation and agreement." Small summarizes this position in the following manner:

Human experience composes an associational process. The elements of that process are interests lodged in the individual. These interests may be reduced to...relatively simple essentials, but in the condition as of actual life, even at the most primitive stages, the interests express themselves in wants capable of infinite variation and combination. The individuals thus stimulated seek satisfactions of their wants, and efforts to this end bring them into contact with each other. At first these contacts are most evidently collisions; interest clashes with interest. The immediate result is formation of groups for offensive and defensive purposes. These groups in time vary more and more from the primitive-animal type. As the variation increases, association becomes an accelerated process of differentiation or permutation of interest within the individuals, of contacts between individuals of conflict and of cooperation among individuals and the groups into which they combine. Incidental to this pursuit of purposes, and to the process of adjustment between persons which results, individuals enter into certain more or less persistent structural relationships with each other known in general as "institutions," and into certain more or less permanent directions of effort, which we may call the social functions. The social structures and functions are, in the first instance, results of the previous associational process; but they no sonner pass out of the fluid state, into a relatively stable condition, then they become in turn causes for subsequent stages of the associational process.... There comes a time when some of the individuals in association begin to reflect upon the association itself in a fragmentary way. They think of their family, their clan, their tribe, their nation, as having interests of its own.... These men coin and utter thoughts and feelings and purposes which become current in their group. There are thence forward more or less distinct group programs, coordinating the instinctive endeavors of the individuals, and producing a certain mass-movement, in addition to the molecular motions, in the associational process .... With this consummation the associational process is in full swing. All that follows is merely differential in detail.[15]

The evolution of society, then, was a gradual working out of the interests of men in more and more complex associations. Unlike the Sumnerian notion, Small felt this struggle was based, in part, on the conscious behavior of individuals and was uniquely human. In another context, Small argued that the phases of struggle took the following forms: (1) unregulated war, (2) regulated war, (3) extension of the area and duration of intermittent strife, (4) legally regulated conflict of interests, (5) fraud, (6) legal trickery, (7) fair rivalry, (8) emulation, and (9) reasoned cooperation.

From this analysis, it is clear that Small believed the conflict of interests was constantly converging toward "minimum conflict and maximum cooperation and sociality."[16] In a word, Small was a disciple of the realpolitik tradition in Germany. This tradition viewed conflict as: (1) the attempt by one or more persons (individuals, parties, nations) to purposefully pursue their interests in the face of hostility and resistance by other persons, and (2) a power struggle between opponents; the manifest or latent function of these struggles was to produce order and unity (i.e., the state, laws) between and within the opposing groups.[17]

If society was an organically linked unity of interest-driven men, and if the movements or processes of history were the working out of these interests toward increasing cooperation in some form of a normative order, then it is not hard to imagine that Small would look for the social bases of knowledge in various interest groups to which a given person belongs. Unlike Marx, however, Small, because of his organic-idealistic, predilection, tended to view an individual as having interests that cut across class lines. Moreover, for Small, it was a small step to his next idea, that past social theories were deficient because they did not analyze the complex network of interaction that actually took place in society. In the next two sections, Small's formulation of these ideas will be examined. For the present, it should be noted that Small also does not fit our social-technological theme perfectly. Although he ascribes certain basic interests to individuals, these interests do not necessarily need to be controlled. Small does suggest, however, that the evolution of interests generates institutions (e.g., the state), which regulate interests for the common good. This evolution was viewed as desirable.[18] However, it also can be imputed that Small did not believe that humans were capable of radical change. In particular, Small "like most of the founders of American sociology (and with the major exception of William Graham Sumner), was opposed both to Marxian theory and socialist politics, and to laissez-faire."[19] In sum, Small, like Ward, was a critic of the status quo, but he did not base his criticism on Marxist premises. The base of his critique will be developed presently.[20]

The Division of Knowledge

I have noted earlier that one of the basic interests of all men was the desire for knowledge. According to Small, this interest was relatively constant, and only the manner in which it was expressed changed. The interest in knowledge, which was a "higher" interest, could not be confined arbitrarily to any type of institution. The knowledge interest was eternal, and the institutions through which it expressed itself were ephemeral.[21] However, he argued that in the modern world at that time, knowledge development was primarily based on occupational interests. That is, each occupation developed a moral code (not an ideology) which legitimized their interests. These conceptions acted as blinders in such a manner that various opposing interest groups could not see the consequences of their views upon the larger social process. The contemporary confusion of moral standards was a product of distinct occupational ethical codes. It follows for Small that the greater the division of labor, the greater the diversity of occupational codes (ethics). Small described this state of affairs in the following passage.

Suppose, for example, we are in the midst of a labor conflict. It is proposed to arbitrate the difficulty. Representatives of the conflicting parties meet. A looker-on, if he happens to be a philosopher, soon discovers that the issue cannot be decided upon ethical grounds, for the conflicting parties, and perhaps the arbitrating board, each have a different standard of ethics. The employers' ethics are found upon conceptions of the rights of the property. The employees' ethics take as their standard certain conceptions of the rights of labor. The arbitrators' ethics may vary from the lawyer's interpretation of the civil code to the speculative philosopher's conception of the ideal rights of the generic man.[22]

Small's solution to this problem was based on the idea that these interest groups lacked a sociological perspective. That is, ethics was basically a judgment about the effects produced by certain actions operating as causes. Only when a comprehensive knowledge of the social process was attained could the cause and effects of certain actions be ascertained. We must be in agreement about the basic nature of life and its social consequences.

Small's ideas of occupational interests determining the structure of thought comes through most clearly in his "novel," *Between Eras From Capitalism to Democracy.* I will sketch an overview of the characters involved and then show the interests they represented. The major characters were: the senior Lyon, one of the early business entrepreneurs at the turn of the century; his son, Logan Lyon, who was working as an administrator in the same firm, Walther Kissinger, secretary to the senior Lyon and a dreamer of utopias; Graham—an ex-entrepreneur who has become prolabor and a social democrat; Halleck, a minister in the Chicago area, who preached to the working classes and who had rejected a secure position in his father's firm to become a minister—he was respected by both business and labor—a mediator of sorts; and Edgerly—an academic. Some minor characters in the story were Elsie, who is Kissinger's daughter, and Kinzie Lyon, the sister of Logan.

The novel utilized as its focal point a crisis in the firm. This crisis was in the form of a general strike for the express purpose of getting labor represented on the board of directors of the company. Graham, the labor leader, has nothing personal against the Lyon enterprise but simply wanted to use this as a test case to expand the rights of labor.

With the above information, Small's formulation of the sociology of interests can be examined. The senior Lyon represented the business establishment, and as such he was unequivocal in his purpose. For example, Small wrote:

He accepted the working world as a scheme of order as unvarying and inevitable as the harmony of spheres. The Newtonian law of this system was, capitalize all the wealth you can, and make it pay every penny of dividends it will produce. The general limitations of the system were defined by the statutes and the recognized rules of competition. Within these boundaries, success belonged to the strongest force.... His whole office philosophy was once packed into a remark to Edgerly: "we can't go into battle without losing killed and wounded, but we must win the fight first and attend to them afterwards. When human sympathies obstruct the operation of business principles, they are as much out of place as lace curtains and bric-a-brac in a foundry."[23]

According to Small, Logan Lyon represented the advantage of a privileged heritage. "By grace of family connections they [Logan and similar types] had learned the business world, through rapid promotion to responsibility that initiated them into commercial relations on a large scale." Life for them was action and not speculation. Their professional milieu required a competitive mentality in which "it had become second nature to choose distinct aims to be reached, and to rate everything at what it was worth as means to those ends." Their occupation implicitly operated with the notion that only the successful will inherit the earth. For them, the market represented the essential idea of the modern world.[24] Kissinger, Lyon's secretary, "was essentially not a man of affairs." Of German heritage, "he was a seer of visions." He belonged to "the race of Klopstock, and Schiller." He lived a dual life, one of routine and one of sentiment. He had always felt somehow alien in the American culture.

Practically Kissinger was an obedient and virtually automatic cog in the conventional machinery of society. In the office his devotion to the company was as unreserved as though the thought of economic evils had never troubled his imagination. Out of business hours he was never quite himself unless he was dreaming dreams of reforming the world. He read the class of literature, and he cultivated the type of acquaintances, that wasted no attention upon feasible improvements, but devoted themselves to theories of an ideal society. Instead of stimulating actual invention, this speculation tended to make him timid and perfunctory. He knew no ways and means but those of his everyday program.... He was not aware of it, but his philosophy actually left room for only two alternatives; either to be content with the established order of things, or to expect a miraculous transformation of the real world into the ideal.[25]

In addition to the visionary and the practical men, Small represented labor through Graham. In a speech to the laborers, Graham suggested something like the following. Modern business was like a system of government in which there was taxation without representation. The laborers do not have any opportunity to make their views known. Moreover, only a radical change in existing business policy would be satisfactory. The aim of organized labor was to transform capitalism into a democracy. In short, labor would refuse to "cooperate any longer on terms that give the lion's share of benefit to the men whose hardest work is the watering of the kind of stock they breed in Wall Street."[26]

The academic perspective on labor was represented by Edgerly. Edgerly was asked to speak at the Patriarch's Club, which was ranked first among the strictly commercial clubs of Chicago. Originally, the Secretary of Commerce and Labor was supposed to speak, but due to illness he could not make the journey. Edgerly, according to Small, was adept "at a peculiar art of linguistic legerdemain." Moreover, Edgerly never believed himself cast in the heroic mold. Yet, he believed that more cross-fertilization was needed between men of theory and men of practice. For that reason, he accepted the invitation to speak on the labor crisis. Edgerly argued that the academic had a moral duty to fit any work or project into the whole scheme of relations, "the whole system of cause and effect, in which it plays a part." Moreover, "It is not this year's nor this decade's wages or profits alone; it is not alone a possible modification of business policies, or redistribution of managerial responsibility; it is not alone the probable influence upon the permanence or proportions of industrial classes. It is all of these together, calculated to their last discoverable effects."[27]

Halleck, to Small, was the image of a secularized prophet. Halleck believed that the important aspect of religion was not knowledge or information but a moral attitude. The church, to his mind, had not distinguished between Jesus' moral attitude and his lack of worldly knowledge concerning how to draft a Russian constitution or an American tariff. Halleck, like Edgerly, spoke to his congregation about the labor problem. He argued that the eighteenth century had misled later social theorists. The eighteenth century believed in the independence of individuals. For Halleck, however, individualistic philosophy is only a "refined selfishness." In actual fact, life was a system of reciprocal interests. Social life can only be advanced by learning to concur and to correlate diverse interests. If we do not learn how to do this, life as we know it will be destroyed. In short, "the peculiar task of our social era is to install the morality of legislating and regulating not for one another but with one another."[28]

Small's novel indicated that there was a converging of men's diverse interests toward seeing life whole. The young Lyon, through his educational background and his association with academics, was finally persuaded that labor represented an emerging consciousness which could not be denied. His sister, Kinzie Lyon, also gained the same perspective through her involvement in charity activities. Kissinger went to hear Graham speak and was convinced that Graham's ideas were right. Kissinger, therefore, resigned his position with the firm. From another angle, Halleck was convinced that the Christian and Judaic tradition meant involvement with the life of one another.

In the last part of the novel, the young Lyon meets with Graham through an arrangement by Halleck. While Graham and Lyon were arguing, Halleck listened carefully and finally synthesized their arguments into a memorandum which satisfied both Lyon and Graham. In essence, the document stated that:

1. The company acknowledges the principle that work in its employ creates an equity in business.

2. There is no way to calculate the exact equity, so the company believes the only way to determine this is through cooperation between the company and its employees.

3. Therefore the company agrees to appoint a committee to work with a labor committee on the affairs of the company.

4. The company agrees that the employees may determine the method of obtaining the committee members, provided they work for the company.

5. The company agrees that committees should cooperate with each other.

6. The company agrees to consider the reports of the committees.[29]

Small's novel represented his ideas about the generation of varying interests and his hope concerning how diverse interests could be resolved. The interests were generated by the division of labor, in which each occupation struggled for its own survival. As industrialization increased, philosophies of life developed centering on individualistic premises. With the segmentation of modern life, more and more interests came into conflict. This conflict heightened mutual awareness. In this milieu, intellectuals, preachers, and others who were morally concerned with the quality of life perceived the need for cooperative associations.

Small used this same analytic approach not only for analyzing strands of occupational thought but for examining the development of sociology as well. The history of the social sciences was rooted in the narrow interests of certain intellectual groups (e.g., cameralists), which were incapable of seeing the organic unity of life.

Small argued, for example, that the development of sociology was dependent upon the physical sciences, the industrial revolution, philanthropy, the French Revolution, various utopian thinkers, (e.g., Fourier, Owen), socialism, political economy, and various other phenomena.[30] It is interesting to note that Small was aware of diverse interests in the sociological enterprise itself. He distinguished between analytic and historical sociologists in the following manner. The historical sociologist, whose interests turn backward in time, will be inclined to doubt that rapid social change is possible. These men are under strong influences which suggest to them that society is bound by the "will of the gods, which grinds so exceedingly slow that men cannot accelerate its motion." Conversely, the analytic sociologist is more tempted to argue for immediate social change. The analytic sociologist tends to forget the importance of time and that "social improvement thus far has been by cooperation of many ameliorative forces." The analytic study of society tends to draw people from the ranks of social radicals.[31]

In the same manner that Small distinguished between the analytic and historical sociologists, he examined the works of early social scientists such as Adam Smith and the cameralists. In the case of Marx and Smith, Small believed that both had been correct in their historical context but that the present time called for a new synthesis.[32] However, cameralism also was rooted in the interests of particular intellectual groups, who attempted to develop theories on the financial solvency of the state. The cameralists were interested in the technique and theory of administering the state. The "object of all social theory was to show how the welfare of the state might be secured." For them, the state was the source of all other welfare. In particular, their interests was turned toward supplying the state with needed revenue.[33] Cameralism, then, as social theory was really an administrative technique for maintaining the interests of the prince. The prince was the state in cameralistic theory. The cameralists were employed in administrative positions surrounding the prince. Their primary purpose was to consider the fiscal needs of the prince. During the period in which the cameralists wrote (middle sixteenth century to the end of the eighteenth century), the chronic condition was war. The cameralists were servants who attempted to aid the prince in administering the estate. The prince was considered the regulator of life, and social theories always ended up in support of him. The great majority of the people in the German states were not considered capable of individual initiative. The major concern of the prince was the self-maintenance of the state and particularly the control of an adequate military force.[34]

In sum, Small did view the genesis of knowledge from the perspective of interest groups. However, his interest-group theory was not based on class differences. As he viewed it, the division of labor in modern life, along with multiple other elements, caused the formation of narrow occupational codes. The fact that he stressed the holistic character of social reality should make us wary of too easily placing him in the critical-emancipatory camp. Small, like most of the men discussed here, clearly argues against any monocausal approach to the study of social relations. It is not surprising, therefore, that even when collective entities are not referred to as the generators of knowledge, a pluralistic tone creeps into the writings. For Small, pluralistic causal factors were simply the reserve side of his holism. Far more than any of the other sociologists discussed in this work, however, Small did analyze past social theories. He was consumed with an interest in intellectual history, and it is to this interest that we now turn our attention.

Totality as an Ontological Principle

Small argued that the only true science of society was the one that objectively represented the totality of phenomena in all their relations. In this context, his reasoning was very similar to that of Comte. Small believed that sociology must build on the results of physiology, psychology, ethics, history, etc. The reason for the existence of sociology was to be found in the assertion that sociology was the study which approached reality with the idea that knowledge must be one and synthetic.[35]

All thinking strives toward a final stage in which the object may be represented, not as it seems to any partial perception but as it is in reality....Nothing more sharply distinguishes the sociologists, as a class, from the specialists whose fragmentary programs promise nothing conclusive, than the explicit aim of sociology to reach knowledge which shall have a setting for all details of fact about human associations as a whole. Demand for the universal is thus the very reason for the existence of sociology....

The problem and the method of sociology was to interpret, "*as a coherent whole, the facts of human experience.*" This method was not metaphysical in any sense; "*it is not symbolical, or analogical, or indirect, in any sense; it is matter of fact generalization of the workings of elemental human interests, as they manifest themselves.*"[36]

What, then, did Small think about past theories? Were they ideologies or true statements? Were they repressive in nature? I don't believe that Small thought past theories were repressive, but only that they were blocked intellectual developments. In his analysis of Adam Smith, Small argued that the economists after Smith had distorted his vision: "It was too much of a task for the interpreters of human experience to develop at once the full logical implications of the progressive principles imbedded in Adam Smith's system." Similarly, Small in his introduction to the cameralist movement stated that: "every theory, system, science is in some way a reflection of the prevailing purposes of the time in which it developed." By this he meant our theories were formed by the dominant interests of that time. And if we removed a system of thought from the activities in which it was involved, we inevitably distorted it. "It is like abstracting a plant from the soil and atmosphere which are the media of its existence, and then expecting it both to

grow and to reveal the abstract process of its previous growth."[37]
Small argued that there was a gradual evolution of human thought.
The reason that we are aware of the organic nature of reality today was because human associations had become more obtrusive
and influential than in any previous epoch. This was due to increases in the intermediate processes of production, consumption,
industrial diversification, the division of labor, territorial competition, and instantaneous communications. "This inevitable contact of man with men has produced confident popular philosophies of association."[38] To bring out Small's position clearly (i.e.,
the type of ideas scrutinized), I will examine his ideas about Plato,
the development of social theory in his *Origins of Sociology,* and
his relationship to the modern socialism of his time.

Small argued that Plato's *Republic* was an exercise in opinion,
not science.[39] The Socratic or dialectical method tended to set up
judgments in the mind of the thinkers as the final test of truth.
Science (Sociology) must rely upon positive knowledge of facts.
This meant that generalizations about society must be tested empirically. Even in the world of morals, Small believed, *The Republic*
could not teach us much. As I have indicated earlier, Small held a
pragmatic theory of ethics which was grounded in the notion that
we could not determine which moral actions were best until we
had discovered the effects of such actions on the whole of society.
Morality for Small was not a series of a priori questions about the
nature of "ought," but rather an empirical question.

The only connection between Plato and sociology was their
bond in a common subject matter. If, however, *"method* is the
chief test of sciences, then sociology and *The Republic* are as far a-
part as mechanics from magic."[40] Method, then, was the key to
differentiating classical political philosophy from the positive science of sociology. In his concern with the methods of modern social science, Small also criticized the socialists.

Small was declaredly not a socialist.[41] He argued that sociology
should not favor any paticular class interests, but should act for
the benefit of all the members of society. It was a false analysis
which divided men into the rich and the poor. The real line of differentiation was that some men were foolish and others sagacious,
some unselfish and others selfish.[42] One of the reasons why social
theories had not been impartially objective was that continually

social theory had been one of the weapons of class conflicts.[43] Reduced, the ideas of men throughout history had two essential elements. First, we had those men who looked at life from the secure vantage of already having arrived at the top of the hierarchy. Secondly, we had men who were struggling for a place on that same secure ground. In the eyes of the former, the world belonged to the chosen few; in the eyes of the latter, the world belonged to the many.[44]

With the emergence of sociology, these partial visions would be replaced by a more rigorous analysis of the whole. In criticizing Marx, Small explained that "from the standpoint of social science any plan at all for correcting the evils of capitalism is premature until the world has probed much deeper into the evils themselves." No well-informed and well-balanced person would assent or imply that the way to accomplish such reform (i.e., the problem of labor organization) had been discovered. On the other hand, a hundred minor plans and policies had been discovered, which made for a *partial* solution to the labor problem. "A hundred means are known, applicable at different points of the industrial system."[45] Small's major arguments against socialism are summarized in the following passage:

Socialism is a programme. Sociology is both science and philosophy....Socialism assumes that which sociology investigates. Socialism may have reached, by shrewd perception, much social interpretation that Sociology will verify; but at present socialism is related to Sociology much as astrology was to the early history of Astronomy, or Alchemy to the beginnings of Christianity.

Toward most of the reorganizations which socialism proposes, sociology is in the attitude of our mechanical engineers toward the practicability of aerial navigation. In relation to immediate social issues the sociologist is rather a referee, while the socialist is an advocate. In contrast with the eagerness of socialism, the policy of sociology is to make haste slowly....Sociology was born of the modern order to improve society. Sociology presumes that right social life is more difficult to understand than the socialistic programme makers imagine.[46]

Small's position on the nature of fractured social visions comes out most clearly in his *Origins of Sociology.* In this work he argued that there had been a gradual evolution of sociological consciousness which was not linear in its development but cumulatively progressive. He limited his study to Germany, but only because he felt that more than any other social science tradition, the Germans had influenced American sociology. In this work the central question is: "What is the meaning of human experience, and to what extent have we developed a technique which may be relied upon to ascertain more of that meaning?"[47] Small believed that science progressed by increased accuracy of observations and comprehensiveness in its interpretation. The latter indicated a type of objectivity which was rooted not in class interests, but in a concern for the whole of society.

Small began his analysis of sociological predecessors with the nineteenth-century German historians: Friedrich Karl von Savigny (1779-1861), K. F. Eichhorn (1781-1854), B. G. Niebuhr (1776-1831), and Leopold von Ranke (1795-1886). Savigny was the first to give a deeper and richer meaning to the idea of *continuity*. He moved closer tó objectivity by treating each object as *"an incident in a causal series of human experiences* reaching back into the impenetrable beginnings of the human career." Savigny in his time was responding to Thibaut's call for a codification of laws applicable to all the German states. Savigny believed that such an undertaking might lead to a Napoleonic regime in Germany. In response to Thibaut, Savigny argued that even if a German code was possible as an abstract proposition, it was not feasible from a practical point of view. Savigny argued that there was not sufficient legal training or legal wisdom to carry out such a task. Savigny's criticism amounted to the contention that "systematic legal codification shall be attempted only by a generation adequately grounded in understanding of the Roman law," which was the basis of German civilization. Savigny, according to Small, believed that laws had an immanent development like language, which could not be introduced a priori. Within the context of Small's study, Savigny contributed the ideas of antecedent causes and gradualism in reform.[48]

Eichhorn added the idea that a given social situation was inherently complex. No one before Eichhorn had successfully outlined "a respectable survey of the interacting social conditions in central Europe, among which constitutional and legal development took shape." To Small, this meant that Eichhorn had made a step toward objective history which was an account of all the different influences which entered into the life of people, "of the ways in which these influences worked, and of the relative effect which each from time to time had upon the total conditions of that people."[49]

While Eichhorn and Savigny contributed the ideas of complexity, continuity, and gradualism, Neibuhr advocated the necessity of "subjecting alleged historical evidence to the severest scrutiny." This critical historical method can be summarized as follows: (1) exclusion of all mythological factors from direct consideration; (2) comparison of all known traditions to discover common material and indicators of the common sources of materials; (3) examination of the credibility of evidence; (4) an examination of the circumstantial evidence to test the reliability of verbal records. Leopold von Ranke continued in the same spirit as Niebuhr and argued that the historian must *"verify by authentic documents,* preferably official documents." History was to be the recounting of occurrences which were primarily the experiences of official people in the church, state, army, etc.[50]

In addition to the historians' contributions, there were the ideas of the social scientists. The first social scientists were the cameralists. Cameralism, as mentioned earlier, was the theory which argued the welfare of the state was the most important concern. And the state was represented by the interests of the prince. In a divided Germany (sixteenth century) the major concerns of the prince were keeping funds to wage war and to defend his provinces. In camerialistic theory the welfare of the state was the supreme concern, and the science of getting money for the state was the corollary to the first premise. By 1765 camerialism had evolved to the point where as a system of thought it was broken up into the divisions of policy, commerce or national economy, and finance.

During the first three-quarters of the nineteenth century the German economists were confused about the proper role of economics. This was partly due to the German confrontation with English laissez-faire economics. The Germans were attempting to integrate Adam Smith's individualism with German ideas of collectivism. According to Small, it took the Germans from 1765 to 1870 to reach the conclusion that "human relations in connection with wealth cannot be truly stated in terms of individuals." Between 1820 and 1870 both English and German economists were converging on a common strand of thought which indicated that "economic determinism" was inadequate as an explanatory device. They were convinced that multiple causation was needed to understand human intercourse in economic settings. According to Small, the idea of multiple causation was an important predecessor of modern sociology.[51]

While the German historians were holding sway over the economists in their country, the Austrians (i.e., Karl Menger, E. Böhm-Bawerk) were developing the idea that economics must be a science of the mind. Economic values must be thought of as "a relation between appraisable goods" and an "appraising mind." Meanwhile, Karl Knies of Germany indicated that political economy must make itself a "theory of persons in their varied activities." Small explained that Knies was introducing the conjecture that economics must be a moral science. That is, human relations were not physical things with spatial boundaries, but "modes of human behavior." Human actions (economic or other) were many-sided and had effects on the whole human condition.[52]

Knies's ethical formulations culminated in the Verein für Sozialpolitik. This organization was stimulated further by A. Wagner's address (1871) to the Evangelical Church of Prussia. In this address, he indicated that poverty, misery, suffering, etc., would always be part of the human condition, but that it was the task of social scientists to diminish these evils insofar as possible. This ideal was to be brought about through the intervention of the state. Small wrote: "If there is one thing more certain than all things else about German civilization, it is that the Germans always believe in the right and duty of society, and particularly of society in the form of the state, to preside over the destiny of the individuals."[53] The Verein für Sozialpolitik became the most influential body of academic men, dedicated to the task that life was an engineering problem which could be worked out through reasonable self-consciousness of concerned individuals.

Albert Schäffle, the Austrian, was one of the first to propose to the Germans the idea of a comprehensive sociology. His thesis was that we must first get an insight into the interconnections of human phenomena in general before "we can have standing ground from which to explain those phases of human phenomena which we label *economic.*" Schäffle's economic theory was one in which the entire system of organizations created by men for the control of natural goods was seen in light of making these goods as useful as possible in realizing the potential of individuals.[54] These ideas culminated in his systematic study entitled *Bau und Leben des Sozialen Körpers.*

Small believed that the development of German social science was more important than the growth of social science in France or England. He argued that America of the 1890s was alive with German thinking, that the Germans were decisive in influencing American sociological ideas. Of even greater interest to us is the fact that Small did not attack these older social-scientific theories of the social world as ideological. He was convinced that these theories were interest-oriented but not necessarily in a repressive manner. The ideas of the past had been organically linked to their particular contexts, and as such, they served the functional interests of those in power. Small's main contention was that the gradual evolution of social-science presuppositions provided the necessary linkage for the formulation of modern sociology. With the ideas of complexity, continuity, rigorous historical methods, collectivism, and ethics, sociology was born. These ideas became part of the assumptive level of sociology which, for Small, meant greater objectivity.

Twenty years prior to writing *Origins of Sociology,* Small had examined the assumptions of sociology. These assumptions, I believe, were then investigated in his later work to support his notion of the evolution of sociological consciousness. According to Small, assumptions "were those aspects of reality which form parts of the background of sociology" and do not necessarily appear in the actual investigation. Today we might say they form the domain assumptions within which interpretation takes place. Small discussed five assumptions.[55] The first was the associational assumption. This was the idea that the human association existed and could be systematically studied. Individuals were not singular atoms but were always involved in cooperation or conflict with each other. The second assumption was the philosophical one, which stated reality was a unified whole. This conjecture was based on common sense and on supposedly philosophical evidence. The third was the cosmic assumption, which indicated that there were fixed physical conditions with which humans interacted. The fourth was the individual assumption of interests. Individuals know, feel, or will something. An individual without interests is not human. The final assumption was teleologic and progressive. There is a process which realizes better proportions in the distribution of health, wealth, sociability, etc.

In the final analysis, then, Small's task was not to unmask repressive ideologies but to demonstrate that modern sociology had venerable roots, which had been gradually assimilated into sociological consciousness. The incomplete visions of the past were due to social conditions that were not yet ready for the development of sociology. Moreoover, Small analyzed the effects of a complex division of labor on various occupational groups. His focus was not on ideology but on the presociological theories suggested by both scholars and the public. He clearly differs from the other sociologists discussed thus far, however, in his concern with past social theories.

Small developed a number of distinct ideas about the role social-science knowledge and intellectuals should play in the development of society. In the first stage of Small's work (1890-1910), he was concerned with keeping sociology distinct from social agitation and mysticism. For Small, the major purpose of sociology was to provide a more comprehensive (synthetic) view of social processes than had been achieved to that time. This first stage blended into the second (1910–17), in which Small advocated a unity of social scientists under some form of organization which would act as an advisory board to the government. The third stage was marked by Small's capitulation to the fact that sociologists were doing many different things and that sociology was one academic discipline among others. By this time, I think, he had reconciled himself to the idea that social scientists would never merge into a unified body to advise the state, even though he still advocated such an action. During all of these stages in Small's thought, he also wrote about capitalism and democracy. In general, his ideas about the latter were congruent with his idea about the role of sociology in society.

Sociology: Neither Active nor Reactive

In his early writings, Small persistently pursued the theme that sociology was not the vanguard of a revolutionary elite. He felt that two dangers were threatening the developing discipline of sociology. On the one hand, he feared that radical ideas would be attached to sociology and thus would cause the popular imagination to expect a revolution. On the other hand, he was afraid that certain mystical preachers would be mistaken for sociologists and their followers would start a cult of obscurantism. In response to these dangers Small proclaimed that the teacher of sociology "must impress the pupil with the belief that this primary task is not to reform society, but to understand society."[56] Socialism, according to Small, had mercilessly exposed social evils but had failed to develop positive programs. At the same time traditional theories of individualism accepted the world in its present state, without possibility of change. Small summarized these directions of thought by writing that "conventionality is the thesis, socialism is the antithesis, sociology is the synthesis." For him the aim of sociology was not the cure of social disease but the development of social health. He expressed his feelings in the following manner:

The most fundamental, and in the end most useful, social service that can be performed by men capable of scientific labor is to collect the social facts that can be discovered in order to derive from them general laws, fundamental principles of social tendency....Men enlisted in this work usually have little time, and perhaps little talent, for direct participation in the work of applying social principles to concrete social tasks. They are none the less large contributors to the final solution of the social problem.[57]

Small believed that the discovery of laws in social behavior was both possible and desirable. He did make a distinction between natural and social phenomena in that social behavior was teleological. However, this did not mean that the discovery of general social laws was impossible. In particular, he noted that the sooner men could determine the effects of certain kinds of behavior upon institutions, the greater the probability of formulating scientific ethics. Ethics would not be based on some essential nature of man or the cosmos but on principles derived from an assessment of certain actions which would benefit all of society. The exact meaning of the good of society was never made clear by Small.

The greatest value of sociology would be its furnishing a *"point of view, a perspective, an atmosphere,* which will help to place all the problems of life with which each has to deal." Sociology would provide a unified view of reality which the laws of the mind demanded. It would involve "alternate analysis and synthesis of the reality, until nothing remains vague, and nothing seems unrelated to the rest." For Small, science was sterile unless it contributed to knowledge of what was worth doing. "Ethics must consist of empty forms until sociology can indicate the substance to which the forms apply."[58] The problem with Small's formulation was that no indication existed that such knowledge, for concrete action was readily available. In general, it can only be said that Small thought sociology should contribute to progressive socialization.

According to Small, socialization was a process of evolution whereby unregulated conflict of interests became regulated through formal laws, recognized morality, etc.,—anything which restrained overt hostility. In short, sociology was to be the science of moral action. It had the legitimacy to do this on the basis of its greater synthetic capabilities in comparison with those of other social sciences (e.g., economics, political science). Much like Comte, Small argued that sociology was to be the highest generalizing science. It would integrate all the knowledge from the various special social sciences. If it failed in this endeavor, sociology was not worth having.[59]

During the period 1890-1910, Small also responded to various attacks on capitalism. His answer was, not socialism, but rather a kind of proprietor-magistrate system to run the large industries. In the first stage, Small, in my opinion, was extremely vague about what concrete form this system would take. In his judgment:

The vulnerable point in our present society is not its permission of large wealth to some of its members, but its maintenance of institutions which, in that last analysis, make some men's opportunity to work for wealth under any condition dependent upon the arbitrary will of other men.

Insofar as agitators for social changes squint toward the notion of equal reward for unequal work, or equal division of the products of industry, they seem to me courteous not only of the impossible, but of the unjust, the unreasonable, and consequently of the altogether undesirable.[60]

Small believed that the problems of lage corporations could be resolved by: (1) increasing our intelligence about them, (2) encouraging legislation which would protect the workers; (3) assuming public control of many properties which belonged inherently to the people. About all these issues Small was extremely obscure and continually argued that we need more comprehensive knowledge of the social process.

Sociologists: Multiple Roles

Small's second stage clarified his thoughts about the role of social scientists in the modern world. Throughout his career Small praised the Verein für Sozialpolitik and finally encouraged the establishment of such an organization in the United States. The ultimate expression of this position appeared in *The Meaning of Social Science* (1910). In this book he continued to argue for the unity of social science, but now it was based on a physical organizational unity rather than on the idea of an intellectual synthesis. "There must be team-work between the social sciences, if they are to advance from the rank of boy's play and consitute serious social science." If academics would forget the administrative partitions which divded them, they could collectively investigate any given event, (e.g., the French Revolution). In his desire for a unified social science, Small was even willing to give up the hard-won professional status of sociology. "I am by no means contending that *sociology* is identical with that unified social science. All I assert is that the sociologists have something to say which is bound to be one of the factors in organizing that unified social science. I do not know, and I do not much care, whether anything or anybody will answer to the name sociology or sociologist a hundred years from now."[61]

The central task of the unified social science organization would be an understanding of the past and the present. In addition, this knowledge would indicate the correct means and ends for the future of the human race.[62] Social science under the unified science program had four distinct phases: (1) descriptive, (2) analytical, (3) evaluative, and (4) constructive. The descriptive phase, for Small, was one in which past facts were described in light of their functions for the "whole experience" within which an event occurred. The analytic phase attempted to connect the facts, while the evaluative phase concerned itself with the worth of the facts. The final, constructive stage was one in which there was concern with control of the facts. Small suggested that the final justification for all knowledge of the social process was the advancement to higher levels of social organization.

Small, then, posed for himself the concrete question: "Should a tendency toward centralization of the control of capital or toward decentralization be encouraged in the United States today?" The proposed institute would be obliged to ask the further questions: "Desired by whom? Encouraged by whom?" He answered the just-mentioned questions by referring, not to the people or particular classes, but to the consensus of the institute of social science. *"In so far as an approximation to reliable evaluation of conduct may be looked for at all from academic sources, not formulas of individual theorists or types of theorists, but decisions rendered by such a composite council as we have supposed, would be the most enlightened appraisal of moral values that science can reach.*[63] [His emphasis.] The most reliable criterion for human values which could be proposed would be the consensus of councils of scientists representing the "largest possible variety of human interests and co-operating to reduce their special judgments to a scale which would render their due to each of the interests in the total calculation." This did not mean that academic men would carry out these policies directly themselves. Small was quite aware of the limitations of the academic mind, and for this reason, the institute of social science was to include practical men in the implementation of these policies. For Small, social science was the holiest sacrament available to men. As he viewed it, sociology would replace religious faith with concrete realistic content. It would show how to operationalize the maxims of Christianity.[64]

In the final stage (1917-22) of Small's concern with the role of social science, he had almost given up hope for an institute of social scientists. It is not clear why Small was despondent about this project. It may have been Germany's return to nationalism and her subsequent rejection of the institute. Possibly it was Small's own disillusionment with Germany during the First World War. Yet again, it may have been his experiences in the university situation, which led him to believe that the insitute was not a realistic possibility. Whatever the reason, it is clear that sociology had taken a different turn from his original conception of the direction it should take. Small, in a somewhat autobiographical portrait, concedes the fact that sociology had become a member of the academic community. "Whatever then may have been the hopes, and the ideals, and definitions of the pioneers, sociology in the United States has come to be, first and chief in one of the numerous interdependent techniques by means of which research into the fact and meanings of human experience is now conducted."[65] In an article entitled "Fifty Years of Sociology in the United States" (1918), Small chronicled the fact that the sociological perspective had been indiscriminately applied to everything. In his schema, he noted that sociology had been used for: (1) promotion of the betterment of immediate concrete conditions, (2) training sciences for different kinds of ameliorative agencies, (3) developing technologies, as distinguished from techniques of social improvement, (4) investigating and teaching abstract phases of social conditions, (5) investigation and teaching of comprehensive syntheses of human relationships, (6) investigation and teaching of group psychology, (7) investigation and teaching the methodology of the social sciences, and (8) investigation and teaching of pure and applied ethics.[66]

While Small was chronicling what had happened to sociology, he also was working on his conception of a utopian democracy. This democracy was based on a purely secular ethic, which meant a conception of ends which were within the realm of actual possibilities. "The beginnings of genuinely ethical conceptions of life are made with the achievement of a sense of responsibility to make one's talents count for what they are worth in a system of reciprocal services."[67] Democracy could be enhanced through already existing institutions, such as education. This institution would be charged with the function of reiterating the facts about social reality. In this way the habits and thoughts of the people would alter the basic structure of society. For Small, democracy was the secularized version of caring about your neighbors.

Democracy will be a way of living together which men will ultimately work out after they have arrived at universal interest in another's well-being. This will be a way of living together in which the requirements of conformity for the sake of assuring the team work necessary for the good of the whole, will be balanced by assurance of a kind and degree of liberty which proves to be necessary in the supreme adventure of achieving the personality of each.[68] [His emphasis.]

Even though Small had faith in democratic processes, he was still concerned that there be a guiding agency to advise the public. The noticeable characteristic now was that this agency had become extremely vague. Nothing was mentioned about who should make up the committee (e.g., academics) or where it would be organizationally based. Small, then, had a lingering hope for the establishment of some intellectual association to guide the will of the people. In a moving passage, Small wrote:

A relatively self-conscious society would provide itself with some sort of a standing committee outlook. It would be a commission charged with the sole function of reading the signs of the times with references to the workings of the social process in the large view which we have considered. It would have the duty of discovering and making known to the whole society where parts of the society were falling behind their indicated functions, and it would be expected to advise society as to the relative urgency of these delinquent functions for stimulus.[69]

Small—like Sumner, Ward, and Giddings—proposed that sociology should be concerned with the discovery of social laws. The discovery of these laws was not to aid in overthrowing the existing state of affairs but to regulate and stabilize the imbalances of modern society. Like the social-technological tradition, he stressed the importance of consulting with other experts. He made a distinction between those who possessed adequate knowledge of the social order and those who did not. In his formulation, only social scientists, and particularly sociologists, were qualified to intervene in social processes. While Sumner wanted intervention from no one and Giddings believed in the necessity of elites, in general, for social order, Ward and Small were more focused in their analyses. They beleived that sociologists were uniquely capable of creating reform policies which would not destroy capitalism but would ultimately transform it into a more democratic order.

Summary

Small's writings exhibit some major differences from those of the other American sociologists examined thus far. First, Small stressed the importance of conflict in social life. He was more inclined to examine social disagreement as a conflict of interests, although he clearly did not maintain that these different interests were based on class divisions in capitalist society. Small shared with Ward the belief that the modern state could help legitimate different interest-groups concerns. Moreover, he shared with Ward and Giddings the idea that a change in the mode of production would not alleviate contemporary social problems. Reform was needed in attitudes and beliefs. Secondly, Small did not accept Sumner and Giddings's assessments of human nature. Small argued that humans were motivated by six basic interests, but these interests were construed so broadly by him that it is hard to identify in what sense they could be viewed in a strictly social-technological sense. It can be argued, however, that he did locate certain generic traits in individual organisms. These traits (desire for health, wealth, sociability, knowledge, etc.) were transhistorical in character.

Small claimed that these interests were and had been satisfied by societal institutions in a variety of ways. He did share with the other social-technological theorists the idea that property, inequality, and hierarchy were necessary conditions for the existence of social order. But the differences between and among men were not simply the product of genetic differences. Small's argument for these differences rests most clearly on a democratic form of elitism. That is, all societies—even democracies—need people at the top to manage them. The division that Small perceived was the separation between the manager and the managed. Small indicated simply that some men were foolish and others sagacious; some unselfish and others selfish.[70]

Small's writings do tend toward a social-technological sociology of knowledge. For example, he argued that the social whole had epistemological and moral priority over the individual. Society had its own order, which was not reducible to individual interests. Moreover, radical change of the existing order was not possible. The complexity of society meant gradual reform, not revolution. Only when men had gained knowledge of the cause and effect of social actions could ameliorative policies be worked out.

Within the social-technological tradition, he pointed out the fallacy of past social theorists in not emphasizing the continuity, complexity, and functional interdependence of social phenomena. The social bases of knowledge were not in homogeneous class-bound interests. The interests were multiple and cross cutting.

Moreover, he argued, social scientists were moving closer to reality by analyzing the social processes as functional units related to the larger whole.

He also stressed the importance of analyzing knowledge of the everyday world. He intended to indicate that (1) cognitive claims based on a modern division of labor had given men fragmentary views of the total situation, (2) these partial visions had to be corrected by social scientists or other interested persons. Although Small did scrutinize past social theories to a much greater degree than the other sociologists we have discussed, he argued that their theories were simply inadequate. They were neither ideological or repressive. These theories were true in their historical context because society had not evolved to the point where men could imagine the organic complexity of life.

Small also made a distinction between natural and social facts. Social phenomena were imbued with telic processes. However, this was a distinction without a difference. Ultimately, he believed that telic phenomena were susceptible to the same kind of regularity as natural phenomena. Small's vision of social science was rooted in two ideas: (1) intellectuals must search for regularities (laws) and indicate the interdependency of social parts on each other, (2) a social organization of intellectuals had to be developed to guarantee the progress of society. The latter prerequisite would aid in avoiding provincial or class biases. Small believed that intellectuals should act as professional advisors. On the one hand a scientific outlook when applied to politics would eliminate the sectarian interests of the politician. When social scientists discovered the general laws of human behavior, it woud be possible to change society on the basis of scientific principles. He also argued that intellectuals should act as advisors to specific governmental bodies. Small argued, in a word, that modern democracy could not function without the benefit of elites. The men of the everyday world simply could not see the reality of their situation—society was a complex whole.

7 / *Edward A. Ross*

(1866-1951)

Biography

Ross was born in Virden, Illinois, in 1866.[1] He was the son of William C. Ross and Rachel Alsworth Ross. Ross's father was a pioneer who had spent time in California during the gold rush of the forties. He then moved to a homestead in Omaha, Kansas, in 1871. Five years later the father died, stricken with paralysis. Ross's mother, originally from Pennsylvania had migrated to Marion, Iowa, to teach high school. While in Marion she had married a local lawyer, Abel Gawdy, who died of tuberculosis in 1859. Two years later she married William Ross. At the end of 1874 she also died of tuberculosis.

Ross was eight years old when his mother died, and his father died two years later. This left Ross an orphan at the age of ten. He was raised by relatives, the Beachs, on a nearby farm. Squire Beach lived four miles from Marion, Iowa, and had raised children who had already left home. The Squire had remarried, and his second wife looked on Ross as her son. Ross remained with the Beachs for five years.

Ross entered the preparatory department at Coe College (Cedar Rapids, Iowa) in 1881. Within a year he was considered a freshman, and four years later he graduated. For two years after graduation he taught at Fort Dodge, Iowa. He instructed such diverse topics as English composition, physics, physiology, logic, and commercial law. Ross then decided to study in Germany to broaden his intellectual horizon, and he attended the University of Berlin during the years 1888-89.

While in Berlin, he studied the works of Hegel and Kant. He claimed to have absorbed much of Kant but could not get past page 171 of Hegel's *Phenomenologie des Geistes.* He believed that the successors to Kant had "opened up vast cloud scapes" which took people's feet off the ground. It was not long before Ross decided not to be a philosopher, so he took a variety of courses. In his words:

After a semester it became plain to me that my profession was to be neither *Vergleichende Sprachekunde* nor phil., so in the Spring semester I sampled freely among the lecture rooms. I used to go to hear Von Helmholtz at the *Physicalische Institute;* I heard Dilthey; Simmel, destined to become a great constructive sociologist; Von Treitschke, the idol of monarchy and reaction, whose lectures in old auditorium 26 were packed with young conservatives; Old Adolph Wagner, the outstanding German economist of his time; Dubois Reymond, stressing always the materialistic phil., and seeming to wag his grey head against God; and Frederick Paulsen whose sun-clear lectures, on Int. to Phil. attracted about 200 listeners.[2]

Ross returned to the United States in 1890 and entered Johns Hopkins for a graduate degree in economics. He studied economics and finance, comparative jurisprudence, politics, philosophy, and ethics. He was granted his Ph.D. with the thesis "Sinking Funds." In the same year he met the niece of Lester Ward, whom he eventually married. In the spring of 1891 President Jordan of Indiana University offered Ross a position in economics, which he took. By March of the following year he had academic offers from Northwestern University, Stanford, and Cornell, and subsequently Indiana offered to raise his salary. He accepted the Cornell offer and shortly afterward took a chair at Stanford.

Ross stayed at Stanford from September 1893 until December 1900. During these years Ross primarily taught economics, although he was beginning his search for what he termed the "linchpins" of society. When he taught sociology, he used the texts of Spencer, Kropotkin, and Ward, but he considered all of these inadequate for instruction purposes. In 1895 Small, at the University of Chicago, was made aware through Lester Ward that Ross had an interest in the concept of social control. Small invited Ross to contribute a series of papers on this topic to the *American Journal of Sociology,* which he did. At the same time Ross was made an advisory editor to the journal, and in 1896 he taught two courses at the University of Chicago. The distinctive feature of Ross's stay in Stanford was his dismissal (1900) from that university because of his anti-immigration policy and his bi-metallism stand. Ross refused to take back his views on certain public problems, and as a consequence he incurred the wrath of Mrs. Stanford, who had him fired. It was very clear that Ross was not a radical but only wanted to test the probity of academic freedom. Ross wrote about his experience:

As secretary of the American Economic Association, 1892-1893, I had gained an inside view of the growing pressure on economists and resolved that I for one would be no party to this fooling of the public. I would test that boasted "academic freedom"; if nothing happened to me others would speak out and economists would again really count for something in the shaping of public opinion. If I got cashiered, as I thought would be the case, the hollowness of our role of "independent scholar" would be visible to all.[3]

Ross then moved to the University of Nebraska in 1901 and spent five years there. In 1906 Ross was offered a chair at the University of Wisconsin, which he accepted and held for some thirty years.

Ross held secure academic positions for most of his life. His voluminous writings, popular and scholarly, gave him enough income to travel extensively. His books grossed some two-thirds of a million dollars, of which he received 16 percent. He traveled to and wrote books about Russia, China, Mexico, and South America. In addition, he visited many other countries, which provided insights and vignettes for his books.

Ross wrote some thirty books and gained international fame. He was president of the American Sociological Society in 1914 and 1915. He also was appointed secretary to the *International Institut de Sociologie.* For our purposes, the following of Ross's works have been examined: *Social Control, Foundations of Sociology, Sin and Society, The Changing Chinese, The Old World in the New, Russia in Upheaval, Principles of Sociology, Social Psychology,* and *Changing America.*

The Derivation of Social Forces

Like the other theorists examined thus far, Ross argued that there were basic drives to human behavior. These instincts were sex, tormenting and teasing others, destructive propensities, passion for domination, wanderlust, hunting and fishing. They had evolved under the auspices of natural selection and had not changed over the course of human history. Each of these instincts had served to aid the survival of the race. It was a fruitless endeavor to ask whether they were good or bad. The major point was that they had survived. The fact of their survival did not mean, however, that they served a useful purpose in modern society. In the present state, the original tendencies of man, could be extremely harmful, and many of these tendencies (e.g., teasing, tormenting, bullying) must be curbed for the sake of social order.[4]

In short, a relatively stable order required that men learn to curb or to control these basic drives. Like Sumner and Ward, Ross argued that these basic wants created derivative social forces. Among them were economic, political, religious, and intellectual interests. These derivative interests were so powerful that they totally determined the attitude and interests of a people in any given time period. These forces, which altered from time to time, were the veritable makers of history. The economic interest had its base in physical hunger and cold. Under these conditions men strove to acquire material resources which alleviated their pain. Religious interest had its root in the desire to experience ecstasy. The experience of helplessness before impersonal forces cast men into a state of submission, which they then acted out in religious ecstasy. The political interest was generated by the need to survive against other enemies, once men had acquired some material resources. The intellectual interest was mainly stimulated by curiosity, but the reason that it had survived was because of its utility. In the modern world, science had slowly become recognized as a form of power. That is, knowledge granted relief from pestilence, hunger, pain, etc.[5]

According to Ross, one of these interests had, at different times, been singled out by social theorists as the prime mover in history. These monocausal interest theories tended to be put forward when some given interest (e.g., religion) reached its broadest influence. Like Small, Ross argued that these theories were one-sided and did not adequately explain past phenomena (e.g., the theory of economic class conflicts makes no sense in a society dominated by religious interests). In lieu of these theories, Ross proposed a "Worry Theory of History." For example, he wrote:

It is reasonable to suppose that men's attitudes and actions depend most in what worries them. When they worry chiefly about what the unseen will do to them, the course of society will be most affected by developments in a field of religion. When they lie awake for fear their property or their lives will be taken, their attitude toward everything will depend on how it is related to the security-furnishing organization, i.e., the state....As soon as one worry is soothed it ceases to shape the course of history and some other supreme worry takes charge.[6]

Ross believed that these drives or instincts of individuals were best harmonized in a society that was a *natural order*. The natural order (an order without design or art), governed by sympathy, sociability, the sense of justice, and resentment, could absorb new aggregates of men coming together from different societies (e.g., the mining camps of California in 1848.)[7] However, these sensibilities were the "mothers" of natural goodness in the human species and derived from the later development of the reproductive function in mammals. The problem of *artificial control* emerged when the issues could not be resolved between man and man. That is, there were offenses which aroused group interests, and this common wrath was the beginning of social control. "Among the earliest signs of collective pressure was the endeavor to make kickers, cowards, and shirkers take part in joint undertakings which benefit all." In every association there were predatory men who lived off the work of others. "The development of mutual aid and higher forms of organization, therefore, necessarily thrusts upon society the problem of controlling the delinquent class."[8]

Ross argued that the traits manifested in a natural social order were not enough to keep the artificial order regulated (i.e., the modern world). He expressed this through a criticism of the function of sympathy in the artificial order and at the same time laid bare the demands of that order.

Success in social organization implies that each man, whether watched or unwatched, sticks to his appointed work, and interferes with no one else in *his* work. Each does his special task, trusting that others will do certain things, at certain times, in certain ways, and will forbear from certain other things. This trust would be sadly misplaced if *affection* and *impulse* were all that could be relied upon to work our complicated social organization. [His emphasis.][9]

The bases of social power in the modern world were located in a variety of agencies. The means of control were public opinion, law, belief, social suggestion, religion, personal ideals, ceremony, art, illusion, ethics, valuations, elites, etc. Each one of these agencies had distinctively negative and positive qualities. For example, Ross explained that religious belief was positive in social control because (1) it was cheap, (2) no concealment was necessary, and (3) it blended with law. Yet it was negative in that (1) it blocked higher and newer forms of control, (2) it prevented the adoption of social commandments, (3) recompenses were not immediate, and (4) it was hard to manage. Law, which was the most specialized and highly developed agency of social control, had to deal with men repressively. "A scientific penology will graduate punishments *according to the harmfulness of the* offense to society, and secondarily, *according to the attractiveness of the offense to the criminal.*" The major purpose of law was to act as a deterrent. In this aim it was the "cornerstone or the edifice of order." Social suggestion also acted as a social-control agency through the institutions of education and custom. The problem with social suggestion was that it changed slowly, reluctantly, and mainly from within. It did not respond to external movements. Art, also, could be used for the benefit of society. Art aroused passions, created sympathy, exploited the aesthetic sense, and perfected social symbols. The greatest service the artist could perform was the transmutation of the realities of hardship, mutilation, and death into some attractive image.[10]

Ross believed that public opinion was the emerging modern agent of social control. Society was an ongoing struggle between classes, parties, and corporations for individual interests. But this conflict was subject to a law of development which indicated that there were "widening areas of temporary pacification, alternating with renewals of discord more centrally organized and on a larger scale, and leading up to a final, at least partial, agreement."[11] This development of public consciousness of collective mentality was expressed aptly by Ross in the following passage, which also summarized his work *Social Control.*

The thesis of this book is that from the interactions of individuals and generations there emerges a kind of collective mind evincing itself in living ideals, conventions, dogmas, institutions, and religious sentiments which are more or less happily adapted to the task of safeguarding the collective welfare from the ravages of egoism....The public composed of living and dead is, if you will, a despot, but still a paternal, benevolent despot. Hence, it is concerned not only with having human community, but with what harms man himself.

Although public opinion exhibited some hierarchical structure, this did not mean that it mirrored the political and social hierarchy. If it did, according to Ross, we could not account for popular movements, peasant revolts, etc. Ross believed that the rise of the influence of public opinion went hand in hand with democracy. It was "the exhaltation of the wisdom and competency of the average man."[12]

This democratization was tied to the decline of class control and the rise of social control. Social control was predicated on the idea of a truly competitive society in which the hopelessly poor and weak had accumulated at the bottom of the social scale because they or their parents were unfit to meet the tests of a competitive system.[13] Ross did not foresee any possibility of elaborate class conflict. He argued that, first, most groups had a stronger will to resist than to initiate acts of aggression; second, there was a law which held that "the more universal the man-to-man struggle, the less pronounced is the group-to-group struggle"; third, "sympathy is strong to the degree of resemblance recognized"; and finally, "the bonds of any group, be it great or small, tighten with danger and relax with security." In addition, the alienation of classes was limited by: (1) common regulative ideas (e.g., common religion, morals), (2) secret hopes of men to belong to classes other than their own, (3) free education for the working class, (4) expansion of national interests, and (5) popularization of a government which did not represent any particular class interest.[14] In this exposition Ross's argument was based on the notion that American society, to some degree, follows the first four general laws and that Ross's description was an empirically accurate picture of existing conditions.

Ross believed that the great middle class was on the rise and its influence would nullify class or caste separations. The middle class was interested primarily in competition. For them, the available positions in society were determined by merit. Moreover, in the age of democracy and anomie, society did not fall into neat divisions. Caste was dead, and the major influences on a person's life came from church, school, press, party, voluntary associations, and public opinion. As man's control of nature and of other men progressed, his sense of security from violence, plagues, calamity, and torment increased. Part of this control over both nature and society emerged from the contemporary attitude of being a by-stander. For Ross, the views of the man on the sidelines were morally superior to those of the engaged actor.[15] For Ross, the state acted as an impartial judge of social conflicts. Social tension was alleviated when law and state did not represent the interests of any social class. "Manhood suffrage ends the open political advantage of one class over another. The servants of the state instead of being drawn from the favored class have now trained men recruited from every social level and therefore in some degree impartial. As umpire the democratic state sees to it that the opposed classes fight it out according to the rules laid down. Consequently one thinks as a citizen rather than as a member of a class."[16]

If society was being operated more and more impersonally, the question of this impersonal control was of central concern. Ross believed that this emergence was the outcome of tested insitutions, beliefs, and ideas which had proved themselves fit for survival. However, as man became more conscious of these processes, he was free to intervene and to shape the nature of social control itself. Ross argued that "when population thickens, interests clash.... It is foolish and dangerous not to follow the lead of superior men."[17] In modern society the situation was too complex to be left either to natural forces or to the average man. The public mentality needed guidance from those who could speak for the whole of society.

Ross was not clear on how the ideal social order should be constructed. He wrote that a variety of forces opted for some sort of control in modern society: rule of the dead, masculinism, clericalism, militarism, commercialism, legalism, and the intellectuals. Only when each group's interests were balanced by the interests of the others could society be correctly guided according to efficient criteria. He formulated the principle of balance as follows: *"In the guidance of society each social element should share according to the intelligence and public spirit of its members and None Should Dominate."*[18] What this means exactly is never made clear.

In sum, Ross argued that men did have basic drives or impulses which needed to be controlled, particularly in modern society. As he viewed it, humans did not need artificial forms of social control in small, natural communities.[19] However, the modern world was too complex and impersonal for the social order to be regulated by a kind of natural community conscience. In this regard, then, Ross assumes a position very close to that of the social-technologist. Modern institutions, also, were considered to be morally and logically superior to the existence of individual concerns. Interestingly enough, Ross like the other theorists examined thus far, does not grant historical priority to institutions. Institutions were the outgrowth of individual needs and wants, and not vice versa. He also argued, like the social-technologists, that authority and inequality were necessary for order and stability. At this point, it is not clear whether he favored radical social change, but we will indicate later in this chapter that Ross was against any kind of radical reform. For now, however, Ross's analysis of the genesis of knowledge will be examined. For the most part, his analysis of American society affected his judgments of other social worlds (e.g., Chinese, Russian)—particularly in terms of his bias toward Anglo-American supremacy. However, it is not clear that Ross was simply a racist.

Pluralist and Collective Modes of Genesis

Ross believed that knowledge was generated by a variety of social forces which were subject to crosscutting pressures. At the root of the generation of knowledge was the interest in knowledge which came, in part, from the concern over forces out of our control. These forces were represented by the predominant worries of a given epoch. In this sense, Ross wrote about a racially inherited mind. What he means by a racially inherited mind is not unequivocally clear.[20] I think Ross meant that through centuries of adaptation to certain physical and social conditions, a race (biologically defined) developed a style of thought which was passed (biologically), in part, to succeeding generations.[21] For Ross, the causes of "racial" superiority were multiple in number: climactic adaptability, energy, self-reliance, foresight, the value sense, marital traits, stability of character, and pride of blood.[22] A number of these elements depended for their development on social organization rather than on blood. Nevertheless, Ross did evaluate other races from the standpoint of the intellectual and moral supremacy of the Anglo-Saxon race. This position can easily be shown in his writings on other nationalities.

For example, Ross divided races into those who reacted immediately to some given stimulus and those who reflected on their initial impulses. The superior races could not be made to act by impulse alone, but only through purposive action. The Chinese, for example, were traditional and purposeful. They were inherently conservative because of the oppressive social consciousness they lived under. Their beliefs were held strongly because they had been successful in attaining order, security, and some happiness for a vast population. But the Chinese culture was an example of arrested development. For Ross, the Chinese had never mastered perspective in painting or achieved harmony in music. Moreover, "their writing is arrested at the level of ancient Babylonia and Egypt."[23] The Chinese, according to Ross, were ignorant and superstitious in some of their actions. They were on a "level with our forefathers in the days of witchcraft, Jew-baiting, the dancing-mania, and the flagellants." Their domestic system was a snare, "yet no Malthus has even startled China out of her deep satisfaction with her domestic system." "It has never occurred to the thinkers of the yellow race that *the rate of multiplication is one of the great factors in determining the plane on which the masses live.* Point out this axiom of political economy to a scholar and he meets it with such comforting saws as, 'One more bowlful out of a big rice tub makes no difference! There is always food for a chicken.' "[24] One of the biggest drawbacks of the Chinese mentality was that they never accepted the principle of efficiency, which demanded that the means chosen were not those that seemed appropriate but those that actually did produce prompt and economic results. "They fail to discriminate *real* from *apparent* fitness, because they have never made the efficiency of agents and processes an *object of inquiry.*" The Chinese were comparable to our Anglo-Saxon forefathers between the fourteenth and seventeenth centuries. In the Middle Ages, the white men also were uncritical. They looked for signs from the heavens and thought that ascetic practices would change the world. However, it was the emergence of the natural sciences which "cleared the fog from the European brain." The natural sciences encouraged the development of hard methods—"observation, measurement, trial and error, experiment—which were as helpful for practical life as for science." The Chinese also had a passive character, which was brought about through the influence of the sages. The literati had stamped their character on the national psychology of the Chinese. For example, the coolies used fans and umbrellas, not from effeminancy, but because they imitated the scholars. Since scholars ruled the Chinese largely by moral force and their strength was primarily in book learning, "they naturally cry down bodily process."[25]

Whereas the Chinese had a gift for concerted reflection, the Russians had the gift of intuition. They were not particularly adept at catching an idea, but in "reading" other human beings they had genius similar to the Celts. Ross explained that the reason Russian soldiers—during the Bolshevik Revolution—were so cruel was because of their imitativeness. "Like all underdeveloped peoples, the Russians are excessively suggestible." When not in a state of war the Russians were extremely patient and not likely to exhibit aggressive behavior. The cossack was not a monster but "just a frontier farm-lad who cannot read and who has been trained to be a soldier in return for a farm." He was an available tool of despotism, "just as a regiment of Montana cowboys who could not read would be a facile instrument of capitalism if projected into a Pittsburg labor-conflict." The Russian muzjiks are normally hard-working, steady people. According to Ross,

This serious-mindedness and depth is probably a product of the savage Russian winter. For generations these people have been exposed to its eliminations, and the scatterbrain, frivolous individuals, who failed to look ahead to winter or who lacked the persistence and self-control to provide themselves always with a tight-shelter and a store of food, fuel, and clothing, were weeded out long ago, leaving no offspring to perpetrate their light minded-ness.[26]

Ross' notion of racial mentality comes clearly into focus when he analyzes the various contributions of immigrant groups to the United States. Ross had a strong aversion to unregulated immigration from "backward lands." His resistance was not based on the immigrants' ability to break up a strong labor movement. Ross was concerned rather with the intellectual quality of foreign stock, which might lower the standards of living, the institutions, and the ideals that America had acquired.

The orignial stock of Americans came from a Puritan heritage in which devotion to an ideal (e.g., political and religious freedom) ruled their mentality. The Dutch mainly came to America out of practical motives. The German Pietists came with high ideals, as did the French Huguennots. "Looked at broadly, the first peopling of this country owes at least as much to the love of liberty as to the economic motive.[27] The first immigrants, then, embodied the following qualities: high endowment of energy, tenacity of purpose, and willingness to take risks. It was from this perspective that Ross evaluated the contributions of later immigrants.

The Celtic Irish had contributed poetry and eloquence to the American mind. "Their gifts of emotion and imagination give the Irish the key to human hearts." The Celtic mentality was not geared toward technical advancement or investigation, however. The Celt had a propensity to see things, not as they were, but as they were to him. The Irish stock furnished orators, salesmen, and traveling men. However, "despite their schooling, the children of the immigrant from Ireland often became infected with parental slackness, unthrift, and irresponsibility."[28]

The Germans had given us good music and drama. They also had contributed to freedom of thought by asserting their right to think or speak on any political, religious, or social matter. The German had a particular quality of mind which was invaluable in an industrial society. Ross described it in the following manner:

> It takes him long to make up his mind and longer to get an idea out of his head. In his thinking he tries to grasp more things at a time than does the Celt. Not for him the simple logic that proceeds from one or two outstanding factors in a situation and ignores all the rest. He wants to be comprehensive and final where the Latin aims to be merely clear and precise. It is this very complexity of thought that makes the German often silent, his speech heavy or confused. But just this relish for details and this passion for thoroughness make him a born investigator.[29]

It was the Slavs and Italians who added virtually nothing to the American stock. The Italians "show a distressing frequency of low foreheads, open mouths, weak chins, poor features, skew faces, and small or knobby crania and backless head." The children of Italian immigrants were twice as "apt to drop behind other pupils of their age as are the children of the non-English-speaking immigrants from northern Europe." Similarly, the Slavs had very low mental ability and seemed to lack the capacity to learn.[30]

In reference to the recent tide of immigration, Ross argued that certain immigrant groups had intellectually contributed more than others. The Germans of 1848 stood out as a super-representative flow as well as that of the Jews from Russia during the eighties. The German inflow since 1870 and the Scandinavians were simply representative. On the other hand, "there is little sign of an intellectual element among the Magyars, Russians, South Slavs, Italians, Greeks or Portugese."[31]

Ross also analyzed other elements in the generation of knowledge. Much like Cooley and Small, he suggested that there were many crosscutting influences which affected the formation of particular knowledge constellations. "Those who would comprehend intellectual or aesthetic advance must consent to take into consideration such factors as the geographical environment, the prevailing occupations, the plane of comfort, town life, the influence of a leisure class, the attitude of the priesthood, the organization of education, the diffusion of learning, and the degree of honor attaching to intellectual and artistic pursuits." Ross speculated, for example, that in the tropics there was no real self-government because the natives of humid zones lacked the energy to provide such government. They inevitably fell under the rule of powers from the temperate zones. These rulers then imposed their rules. "The descent of the Aryans into India, the conquest of Chinese by Mongols and Manchus, the recurrent barbarian invasions of Greece and Italy" were examples of this phenomena.[32]

On another level, Ross argued that thought was, not the working out of a single mind, but part of a cooperative process. Common sense, group opinion, and public opinion were the results of many minds. A school of thought often began "with a band of like-minded rebels against the conventional, who stimulate and influence one another until they work out a creed, a style or a manner which can make its way."[33]

Imitation was another influence in generating knowledge. More particularly, "in democracies majorities are imitated." In aristocratic periods men molded their opinion after that of their superiors, but in democratic situations the average man placed his faith in the opinions of others like himself. As Ross viewed it, men's beliefs were swayed by conventionality and custom. Conventional imitation was essential for controlling beliefs and worldviews. These belief systems, in turn, shaped our attitudes toward the world and

other people.[34] These conventions had their roots in the traditional attitudes of the leisure class toward work, pecuniary success,
conservatism, and art. The aristocratic beliefs spilled over into the
everyday world and took hold in classes which accepted them for
simply imitative reasons. Similarly, cities were imitated by country
villages. The country mind (e.g., farmers' wives, peasants) was a
slave to an imposed sense of obligation. "Prolonged exposure to a
circle or groups that speak always with the same decision, the same
command, benumbs the will over whole areas of choice." The rural
immigrant in the city was exposed to the provinciality of his rural
sentiments. "A type of mentality emerges more impressionable and
plastic than that of the farms." This was not to say that the city
mind was superior. Ross argued that the city created hysteria in its
dwellers. "The continual bombardment of the attention by innumerable sense impressions" created a mental state similar to that of
the mob mind. The city deweller was likely to be impulsive, to exaggerate his feelings, to tend toward fickleness, and to have a general inability to reason. An example of modern stimuli which bom-
barded the individual was the newspaper. Newspaper reading cultivated what Ross entitled *paragraphesis*. This was the "inability to
hold the mind on a subject for any length of time."[35]

His age, according to Ross, was one in which public opinion played a large part in the formulation of collective consciousness. Public opinion was rooted in the crosscutting interests of various
groups. Of course, Ross was aware that some of the agents of public opinion (e.g., newspapers) were controlled by private interests.[36]
But he optimistically believed that public opinion in its widest
sense had socialized Americans not to identify with any particular
group interst. Thus, even the workingman could not be politically
radicalized. In the following passage Ross exhibited his particular
analysis of crosscutting influences on the mentality of the American worker.

These wage-earners have been so well socialized as "American" that it is
not easy to persuade them to think of themselves as exploited proletarians.
Contrary to the socialist assumption they do have much in common with their
bourgeois fellow-citizen—patriotic memories, aversion to kings and nobles, belief that "a man's a man for a that," respect for hard work, pride in the spread
of American ideas over the world, a certain chivalry toward women, sentiment for children, affection for the public school, enthusiasm for base-
ball. . . . Moreover, manners in America are genial and democratic. The wage-

earners have not been discriminated against politically. . . . Thanks to free public education the children of the working men may be found at any social level. Hence, only those native wage earners take freely to syndicalism who in remote mining camps, or as homeless, womanless, voteless, floating laborers, come into contact with the ugliest side of private capitalism.[37]

In one sense, Ross does not fit our conception of the social-technological tradition in the sociology of knowledge. He argued that knowledge generation in the modern world was a product of an internally complex society. Because of this, it was impossible for knowledge to be controlled by any one interest group (political or economic). His analysis of other societies (e.g., the Chinese) suggests, however, that he did believe that various elites could determine knowledge interests. He comes closest to our conception of the social-technological tradition in his discussion of national or racial minds, yet, when scrutinized carefully, he seems to argue that these national minds are a product of multiple factors—geography, climate, elites, internal organization. If these multiple interests are to be taken in a holistic sense, however—as they have been in Sumner, Giddings, Ward, and Small—then Ross writings do fit our social-technological conception. Without making a final decision, we will analyze the type of knowledge he was concerned with.

Common Sense and National Thinking

To understand the types of knowledge that Ross analyzed, we must first get a grip on his idea of sociology, and more particularly, on the kind of sociology that he thought he was engaging in. Sociology, for Ross, had for its subject *social phenomena.* Social phenomena meant "all phenomena which we cannot explain without bringing in the action of one human being on another." Sociology, then was the science of the unity of the relationships between and among social phenomena. Ross wrote,

This adjacent science [to economics] that buries itself with imitation and custom and tradition and conventionality; that seeks the origin, meaning, and authority of the standards and ideals shaping individual action; that traces the connection between the constitution of a society and the opportunities and ambition of its members; that inquires into the causes and the consequences of the spontaneous sentimental groupings of men; and that deals with the development of the social mind and the means and extent of its ascendency over the desires and valuations of individual minds, this science is sociology.[38]

Ross adhered to the belief that sociology would someday exhibit a unified system of inquiry. More particularly, it can be noted that Ross was interested in social psychology and not in the general field of sociology. Social psychology studied the psychic planes and currents that existed among men because of their association with each other. It sought "to understand and account for those uniformities of feeling, belief, or volition—and hence in action—which are due to the interaction of human beings, i.e., to social causes." Social psychology differed from sociology in that "the former considers planes and currents; the latter groups and structures." Social psychology examined behavioral uniformity which was due to "mental contacts or mental interactions." Social psychology, as Ross understood it, was the study of the influence of minds on other minds in terms of what was common to them. In particular, Ross explained that "a wide uniformity in belief, practice, or institution is either the manifestation of an affinity or the outcome of imitation."[39] If Ross was consistent with what his writings on social psychology suggest, then we should expect that he would not be interested in differences as much as in commonalities. I will show that this is indeed the case in Ross's analysis of knowledge systems.

Ross, like Small, argued that past social theories were wrong because they did not take the complexity of human affairs into consideration. In the study of social life, there could only be one master science—sociology. Philosophers and moralists were inferior to sociologists, not in their intellectual power, but in their methods. Sociology had a fondness for objectively observable facts rather than for subjective interpretations. Philosophy had a propensity to rely on superficial analogies rather than on the facts as they were. The value of science was in its method of verification. Speculation was unfounded unless it could be supported by some analysis of the facts. Ross criticized Comte, among others, for espousing linear laws of succession and the notion that societal development followed the lead of the mind. The various institutions in society (e.g., industrial, military, political) do not follow the same course of development in different nations. As Reinhard Bendix was to argue much later, Ross suggested that the particular development of nations was dependent upon both external and internal conditions. The physical environment, through demographic and economic factors, "moulds a social type which will undergo certain transformations of its own." Of course, internal development is dependent also upon exposure to alien groups as well as to the peculiar internal mix of institutions in any given society.[40]

Ross did not argue that Comte was an ideologue supporting some particular class or interest group. Rather, Ross was inclined to evaluate past theorists as simply lacking the facts available at the time he was writing. The only group he severely criticized were the rationalists of the Enlightenment period. They had stressed far too much the rational element and had neglected the emotional, cohesive elements of society. "Rationalism failed for several reasons. It clipped the wings of imagination; it cramped the emotions; it misinterpreted the social impulses; it robbed religion of all wonder; it neglected the ebullient side of human nature. But its cardinal sin was failure to furnish a good cohesive principle for society. Its cement would not hold, and the bankruptcy of its moral method soon became apparent."[41] According to Ross, rationalism failed and so did laissez-faire philosophy. *Laissez-faire* was the philosophy worked out by honest European thinkers, "wishful of social progress, who thought nothing would help so much as the removal of such barriers and hindrances to the operation of beneficient, social forces." It failed because extensive social reconstruction was successful with the aid of interventionalist theories (i.e., that of Lester Ward). In particular, interventionist policies created: (1) universal education at the public expense, (2) workingmen's insurance, (3) public libraries, (4) public facilities for recreation, (5) restriction of industrial labor for children, (6) reform treatment of juvenile and first offenders.[42]

For the most part, Ross did not analyze past social theories. As a matter of fact he was critical of Small for examining the history of sociological theory rather than formulating new theory. Ross, in fact, scrutinized knowledge of the everyday world, the public mind, and a kind of racial consciousness which I have examined earlier in this chapter.

If the immediate causes of social action were to be sought in the interaction of human minds, then there was no reason to appeal to material or cosmic forces for explanation. In *Sin and Society*, Ross argued that "the sinful heart is ever the same, but sin changes its quality as society develops. Modern sin takes its character from the mutualism of our time." In the modern world the individual must contrast his interests with those of many others. Modern-day sin was impersonal and not punished by the public because they did not perceive it as sin. This was because businessmen insisted on a laissez-faire policy in their work. Because businessmen were influential, they shaped many policies of the nonbusiness world as well. Consequently, "The leisured, the non-industrial employees, the bulk of professional men, and many public servants, hold to the unmitigated maxim of *caveat emptor,* and accept the chicane of trade as reasonable and legitimate."[43] Moreover, "it takes imagination to see that the bogus medical diploma, lying advertisement, and false testimonial are death-dealing instruments." Social defense was coming to be a matter for the professional trained to see these sins. Sin was conduct, unlike vice, which harmed other individuals. "Sin grows largely out of the relations into which men enter, and hence social development, by constantly opening new doors to wrongdoing calls into being new species of sin." One modern form of sinning was through the syndicate (i.e., the corporation). The modern corporation did not hold a grudge, feel anger, have political ambitions, or indulge in petty tyranny. Yet the corporation gravitated toward one goal: gain. The problem with the corporate mentality was that it did not feel the restrainment of either personal or public conscience. Its impersonality alienated it from patriotism, dread of hellfire, or love of social service. "In short, it is an entity that transmits the greed of investors, but not their conscience: that returns them profits, but not unpopularity." Ross was critical of Socialist answers to the problem of corporate greed, although he was in agreement with them that something had to be done. The social revolutionary made too many mistakes in his thinking. He charged too many ills to the competitive system when they really only belonged to monopoly. Inequalities of wealth had arisen, not from capitalism, but from the outgrowth of privilege. Ross's answer to the problem of monopoly was enforcement of the rules. "Without pressure from the outside, the moral level of practice will be low, and the good man will have to stagnate or get out."[45]

Business norms had not been held in check in America, because there was no landed aristocracy. In Europe the upper classes had traditionally despised the trader's perspective. The upper class tended to judge a thing or an activity on how much it added to the worth of life. Since this aristocratic emphasis on living rather than on money-making "leeches down through the general community, commercialism is in Europe more confined to the business class." Part of the reason for commercialism had been the influence of business on newspapers. The editor-owner has given way to the capitalist owner. The capitalist's major interest was in making money. The more the newspaper depended on the subsistence of advertisers, the less autonomy it had from business interests. "On the desk of every editor and sub-editor of a newspaper run by a capitalist promoter now under prison sentence lay a list of sixteen corporations in which the owner was interested. This was to remind them not to print anything damaging to these concerns. In the office these corporations were jocularly referred to as 'sacred cows.' "[46]

Ross's analyses of the everyday world also were exemplified in his writings on the attitudes of different groups toward the idea of change. The intellectuals had the least fear of change and understood the need for it. The commercial class was in favor of change as long as it did not conflict with their interests. The wage-earning classes were often slaves to tradition. However, "once their minds are set free, they stand for radicalism, i.e., the rational and thorough-going adaptation of institutions to the needs of society." The farmers were also inclined to be extremely conservative. "Of all the economic classes the propertied is least sympathetic with the rational transformation of time-hallowed institutions." Its economic performance was predicated on inheritance, therefore it could not allow the past to be deprecated. In the long run: "The domination of the farmers or the propertied therefore makes society like a stiff-jointed rheumatic, while the shifting of power from these classes in the direction of the intellectuals, the business men, or the proletariat, is apt to make society more supple and adaptable."[47]

Complex social organization presented the individual with the problem of finding his place in it. Men discovered what they were fit for by the experimental method. "By a series of competitions we test the impression we make on others, rate our powers in terms of other men's powers, and determine whether or not we may aspire to the more eligible occupations and posts."[48] Each occupation demanded different intellectual and emotional characteristics. For example, it can be expected that the man of science, the soldier, and the section boss will exhibit different emotional traits than the diplomat, the nurse, and the grade-school teacher. The pastor's duties and demands are not to be equated with those of the businessman. In short, different tasks demand varied emotional and intellectual responses.[49] Organizations, also, were shaped by the nature of their task. If the organization was geared toward physical matter rather than psychical material, then the spirit of the workers was not so important. Strict obedience was necessary within organizations which deal with crisis situations (e.g., hospitals, epidemics, fires). Unfortunately, military organizations had served as a model for noncrisis institutions such as government bureaus or business administrations. Both such institutions perpetuated the false idea that the "usefulness of the subordinate to his superior consists in executing orders and furnishing reports. It is irrational, however, to repress the natural doubts, queries, or demonstrances of the intelligent and loyal subordinate in a non-fighting organization."[50]

Ross also argued that psychic beliefs were passed on in two different modes. One was by conventional imitation, in which a belief radiated from some prestigious source and was copied by others. The second was custom imitation, which was generational and passed from father to son. An example of the former was the fact that the laboring classes looked down on manual labor and tried to advance their children out of the factory. They also accepted uncritically the idea that monetary success was the only success. If the workers had examined these beliefs, they would have seen that these beliefs were imposed on them by sources of evaluation other than their own. Conventional imitation was best illustrated in the long period of childhood happiness. Through long association with their parents, the children absorbed spontaneously and unconsciously the knowledge, practical wisdom, arts of life, beliefs, and values of those parents. The longer these traditions had been transmitted, "the more precise they became and the more fearful is each generation of departing from them.[51]

I have indicated that Ross examined many types of knowledge and their functions. He tended to concentrate especially on racial consciousness, the foundation of the everyday world, and public opinion. In particular, he believed that the wrong type of belief system permeated modern American life. The belief in laissez-faire was a kind of collective sentiment which needed to be modified. The prevalence of this belief was due, to the influence of business. As Ross saw it, only a change in the collective belief system would make America better. In short, Ross's analysis is amenable with our conception of the social technologist. However, for final proof, we will turn to his analysis of the role of sociology.

Sociology and Interventionist Policies

Like Giddings, Ross was convinced that modern democracy did need the advice of experts or of those he considered rational imitators. In an advancing industrial society "there will be, in the earlier stages of every discussion, a minority that is nearer right than any majority." In the United States "the plain people have a great respect of those of exceptional achievement, and confidence in the expert is rapidly growing." Part of the role of rational imitators was to increase the number of those who imitate rationally. The problem with elevating rational imitation was that it demanded "the purging of the mind from every kind of prepossession," which left room for origination that only few people could attain. It seemed that rational imitation would always be the privilege of a few men. "The rational imitator is not fascinated by the great man or the crowd."

He is impressed neither by antiquity nor by novelty. He is as open to what comes from below him as to what comes from above him in the social hierarchy. He is conservative in that he keeps every precious inheritance from the past until he has found something better; he is radical in that he goes to the root, instead of judging by mere surfaces....seeing the bases of society in incessant flux, he realizes that the super-structure must change. He accepts the relativity of our dearest mental furniture, our moral standards, social theories, political philosophies, and party programmes. He distrusts yesterday's thought, not as unsound, but as unfit for today's occasions. Most institutions he knows are in the grasp of a current of change which relentlessly antiquates not only the wisdom of the fathers, but even the conclusions of his own youth.[52]

According to Ross, certain elements of the cultural realm were more amenable to the growth of rational imitation. The practical arts and the sciences were two of those elements. Rational imitation spread in these disciplines because competition tested the fittest tool or machine and science evaluated the truths of its doctrines. Exact measurement enabled us to discover the better of two practical types, and science tested the verifiability of such judgments.

Sociology had its place in the sciences because it searched for the regularities in social processes that could be verified. If physical sciences attempted to improve the usefulness of certain species and plants—why couldn't the social sciences attempt to better the human species? For Ross, even though sociologists followed the methods of nature science, they were not interested in knowledge for its own sake. Like Small and Ward, he argued that sociology existed to improve human relations. "They confess that they are studying how to lessen the confusion, strife and mutual destruction among men and to promote harmony and team work." However, sociology does not suggest any one plan for human improvement. "Knowing that humanity must advance along many roads they keep their program broad."⁵³ The consequence of the development of the social sciences was an inevitable attack on the maladjustments of men. If nothing was attempted society would be left in ignorance. We could reasonably hope as the laws of social phenomena were developed that most radical proposals would be eliminated and that the public would focus its attention on smaller issues rather than on structural ones. For Ross, ideas like autocracy and anarchy had already been eliminated from serious consideration.⁵⁴

The major role of social science was to anticipate anticipations in formulating interventionist policies. The principle of anticipation was stated as follows: *"Any established and known policy, whether of government, or a corporate body, or of an individual, which affects people favorably or unfavorably according to their present conduct, will come to be anticipated and will result in modifying behavior. Favorable action will call forth more of the conduct, condition, or type of character favored, while adverse action will tend to repress it."*⁵⁵ [His emphasis.] "The social scientist ought to *anticipate these anticipations* and thereby arrive at a judgment as to how particular policies will work *in the long run."* Ross recognized the problem that some people might anticipate the anticipations of anticipations. He resolved this problem with the Machiavellian solution that "we should shun publicity for things we do not wish people to anticipate."[56] "In the taming of men there must be coil after coil to entangle the unruly ones. Manquellers must use snares as well as leading string, will-o-wisps as well as lanterns. The truth by all means if it will promote obedience, but in any case, obedience."[57] Only those intellectuals who could keep their emotions in control would be best able to anticipate developments. Ross distinguished the attitudes of the emotionalist and the intellectual in the following manner. The emotionalist would most likely suggest that an unhappily married couple simply get a divorce. The intellectual, on the other hand, would suggest that if divorce becomes too common, then in fact there will be fewer happier marriages. "Few people will form risky and unstable unions because they know that they can obtain a divorce if the union does not turn out well."[59] The intellectual is more concerned with the long-range effects as well as the possible dysfunctions resulting from policy changes.

Sociologists and Public Welfare: The University as Nodal Point

Ross argued that leisurely reflection was necessary for wise intervention policies. "Where there is cool discussion and leisurely reflection, ideas contend and the fittest are accepted by all." The natural rendezvous of such experts was the university faculty. "Nothing could be more fortunate than the fact that at Madison [University of Wisconsin] the demand for experts on Capitol Hill and the supply of experts on University Hill, a mile away, should meet and satisfy each other." If the experts came from the University, then we could expect that they would play an important role in intervention policy making. The next question that emerges is: What did Ross mean by wise intervention policies?[59]

Ross argued that men tended to overlook the fact that selection adapted men to yesterday's conditions. "When the requirements of the social environment are changing a gap is bound to appear, and this will be closed, when possible by artificial means." "Thus as civilization develops, social institutions are moulded more by the products of human thought and less by impressions from nature. Ideas play a greater role, climate and scene a lesser role. Man becomes a citizen of the world rather than a parish and *psychology* rather than *geography* provides the keys to social evolution."[60] In keeping with his strong ideas about natural laws and their relation to social existence, Ross endorsed intervention only when it followed the social forces.[61] Abstractly stated, the ends of social intervention were (1) each increment of social interference should bring more benefit to persons as members of society than it entailed inconvenience to persons as individuals, (2) social interference should not hinder passion for liberty, (3) social interference should respect the sentiments that were the support of the natural order, (4) social interference should not be so paternal as to check the self-extinction of the morally ill-constituted, (5) social interference should not so limit the struggle for existence as to nullify the selective process. The experts should apply their knowledge with economy, inward simplicity (i.e., control by example), spontaneity, and a capacity for diffusion. In this schema Ross's values are elaborated. It was not normal for people in the modern world to live in Fourierite communities, since man was not inherently a gregarious creature. Therefore, social competition—not private capitalism—should be encouraged. The interventionist should not block men's natural propensity toward moral feelings, which were rooted in religious traditions. These ideals had evolved over a long period of time and were part of what constituted public moral consciousness. Reforms should not cater to those who were ill-suited for competition. Poverty programs must be tempered by the realization that some men would take advantage of the situation. In addition, Ross believed that reforms should be adopted on a small scale before adoption on a large scale and that these reforms should be the outcome of a social movement. Moreover, in a democracy reform should not be sought except by legal and constitutional methods.[62] It is clear that Ross saw no value in violent revolution. He wrote that,

The conclusion is irrestible that violent social change is a desperate policy which has no place where speech is free and elections are honest. Any good thing which might be established by the arms of a minority will, within a few years, be voted in by the majority, if only its friends will keep agitating. Therefore the impardonable sin in a would-be reformer is *impatience*....The principle that if a certain minority has the right idea it will be able to make itself the majority is the only safe principle to follow. In the end society will get on faster on this principle than on any other.[63]

Ross wrote in 1918 that the most serious problem the statesman had to contend with was estrangement. The statesmen and educator had to counteract estranging tendencies whenever and wherever they appeared. A self-conscious society had to limit sect-formation, particularly that of religious sects. The increase of secular knowledge and the public-university system should lessen the chances of a false prophet "to gain a following." "The public university, moreover, rears up a type of leader who will draw men together with unifying thoughts, instead of dividing them, as does the sect-founder, and his private imaginings and personal notions."[64] The ethical concern for order was maintained by tradition, the party of order (e.g., professionals, teachers, editors, lawyers), stabilists (e.g., property owners, teachers), and ethical elites. The ethical elite was superior to the others in that it had at heart the general welfare of society. "They must be wise enough to perceive the social value of sobriety, monogamy, or veracity, and disinterested enough to champion the standards that make for these practices." The spread of superior ideals did not happen by contagion, but through a few superior men pressing their desires, tastes, and opinions upon the many.[65]

It is clear that Ross desired a democracy in which the "educated elite" from the universities would diffuse their secular knowledge to government, newspapers, students, or other such agencies. It also is the case that Ross evaluated foreign cultures on the basis of their propensity toward intervention in the social process. In Ross's mind America was the leader in this evolution, and most other nations were far behind. It was his hope that Russia and China, for example, would follow the lead of the United States. Ross believed that the older and maturer social minds should impose more rational social standards on the underdeveloped countries.[66]

In the final analysis the phenomena that Ross feared most was the decay of social products (e.g., uniformities, standards, groups, and institutions). The causes of decadence were many: changing of climate, immigration, patronage, red tape, indifferentism, obsolescence, absolutism, etc.[67] The decadent society would be one that sunk below a former level of unity, vigor, and efficiency. "Society decays when the laws, customs, and beliefs tending to keep within bounds the selfishness of individuals are not respected as yore."[68] In part, then, the role of the social scientist was to prevent the decay of society through the formulation of intervention policies.

For Ross, the role of sociology was the establishment of social laws or regularities. In the social-technological tradition, he stressed the importance of positive thinking. His major concern was for social order or stability. Ultimately, like Ward, Ross suggested that sociology should help to create new forms of social control. Although he was not fond of laissez-faire policies, he did believe in the moral value of a competitive system. Like Ward Ross also suggested that sociology should try to improve the human condition. It was not knowledge for the sake of knowledge which was sought. Like Small and Ward, he argued that sociologists should work with others leaders or governmental agencies in formulating policy. Like the other sociologists discussed thus far, however, Ross did not believe that sociology was politically biased. Somehow, with the aid of their laws, sociologists could speak for society as a whole.

Summary

Ross also formulated a social-technological sociology of knowledge position. Ross viewed man as being moved by basic instincts or impulses. In the early history of man, these instincts had helped man to survive, but in modern society many of these impulses (e.g., aggressiveness) were of questionable value. These drives had to be brought under artificial social control if a viable social order was to be maintained. The major value of the instincts was the creation of secondary interests which culminated in the development of modern institutions such as religion, law, economics, and government.

Like the other sociologists examined thus far, Ross also believed that society had priority over the individual. This was particularly clear in his concern for maintaining social control. He argued that some kinds of hierarchy, inequality, and property were necessary prerequisites for a stable society. In the liberal tradition, Ross considered society as a complex, interdependent, and organic network of social actions. If one part was altered, then we could expect ripple effects throughout the rest of the social body. Society also was subject to immanent laws of change. Change should originate from and within already existing legitimate institutions, however; Ross was against any kind of radical change.

Ross argued that knowledge was generated by societal totality generally, and, in particular, by a kind of racial mind. The knowledge interest itself was rooted in primitive man's concern for control over the forces of nature and society. As man evolved, caste and class divisions were no longer decisive in the formulation of thought. The modern complex division of labor created crosscutting pressures on the individual. In America, these multiple influences were particularly prevalent because of the mixing of vastly different racial minds.

For the most part, Ross did not analyze past theories as ideologies of various dominant groups or classes. His major focus was on: (1) racial or cultural minds, and (2) the everyday mentality of different groups. He tried to explain the latter as a product of imitation, occupational differences, historical worries, and organizational proclivities. When he did scrutinize past theories, his point was much like Small's—there had not been enough concern for the complexity of social interaction.

Ross believed that the discovery of social laws was possible and desirable. The purpose of social science was to formulate general laws about the nature of order in society. In particular, its major task was to extend the knowledge of artificial social control. The more that was discovered about social life, the sooner we could get control over these forces. The role of the social scientist was to act as an expert on guidance (e.g., as an advisor to governmental bodies). Ross did not particularly want a group of social scientists to control society as Comtean high priests. But it is clear that he desired social scientists to act in conjunction with other leading groups in society to maintain control over the social order. In his writing, even a democracy needed the guidance of expert minds. Like Giddings, Ross also espoused a form of democratic elitism.

8 / Charles H. Cooley

(1864 - 1929)

Biography

Cooley's grandfather Thomas Cooley was a direct descendant of Benjamin Cooley, who had settled near Springfield, Massachusetts, in 1640,[1] where he was to become a selectman. In a sense, he set a precedent which his lineage would pursue to even higher social status. By 1824 the family had migrated to a farm in western New York. The life was hard, and it was difficult to make ends meet with eight children. The eighth child was Thomas McIntyre Cooley (C. H. Cooley's father), who seemed to be the most ambitious of the group. Thomas was working in a law office at the age of eighteen in Palmyra, New York. In 1846, he was admitted to the bar in Attica, New York.

Thomas soon moved to Adrian, Michigan, where he was admitted to the bar in short order. During his first years there he formed a partnership with Charles Crosswell, who was later governor of the state. While in Michigan, Thomas was also involved in real estate. However, by 1850, when he was appointed court commissioner, he was devoting himself entirely to law. In 1857 he was made compiler of the laws for the state. Two years later he received one of the three original appointments to the faculty of the University of Michigan Law School. Within five years (1864) Thomas was appointed a justice of the state supreme court. By this time the family was living in Ann Arbor, Michigan, and it was here that Charles Horton Cooley was born, in the same year that his father was appointed a State Justice. Following his migration from the farmlands of New York, Charles's father not only distinguished himself as a lawyer and justice but also was the author of several famous legal treatises and the first chairman of the Interstate Commerce Commission. Charles Horton Cooley inherited a legacy that would be hard to surpass.

Very little is known about Cooley's early life except what he had written in his notebooks. Much of the material Cooley had preserved about his early life he later destroyed. Unlike Ward's forty-three journals, which were destroyed by his wife and his sister after his death, Cooley himself decimated his childhood journals. From his later correspondence we detect a sour note that his early life was not something he particularly wanted to remember. "From early childhood—perhaps the age of 8 or 10—until I was over 20, my health was miserable, so that my youth was in the main very dreary. I desire nothing less than to live it over again. There is scarcely any period of my past life that I would care to repeat."[2]

Cooley entered the University of Michigan at the age of sixteen (1880). It took him seven years to finish, which he attributed to his physical condition. During the summer months of these university years, Cooley would take trips to the mountains both east and west of Michigan. He found that hiking and camping in the mountains of Colorado stimulated better health. In 1884 he made a trip to Europe for a year. During that time he visited London, Munich, Switzerland, Berlin, and Dresden. At the Ludwig-Maxmillian University he studied general natural history, climatology, meterology, and philosophical tendencies of the present. Cooley was not particularly enamored of the German university professors and often wrote about the value of America from the perspective of his dislike of Europe.

When Cooley finally did graduate from the University of Michigan in 1887, he had acquired a degree in mechanical engineering. His university record consisted mainly of courses in language (Greek, Latin, French, German), history, and engineering. With his engineering background, he worked as a draftsman in Bay City, Michigan, for six months. From the winter of 1880-81 until 1892 Cooley lived in Washington, D.C. He worked with the Interstate Commerce Commission, Census Bureau, and prepared a report on the safety of appliances for the Commerce Commission. We may note that except for these three years and his two trips to Europe (in January 1884 for one year and in November 1891 for six months), he never left Ann Arbor, Michigan. During his years in Washington, Cooley was thinking about what career to pursue, and he finally decided on a doctorate in political economy with a minor in sociology at the University of Michigan. His cover letter to Luther Bernard in February of 1928 indicates a natural necessity in this decision. Cooley wrote,

I formed in early youth the idea of devoting myself to the increase of social knowledge. This idea was, I suppose, the product of a natural curiosity about life, of hearing and reading about social and economic problems and of the intellectual environment in which I lived. My father was a jurist and a man of wide knowledge and great public spirit; Henry C. Adams, a pioneer of the newer and more humanitarian economics, was a friend of the family and so also were president James B. Angell and other men of broad outlook. It was almost a matter of course that I should aspire to count for something in what appeared to be the most urgent moral and intellectual problem of the time.[3]

While pursuing his doctorate, Cooley met and married Elsie Jones in 1890, at the age of twenty-six. His father-in-law was a highly esteemed man. Mr. Jones was the first dean of the Homeopathic Medical College, at the University of Michigan. Soon after their marriage, the Cooleys spent a six-month holiday in Florence, Italy, and Cooley remembered this as one of his happiest periods.

By 1894 he had finished his doctorate in political economy and was seeking a position. Fortunately for him, he had been hired in 1890 as an instructor at the University of Michigan, while pursuing his graduate studies. From 1899 to 1904, he was an assistant professor of economics, and from 1904 to 1907, an associate professor. Finally, in 1907 he was appointed a full professor of sociology. Before receiving his last two appointments, Cooley had had to remind the administration that he was due for promotion.

Cooley was consistently productive throughout his lifetime. He wrote *Personal Competition* in 1899, *Human Nature and the Social Order* in 1902, *Social Organization* in 1909, *Social Process* in 1918; *Life and the Student* in 1927, and *Sociological Theory and Social Research* in 1930. In addition he wrote some twenty-five journal articles, of which the most important are reprinted in the last-mentioned book.

Cooley declared that he had no living teachers in sociology. Although he was acquainted with Giddings and Ward, their writings did not inspire him as much as those of Goethe, Thoreau, Emerson, and Darwin. "From Emerson he drew moral inspiration and a love for democracy, from Goethe the notion that one's life should be a work of art, and from Thoreau a taste for the simple life and the willingness to be a nonconformist."[4]

In summary, Cooley led a successful, shielded life at the University of Michigan for most of his life. His status within the sociological profession was secure. In 1910 Giddings offered Cooley a job at Columbia University, which he refused. He was elected president of the American Sociological Association in 1918.

Idealistic Organicism and the Primary Group

Like Small, Cooley developed his notion of organicism against the particularistic theories of his day. He believed that the world was organic in nature. In the organic view of society, neither the individual nor the society were the primary unit of analysis. "A separate individual is an abstraction unknown to experiences, and so likewise is society when regarded as something aprat from individuals." For Cooley the real thing was in his words "Human Life." By this he meant that we can never get at the ultimate nature of life, but can only approach it indirectly. He argued that there was no simple method to approach the facts. Whether one started with an analysis of the individual or of society depended on the observers and the limits of their perception.[5] However, he intuitively argued that the organic method was the best method because it was contemporary and it seemed more in line with our commonsense notions about life. Cooley had to argue ad hominem for this position, because he mixed metaphors. On the one hand he tells us that the observer is the limiting force in interpreting life and that this could not be escaped. In this regard, he argued contextually that there were many threads to follow and we could not pursue them all at once. Yet, at the same time he indicates that the organic perception was more adequate to the nature of the facts. To argue the latter point he had to assume that we know the nature of social reality a priori.

Cooley believed that particularist theories (e.g., economic determinism) were wrong because they supposed that life was built up from one single point.[6] Everything was plastic and took influence as well as giving it; therefore, it was ridiculous to assert causal priority. Cooley argued that the organic view was not merely an abstract theory but was more verifiable than particularistic notions in giving an adequate description of the world. It was not clear what the criteria of adequacy were, but they seemed to include some ideas about seeing life whole. In this sense Cooley's argument was circular.

More importantly, we may note that Cooley elaborated a number of reasons why he thought particularist theories were so prevalent. First, he argued that the popularity of material and economic determinism was due to the industrial character of our time. "A society like ours produces such theories just as a militarist society produces theories that make war the dominating process." Second, there was a certain psychological convenience in having a fixed beginning point for thinking. "Our minds find it much easier to move by a lineal method, in one-two-three order, than to take in action and reaction, operating at many points, in a single view." Finally, Cooley argued that the root of particularism was in the impulses of self-assertion. "After we have worked over an idea a while we identify ourselves with it, and are impelled to make it as big as possible—to ourselves as well as to others."[7] If it was the case that organic theories were better descriptions, then we may well ask about how to apply such theories. In concrete application how did Cooley apply the notion of seeing life whole?

It is interesting to note that Cooley's application of organicism was primarily used to explain the genesis of the self in the everyday world and not as a critique of intellectuals and class hegemony. He was more concerned with the social grounding of knowledge in the everyday world than with ideological analysis.

For Cooley, the self was generated through interaction with other persons. "It reaches him at first through his susceptibility to touches, tones of voice, gesture and facial expressions; later through his gradually acquired understanding of speech." We may be born with the need to assert ourselves "but whether we do so as hunters, fishermen, traders, politicians, or scholars, depends upon the opportunities offered us in the social process." The self idea included the following components: (1) the imagination of our appearance to the other person, (2) the imagination of his judgment of that appearance, (3) some sort of self-feeling.[8] Knowledge of social life (i.e., genesis of self) was not something that existed outside of us, but was the very foundation of society itself.

Society exists in my mind as the contract and reciprocal influence of certain ideas named "I," Thomas, Henry, Susan, Bridget, and so on. It exists in your mind as a similar group, and so in every mind. Each person is immediately a- ware of a particular aspect of society and so far as he is aware of great social wholes, like a nation or epoch, it is by embracing in this particular aspect ideas or sentiments which he attributes to his countrymen or contemporaries in their collective aspect.[9]

In a word, "the imaginations which people have of one another are the *solid facts* of society, and...to observe and interpret these is the chief aim of sociology." The question immediately arises as to changing historical situations. Are social selves always the same? For Cooley, "the object of self-feeling is affected by the general course of history, by the particular development of nations, classes, and professions." He wrote about the relativity of the self in the following manner: "It is a truth, though hard for us to rea- lize, that if we had lived in Dante's time we should have believed in a material Hell, purgatory, and Paradise, as he did, and that our doubts of this, and of many other things which his age did not question, have nothing to do with our natural intelligence, but are made possible and necessary by competing ideas which the growth of knowledge has enabled us to form."[10]

Given that our thought was limited by historical periods, na- tionalities, etc., from what vantage point could we examine our- selves or others? For Cooley there was a limit to reflexivity in the sense that the more thoroughly American a man is, the less he can perceive Americanism. He will embody it; all he does, says, or writes will be full of it; "but he can never see it, simply because he has no exterior point of view from which to look at it."[11] What then can the sociologist do in the face of this relativity? Cooley's answer went in the direction of finding the universal in the parti- cular. He surveyed the social world and came to the conclusion that the primary group (i.e., family, play group) was the funda- mental root of all later social and institutional development. The sociologist—Cooley, in particular—could examine the universal features of the primary group and its effects on the shaping of the human mind.

The social nature of man (i.e., his teachability) was developed by the simple forms of intimate associations, or primary groups. These groups were found everywhere and worked upon the individual in somewhat the same way. This basic social nature simply meant consciousness of one's self in relation to others, love of approbation, resentment of censure, emulation, and conscience.[12] More importantly, Cooley wrote:

Where do we get our notions of love, freedom, justice, and the like which we are ever applying to social institutions? Not from abstract philosophy, surely, but from the actual life of simple and widespread forms of society, like the family or the play group. In these relations mankind realizes itself, gratifies its primary needs, in a fairly satisfactory manner, and from the experience forms standards of what it is to expect from more elaborate association. Since groups of this sort are never obliterated from human experience, but flourish more or less under all kinds of institutions, they remain an enduring criterion by which the latter are ultimately judged.[13]

It was in the primary group, then, that Cooley located not only the genesis of self but all social knowing. Cooley realized that he was violating his own notion of organicism by locating one particular institution as the basis for all others. In part, he attempted to circumvent this by arguing that primary groups changed slightly with race, civilization, institutions, etc. In the final analysis, however, he believed that primary groups were relatively independent from other movements or institutions. These groups, then, were the springs of life, not only for the indiviudal but for social institutions as well. "They are only in part moulded by special traditions, and, in larger degree, express a universal nature."[14] This, then, was Cooley's answer to the problem of relativity. We must locate the universal through an analysis of primary groups which expressed universal human nature. And, indeed, this was what Cooley did in his own work. He examined the ideas of love, hostility, sympathy, sociability, leadership, and conscience. If the primary group was the starting point, then Cooley had to discuss the role that primary-group ideals played in the evolution of societies.

Cooley argued from an evolutionary perspective. He suggested that part of the evolutionary process was beyond human control, but in some small ways the human will participated in this movement. For Cooley, the central fact of history from a psychological perspective was the gradual enlargement of social consciousness and of rational cooperation.[15] By this he meant something very close to Durkheim's conception of mechanical and organic solidarity. For example, he wrote: "The differences between tribal society and the modern system of life lies mainly in the large-scale organic character of our whole social process. Formerly we lived in many small societies the relations among which were comparatively external and mechanical; now we live in one great society the parts of which are vitally and consciously united."[16] This meant that modern life fostered a kind of individuality which favored increased choice and not isolation. That is, modern conditions, "tend to make life rational and free instead of local and accidental." At this point Cooley was not violating the importance of primary groups, because he argued that "self-feeling, self-assertion and the general relation of the individual to the group are much the same at all epochs....Change has taken place chiefly in the extent and character of the group to which the individual appeals, and in the ways in which he tries to distinguish himself. The Germanic tribesman, the medieval knight, the Renaissance artist or scholar and the modern captain of industry are alike ambitious; it is the object that differs."[17]

How is it, then, that new ideas, institutions, or sentiments change? What is the mechanism of change? For Cooley, the answer was twofold. First, new ideas evolved simply because of man's creative linguistic capacity to evolve new meanings from old words. The higher activities of the human mind were, in general, more like a series of somewhat fortuitous explosions than a uniform force. Second, change involved selection which came about through competition of influences and the propagation of opportune innovations in thought and action. The selective principle, the arbiter of competition, was ever human nature—but human nature conditioned in its choices by the state of communication which determined what influences were accessible, as well as by the constraining momentum of its own past. In the final analysis what was selected—consciously or unconsciously—was that which tended to work. The actual process was a method of trial and error in which the more a thing worked, the more it was enabled to work, since the fact that it functioned drew more and more energy to it.[18]

Unlike the other theorists examined thus far, Cooley did not argue that man had certain physiological traits which needed to be controlled. He held a much more optimistic view of human nature. He stressed the plasticitiy of human nature. If Cooley can be said to have a theory of human nature, it certainly centered on the traits that one acquired as a member of some primary group. However, the characteristics that one acquired as a member of a primary group were universal. They were, in somewhat Simmelian terms, the a priori forms which made social interaction possible. Likewise, Cooley did not ascribe cognitive or moral superiority to the idea of society, as the other theorists did. As he said, you can focus your analysis on the individual or on society, since they were the reverse sides of the same reality.

In the above sense, Cooley's image of man and society does not fit the social-technological tradition. However, Cooley also believed that the existence of class systems was inevitable. There would always be an upper class, and as a consequence a lower class also would persist.[19] Moreover, Cooley did not believe in the necessity or the possibility of radical social reform. "Cooley's advocacy of gradualism in social reform was in keeping with his conception of the ameliorative nature of the evolutionary social process. Progress rests in the order of nature." Finally, Cooley suggests in other parts of his writings the importance of nonrationality in human action. He stressed the importance of sentiment—loyalty, service, kindness, rightness.[20] In these three senses, Cooley does fit our conception of the social-technological tradition in the sociology of knowledge. However, for a fuller exposition, we will turn to his analysis of knowledge.

Multimodal Genesis

Knowledge, for Cooley, was organized within and among many types of associations and institutions. In this section I intend to examine Cooley's writings in relation to communication, sentiments, institutions, values, classes, groups, and leaders. For the most part these categories belonged to Cooley's typology of the organizational bases of the modern world.

Cooley believed that communication was the basis of what he considered human nature. Without man's teachability, particularly, his symbolic activities, he would never have been able to rise above the level of the animals. Man's capacity for sympathy, honesty, and virtue evolved from the ability to imagine the plight of another individual through symbols. The central characteristic of the modern world in particular was the changing role of communication. "The system of communication is a tool, a progressive invention, whose improvements react upon mankind and alter the life of every individual and institution." All communication was characterized by the following components: (1) expressiveness, (2) permanence of record, (3) swiftness, and (4) diffuseness. The modern world had been altered primarily by the last two elements. Knowledge was made available through newspapers and the like more rapidly than ever before. And the newspapers also diffused knowledge among greater numbers of people than previously. For Cooley this was a good development because "printing means democracy, because it brings knowledge within the reach of the common people.... It brings to the individual whatever part in the heritage of ideas he is fit to receive." Increased communication meant democracy for Cooley because the possibilities of human development presupposed opportunity and choice. Whatever enlarged "the individuals's field of selection without permanently confusing him added to his liberty."[21] In line with this philosophy Cooley argued that there was a natural selection process involved. A man could not receive ideas which he was not capable of assimilating. And, in part, this selection was unconscious and based on sentiments.[22]

The larger historical processes, mainly made up of sentiments, were less open to conscious manipulation. In a sense, they constituted underground currents that shaped the general character of life. Sentiments were the chief motor forces of life and inherently less subject to change. I believe that sentiment, in Cooley's usage, simply meant the socialized feeling that we acquired for each other—sympathy. And "our moral sentiment always reflects our time, our country, and our special field of personal imagination." The two traits of modern sentiment were diversification and humanism. In the latter category, Cooley was writing about the extension of primary-group ideals into all spheres of life. By the former, he suggested that the scope of our will increased with the intensification of life. And "this change is bound up with the extension and diffusion of communication opening up innumerable channels by which competing suggestions may enter the mind." The main thing to note about sentiment was its obstinacy to change. "We all cherish our habitual systems of thought, and anything that breaks in upon it in a seemingly wanton manner, is annoying to us and likely to cause resentments."[23] Sentiments maintained themselves by crystallizing in the institutions and values of the everyday world in which traditions proved their worth. Institutions were simply definite and established phases of the public mind. They were typified primarily by their relative permanence and visible symbols.

The mechanical working of tradition and convention pours into the mind the trained wisdom of the race, a system of thought every part of which has survived because it was, in some sense the fittest, because it approved itself to the human spirit.

The great institutions are the outcome of that organization which human thought naturally takes on when it is directed for age after age upon a particular subject, and so gradually crystallizes in definite forms—enduring sentiments, beliefs, customs and symbols....Language, government, the church, law and customs of property and of the family, systems of industry and education, are institutions because they are the working out of permanent needs of human nature.[24]

The major value of the institutional organization of knowledge was its psychic utility. Institutions as organized modes of thought prevented mental overload. When confronted with new or changing situations, the individual had recourse to established institutions for explaining the problematic world as well as that which was unproblematic or secure. In a word, institutional thought was psychically inexpensive. Institutions, also, generally expressed a system of values.

Values or systems of values were organized practical ideas or motives to behavior. His conception of the working of values could be schematized in the following manner:

Organism ————————⟶ Situation ————————⟶ Object
(gives meaning)   (may be passive
                                                                            or unconscious
                                                                            of its value)

As shown above, the organism is what generated value, and the generation of value was mental although not necessarily conscious (e.g., suggestion, sentiment). The important idea was that each organized tendency always involved some set of values in relation to its object. These conscious or unconscious values acted as a grid for our perception of the social world. But more importantly, valuation itself was a social process and did not belong to Plato's ideal realm. The values that limited our perspective were the ones that allowed us to see at all. Values were relative in the sense that they varied with time, the group, the nation, etc. Values were also multifarious because they expressed differentiated phases of the social system. We could classify values arbitrarily along religious, aesthetic, economic, or legal lines.[25]

For the most part, Cooley did not concretely analyze any specific set of values and show how they related to corresponding actions. He did suggest that values were promulgated by the upper classes. The lower status groups, in turn, imitated the upper class, and as a consequence values were diffused throughout the population. Cooley believed that there was one certainty which social psychology taught: "if there is a man by whose good will we desire to profit, we are likely to adapt our way of thinking to his." We may note that Cooley, following Veblen, did analyze the business and technical interests in pecuniary consumption.

The pecuniary market taken as a whole, with its elaborate system of money, credit, bargaining, accounting, forecasting of demand, business administration, and so on involving numerous recondite functions, requires the existence of a technical class.... They have an intimate knowledge and control of the system which enables them to guide its working in partial independence of the rest of society. They do this partly to the end of public service and partly to their own private advantage.[26]

Unlike Marx, Cooley argued that the self-interest of modern economic institutions was not due to capitalism alone. In fact, there were simply no general restraining rules of public morality which inhibited the Machiavellian opportunism of most groups. The period was one of intense change, in which absolute values had been decimated. Once settled lines of thought were reestablished, this opportunism would disappear.

Unlike Marx, also Cooley stated that classes were like overlapping circles. Like Small, he suggested that we could cut the social world up any number of ways. The divisions, in part, were our own creations, and as such Marx's analysis of class conflict was only one possibility among many. Moreover, since individuals never exist in isolation, insofar as groups exist and "stand out from one another with some distinctness, they constitute social classes." Cooley essentially did not agree with the Marxian analysis of class because it ignored the solidarity of the present order, "which ensures that any change must be gradual and make its way by reason." Hostility between classes would never become bitter as long as the service ideal was present, and the service ideal was more possible in a democracy than anywhere else.[27]

Following an idealistic philosophical analysis, Cooley argued that the distinct difference between the propertied class and the poverty stricken was a matter of cognitive organization. The poor had no spirit or surplus energy adequate to a cooperative endeavor. "It is this lack of common consciousness and purpose that explains with which, in all ages, the poor have been governed, not to say exploited, from above." Moreover, at present the "common man is impoverished not merely by an absolute want of money but by a current way of thinking which makes pecuniary success the standard of merit." For Cooley, the bourgeoisie would always remain. First, he believed that property was the basis of economic stability and that there was nothing practical enough to take its place. Second, the bourgeoisie were always taking new members into that class. As these members moved into the new class, they assimilated its values.[28] And, finally, the bourgeois class made sure of maintaining their interest by propaganda. Cooley wrote, for example, about the newspaper interests in the following manner:

Newspapers are generally owned by men of wealth, which has no doubt an important influence upon the sentiments expressed in them; but a weightier consideration is the fact that they depend for profit chiefly upon advertisements, the most lucrative of which come from rich merchants who naturally resent doctrines that threaten their interest....And even that portion of the press which aims to please the hard-working class is usually more willing to carry on a loud but vague agitation, not intended to accomplish anything but increase circulation, than to push real and definite reform.[29]

Innovative knowledge, according to Cooley, was mainly developed by individual geniuses. They seemed to possess an extraordinary ability to transcend the constraining situation of the present. However, the reason they achieved fame was due to social conditions beyond their control or ability. Cooley wrote that all individuals were born to action and whomever is capable of guiding our action had power over us from the beginning. Every occupation had its heroes from which the ideals of service were formulated. More importantly, "works of enduring greatness seem to depend, among other things on a certain ripeness of historical conditions."[30]

For Cooley, the generation of knowledge was not the outcome of interest-group struggles. In the social-technological tradition, he stressed the importance of the societal totality. As he saw it, the production and diffusion of knowledge was a consequence of numerous activities. Communication systems, institutions, values, classes, and individual geniuses were the main generating units. And, more importantly, these units in Cooley's analysis could not be simply rephrased to represent the idea of interest groups. On the contrary, he argued, these elements must be taken together, in a gestaltlike fashion, if we are to understand the genesis and diffusion of knowledge.

The Spatial and Social Sciences

It already has been indicated that Cooley analyzed the genesis of thinking in the everyday world. His major focus was on the emergence of the "self." However, in the critical tradition, he also analyzed the foundations of the natural and social sciences. The emphasis was on the idea that there were no ultimate starting points for investigating society. He believed that the understanding of anything presupposed the existence of the everyday world.[31] Like Small, Cooley's critique of social theory was based on the failure to see life whole.

Contrary to the rationalist tradition in philosophy, Cooley wrote there were no philosophical escapes from our basic sociality.

It was a Rule of Descartes "never to receive anything as true which I do not know clearly (evidemment) to be so, that is to avoid carefully haste and prejudice, and not to include more in my judgments that what presents itself so clearly and distinctly to my mind that I have no occasion to doubt it."

This is no safeguard against illusion. The ideas we get by suggestion from the crowd, or from the universal opinion of the hour, have precisely this distinctness, and as they come unconsciously we are unaware of haste or prejudice.

And

I do not know that there is any one principle more essential to the understanding of human life than this: that the premise of our thought, the things
that appear to us as matters of course, so that to question them is merely ridiculous, are just those things which we believe only because we are used to
them, and have no other foundation whatever.[32]

Extending this thesis, he argued that in one sense all scientific
knowledge was, in part, socially based. Even in the physical sciences, the notion of perception was not merely raw physical
datum but "the outcome of an extended process of education, interpretation, and social evolution." In this sense Cooley's sociology of science anticipated the later formulations of Thomas Kuhn.[33]

Cooley was aware also that the assumptions with which we started an investigation affected the end product of a research activity.
The weakness of Cooley's position in this regard was that he did
not elaborate clearly or systematically which assumptions, if any,
were the best ones to start with. For the moment, it can be indicated that Cooley argued that sentiments or trends of thought
which made up the assumptive level of investigation were not conscious choices. They came to us through the weight of tradition.
He argued:

Every scientific inquiry is based on theoretical assumption: you accept (often) unconsciously some general idea to be true and inquire as to some more
specific hypothesis related to this. Your assumption passes over into your results; and it is easy, therefore, to "prove" by the most exact methods, something essentially false. Medieval students proved a world of things which we
regard as nonsense, and it is impossible to say how much contemporary science will later appear to be of this character. I believe that most that has been
done in psychology and sociology under the influence of physical and biological science will prove to be so—elaborate building on rotten foundation.[34]

Cooley distinguished, in his methodological reflections, between
two types of sciences. One type he called spatial science, and this
group included what we generally call today the natural sciences.
The other was called social science and was represented by such
disciplines as history, sociology, psychology, economics. Unlike
later critical theorists, Cooley believed that sociology did not need
to make a distinction between critical social science and verstehen
social science.

Cooley recognized that the spatial (physical) sciences were constrained by their interest in controlling their object (nature). Ac-

cording to him, "the practical success of spatial science in enabling us to predict, and even to control, the behavior of the material world about us has given it vast prestige." The key to the success of the spatial sciences had been in the refinement of measurement. Spatial knowledge, generally, had been considered as verifiable and cumulative. Cooley, however, was wary of truths of spatial science. In this regard, he wrote:

If, then, a group of investigators can agree upon a technique of measurement they may go ahead, achieving results and passing them on from man to man, from generation to generation.... But we must, of course, discriminate between the immediate results of measurement and the body of hypothesis and theory which is constantly arising out of them. Science gives us fact out of which the intellect endeavors to build truths, and what we judge to be true, even in the spatial sciences, is largely a social matter dependent upon the general movement of thought.

There was nothing inherently true about the discoveries of spatial science. For their discoveries had to be evaluated in light of other considerations. Cooley argued that most well-organized groups, scientific or otherwise, had a body of beliefs which generally went unchallenged. Conformity in these groups was brought about by processes not unlike that of religion or politics. For Cooley, no group was a "trustworthy critic of its own conclusions, and only the test of time and exacting criticism from whole different points of view can determine the value of its contribution."[35]

Cooley argued that social sciences, like the spatial sciences, were affected by the general movement of thought. But the social sciences operated under different methodological canons, which had to do with the object that was being investigated—social processes. The basis of our knowledge of men was in sympathetic or dramatic perceptions. The social processes of actual life could be embraced only by a mind participating through intellect and sympathy with the many currents of human forces. In this activity the researcher must dramatically imagine the meaning of some given behavior.[36]

Cooley stated that the methodology of the social sciences was different for two reasons. The object of investigation was concerned with meaning and to a certain degree with man-made processes. Contrary to the behaviorists, Cooley explained that the symbol was nothing in itself, "but only a convenient means of developing, imparting and recording a meaning" and that meanings were a product of mental-social consciousness.[37] In the final analysis, we must ask: What does it mean? Cooley's notion of meaning was based on the twin ideas of communication and historical record.

The social sciences were more fortunate than the spatial sciences because men had left a history of their activities. Since men, to some degree, made their own history, we could understand our present consciousness through a study of the past; and because our meanings were derived from the past, the possibilities for the present and the future could be anticipated. The important thing for the social scientist to keep in mind when doing his research was the role of the symbol. The human mind was not simply a mediator between a fact and the measure of it, but the symbol was actually the means of grasping the fact. Another dimension of Cooley's particular social science methodology was the idea of process or social change. Cooley believed that life was inherently processual. Society required by its very nature a continuous reorganization of persons.[38]

It is interesting to note that Cooley applied his organic framework to critique the political economy that was prevalent in his day. Knowing that assumptions played an important role in scientific research, Cooley argued that the political economists tacitly assumed a narrow ethical concern, and their analyses were deficient in larger contexts.

Cooley believed that the economists of his day only studied the short range mechanism of supply and demand. They did a good job within the narrow areas they allotted themselves, but they were not very good at throwing light on wider economic processes and the "social significance of the mechanism which it treats."[39] The economic theorist appeared as a man who counted the seconds with care but was incapable of telling the time.

In examining demand, Cooley argued that it should not be the ultimate datum for economists. Demand was an effect as well as a cause. Demand was not simply a part of human nature but was the outcome of past historical configurations as well. Also, demand was a class phenomenon. If one-tenth of the population received half of the disposable income, then "demand is preponderately determined by the conomic power and will of about this fraction of the people—a condition to be explained only by taking a view of economic process large enough to include the many forces tending to such a concentration of power." Uncharacteristically, Cooley wrote about the political economy that "There could hardly be more vicious method than to confine attention to the process which mediates between supply and demand, leaving readers to infer, if not telling them in so many words, that economic good or ill is to be looked for wholly or chiefly in the greater or less efficiency of this process."[40]

Cooley criticized American economists, in particular, for considering "productivitiy as judge on the market as the righteous or approximately righteous basis of distribution, and in so doing of course they accept demand with all its implication, as the standard of economic justice." He argued that the ordinary economic analysis could not provide a foundation for "a judgment of the social value of the present distribution of wealth...It is the more or less veiled ethical pretensions of the narrow school of economic analysts that make it doubtful whether their influence is good or otherwise."[41]

Cooley also criticized the economists for their treatment of public control. He argued that "political economy assigns a great sphere to rational control in its individual aspect, making this part of its system, but ignores, or sets apart as interference, the same thing in its collective aspect."[42] Political economy tended to exaggerate rationality as being ideally efficient, but to deny the reality of public rationality. To Cooley, public control was a gradual enlarging of human consciousness toward a more equitable distribution for the whole of society.

Cooley tends to analyze the knowledge of everyday life, although he does show a concern as well with the presuppositions of natural science and political economy. Like Small, he exhibited an interest in other social theories. However, like many of the other sociologists discussed thus far, he did not suggest that the political economists were simply promulgating ideology. From this position, the major thing wrong with contemporary social theories was their failure to see life whole. In this regard, then, Cooley shows a tendency, like Small, toward the social-technologist position. There is one other aspect of Cooley's work that should be examined before he can be simply declared another social-technologist—the role of social science.

Social science, for Cooley, was the unity of theory and practice, but not in the Marxian sense. His sense of social theory included a concern with art, ethics, and criticism. Cooley proposed that a social science without practical implications was a futile endeavor. If it is the case that Cooley stressed the differences between the social sciences and the spatial sciences, then we can expect that the social sciences as a study of man would be subsumed under some other purpose than instrumental control. For Cooley, sociology assumed both an interpretative and a progressive function.

Sociology: The Science of the "Primacy" of the Primary Group

Cooley argued that social-science knowledge was different from the knowledge garnered in the natural sciences. The task of social science was to discover the "essential" relations in social interaction. The problem of "essential relations" was that they were not subject to numerical measurement. Cooley adhered not to the metaphysics of mind-body dualism, but to a kind of parallelism. All social knowing was simultaneously connected with brain and the nervous system. "It is their minuteness and inaccessibility," however, which make it unlikely that these processes will ever be measured. The distinctive quality of social-science knowledge is its dualistic character. It is both behavioristic and symbolic. "Strictly speaking, there are no yardsticks in social knowledge, no elementary perceptions of distinctively social facts that are so alike in all men, and can be so precisely communicated, that they supply an unquestionable means of description and measurement."[43] This did not mean that objectivity and social cooperation was impossible in the study of social phenomena. The basis of cumulative and objective social science was rooted in: (1) the general similarity of mental-social complexes throughout the human species, (2) the closeness formed by a common language and culture, (3) the competence of particular minds. The last-mentioned required native ability, factual knowledge, social culture, and training in particular techniques.

Cooley also argued that the purpose of social science was to aid in the practical development of man. It was to do this in two ways. First, social science was to broaden man's understanding of man. Cooley wrote:

Human life as a whole is much like the particular enterprises that make it up; it is something that we may hope to work out successfully by constancy and intelligence. This intelligence, on a large scale is social science.

We understand another person, in some measure, through the process of our own development, which is similar to his, enabling us to participate in his life and observe where it is like or unlike ours. It is the purpose of social science to extend our mental development and participation so as to embrace groups and processes in a similar way.

Secondly, social science must concern itself with world of "ought." In criticizing the political economy of his day, he stated that practical guidance should be a part of every social science. To ask for this guidance, however, means that "special phenomena must be seen in light of their larger relations."[44]

For Cooley there was no dividing line between intelligence and ethics. The intelligent view attempted to take all the interests that were at stake into a synthesis which became an ethical view. He believed that "we get on by forming intelligent ideals of right, which are imaginative reconstructions and anticipations of life, based upon experience." A social science in its central principles had to be an ethical science, or it was "unfaithful to its deepest responsibility, that of functioning in the aid of general progress." He believed that we were all agreed in desiring a just, kindly, and hopeful society, and any social science that serparated the principles of his science from those of social philosophy was fatally wrong.[45]

Cooley believed that "conflict, of some sort, is the life of society, and progress emerges from a struggle in which each individual, class or institution seeks to realize its own idea of good." However, conflict as such, was not something that would increase hostility. The real "trouble with our industrial relations is not the mere extent of competition, but the partial lack of established law, rules, and customs, to determine what is right and fair in it."[46] And this lack of standards was simply due to recent rapid changes in industry and industrial relations. In the long run, integration would be established along the lines of some vague service ideal. Moreover, in America, it would be difficult to have class warfare, because the state was founded upon the thought of the people. Therefore, it would be difficult to develop a hostile attitude toward it. Energies of discontent would be absorbed in only moderate agitation.[47] Cooley wrote:

I do not anticipate that the struggle of classes over pecuniary distribution will go to any great extremes. It seems more probable that facility of intercourse, democratic education, underlying community of interest, and the large human spirit that is growing upon us, will maintain a working solidarity. Common ideals of some sort will pervade the whole people; and they cannot be ideals dictated by any one class. They must be such as can be made acceptable to an intelligent democracy....Whoever has wealth, whoever has power, I am inclined to think the sway of the public mind will be such as to insure the use of these in the main, for what is regarded as the common welfare.[48]

According to Cooley, only large and complex systems like the United States had advanced freedom. Freedom or a good social order meant that the individual has: (1) a good family life from infancy, (2) good schooling, (3) free technical and professional education, and (4) the possibility for travel. Cooley did not analyze what was necessary for these conditions to exist but simply stated that they were available in the United States. Underlying Cooley's notion of a good society is moral integration. "The creation of a moral order on an evergrowing scale is the great historical task of mankind, and the magnitude of it explains all shortcomings." How can we achieve this moral order? In answer to this question, Cooley wrote that: "The aspirations of ideal democracy—including, of course socialism, and whatever else may go by a special name—are those naturally springing from the play ground or the local community; embracing equal opportunity, fair play, the loyal service of all in the common good, free discussion, and kindness to the weak."[49]

We have come full circle now with Cooley, for "the heart of reform is in control of the conditions which act upon the family and neighborhood." Social science was to aid in the extension of primary ideals into the larger community. Cooley believed that modern democracy was "traceable back to the village community life of the Teutonic tribes of northern Europe."[50] We can now see that his concern with the universal aspects of the primary group hang together with his social ethics. The role of social-science knowledge was not a negative one. It did not exist to rid itself of the dominant property class or to examine authoritarian relations. Its major role was to aid in the extension of familial ideals into other, more formal, pecuniary institutions. When that was accomplished by intention or unconscious processes, man will have taken a large step toward his ideal society.

Sociologists as Critics

Cooley also argued for broad bases for social criticism. He believed that cultural achievements inevitably produced their own critics. Therefore, we need criticism from political radicals and literary artists as well as from social scientists.

He argued that a critique of the present social system was necessary. The critique should be based on assessing the value of various activities. The critics had to be well educated in history, social science, and practical conditions. This I take to be the task of social scientists. Second, the literary artist by depicting an ideal life could be the cause of radicalism in others. He also could write plays and novels in which the villain had to give way when confronted with truth, justice, etc. Finally, it was essential "that radical groups however small and umpopular, should develop and express their views."[51] Radical groups tended to force discussion to the assumptive level, which was always necessary for further illumination of social ideals.

Cooley further believed that science without art or some vague sense of the ideal was a barren endeavor. He argued that "science steps more assuredly than art, but its path is narrower, it cannot deal with life in its fullness. And so the humanistic studies—history, literature, psychology, sociology—can be sciences only as to detail; when they interpret life largely they are arts." He had faith that art promised the freedom of which most men dreamt. Art was a personal treatment of life beginning in the senses and moving to the imagination, and Cooley asked "Is not the creation of a fair society the supreme and inclusive art?" In criticizing the prevalence of economic values in modern society he wrote:

Perhaps we shall succeed in achieving the higher values only as we embody them in a system of appealing images by the aid of art. We need to see society—see it beautiful and inspiring—as a whole and in its special meaning for us, building up the conception of democracy until it stands before us with the grandeur and detail of great architecture. Then we shall have a source of higher values from which the pecuniary channels, as well as other, will be fed.[52]

In the final analysis Cooley never answered the question of who will benefit from social-science knowledge and criticism. He seemed to have faith that progress would benefit the whole of human life. Exactly what or who progress refers to was not made very clear. Indeed, Cooley himself stated that progress was tentative and processual in nature rather than a fixed goal. He argued that "rational control calls for an intelligence and idealism that understands how the whole ought to work, and exerts the necessary authority at the right time and place."

In short, the reality of progress is a matter of faith, not of demonstration. We find ourselves in the midst of an onward movement of which our own spirits are a part, and most of us are glad to be in it, and to ascribe to it all the good we can conceive or divine. This seems the brave thing to do, the hopeful, animating thing, the only thing that makes life worthwhile, but is an act rather of faith than of mere intelligence.[53]

If life had a tentative growth that could not be foreseen, what then, could social scientists do to aid in this progress, assuming that we were committed to an act of faith. Cooley answered by arguing that:

At bottom any science is simply a more penetrating perception of facts, gained largely by selecting those that are more universal and devoting intensive study to them....Our study should enable us to discern underneath the apparent confusion of things the working of enduring principles of human nature and social process, simplifying the movement for us by revealing its main currents....This will not assure our control of life, but should enable us to devise measures having a good chance of success. And in so far as they fail we should be in a position to see what is wrong and do better next time.[54]

Interestingly enough, Cooley's conception of social science comes much closer to that of the critical tradition in the sociology of knowledge. He does see an important role for criticism and evaluative judgments in social science. In fact, Cooley argues that sociology "ought" to create ideals which will not only act as guideposts but also serve as a base from which to criticize the existing set of social arrangements. Moreover, he does not argue that the role of sociologists should be to discover social laws. Although he does come close to this position in suggesting that one must discover the "essential" elements in the shifting matrix of social life. The major element of Cooley's writings which does not fit the critical tradition is his abhorrence of radical social change. Otherwise, his views on the sociology of knowledge come closer than that of any other theorist discussed to a critical stance. In part, this can be attributed to Cooley's concern for a practical social science and a just social order which is based on ideals.

Summary

In comparison with the other theorists examined thus far, Cooley held a more optimistic view of human nature. He did not believe that man had some evil or impulsive nature which had to be controlled. But he did reify the idea that primary groups socialized individuals at diverse times and places with the same characteristics. Communication was the heart of what it meant to be human, and only an ongoing society could provide the basis for this development. He stressed the idea that man acquired his social being only from already established norms. In this sense (i.e., the lower classes) he was not critical of the existing order. He realized some people did not have as much opportunity as others, but this was because the lower classes lacked organizational abilities. In addition, pecuniary valuation was the incorrect standard for the lower classes to apply to themselves. In any case, we could always expect some men to exist at the bottom of the social ladder.

From another angle, he argued that hierarchy, inequality, and property were necessary for the maintenance of society. Leaders developed naturally in various occupational groups, and the leaders could not be suppressed. The progress of the human race was based, in part, on the evolution of creative leaders. Cooley adopted an evolutionary perspective, from which he argued that modern society was characterized by: (1) contractual arrangements, (2) increased communication, (3) formal organizations, and (4) business sentiments. Like Small, his major criticism was that various groups spawned by the division of labor had emerged with fragmentary views of social ethics. The modern division of labor had cut off the possibility of formulating a noneconomic ethic. Until a public morality was reestablished on a massive level, the pecuniary self-interests of most groups would continue to multiply. In the final analysis, Cooley thought that primary-group beliefs carried into formal organizations could help recreate a larger, more embracing public morality.

His analysis of knowledge focused on societal totality as the main generating unit. Within modern society there were multiple influences which shaped man's mind (e.g., collective sentiments, class, occupation). Moreover, the organic unity of modern society was not simply a product of a particular class or group of men. Evolution was a process beyond the control of any one group. Evolutionary vectors had deep roots in the collective sentiments of the past and were mainly unconscious processes. The ideas which had emerged from the collective sentiments (e.g., theory of evolution) survived because they were useful to the totality of society and not to some particular class.

Cooley did examine the assumptive levels of social and natural science. However, most of his energy was expended in trying to account for the genesis of "self" in the everyday world. His major point was, not to indicate the repressive nature of some thought, but rather to show how thinking was possible at all. In this sense he was characteristice of much modern thinking in his lack of ability to see life whole.

Like Small, Cooley argued that social science investigation was different from natural science investigation. The social scientist could never step out outside himself, because he was involved in the social process. The social scientists, also, must take into consideration the role of symbols in the interpretive process, and, Cooley argued, we must find the universal in the particular. The methodology appropriate for finding essential relations was one of intuition, proper training, and sympathy.

The task of social science was to extend our understanding of the everyday world and thereby get better control of it. The major emphasis of social science was to discover under what conditions primary-group ideals could be extended into other spheres of life. The particular role of social scientists was to discover the universal elements in human nature. The discovery of this universal nature would not assure the control of life but would enable us "to devise measures having a good chance of success." In this sense, Cooley adhered to the idea that social science experts would help society with their technical application of knowledge. If only social-science knowledge could be applied, primary ideals would gradually inundate the social world and thereby the ideal society could be brought into existence. As Cooley indicated, primary groups are the mainspring of civilizational development.

From our perspective, Cooley is an ambiguous case for the critical sociology of knowledge tradition. He did not emphasize the importance of "real" material-economic interests, and his idealistic-organistic framework leads him to view analytic distinctions as, in part, arbitrary. Yet he clearly saw the linkage between social theory and philosophy. And, unlike the other early American theorists, he stressed the importance of "ideal formulations." Cooley did not take seriously the claims of natural science. As he said, we must evaluate the "progress" of natural science in relation to the larger social whole. He also stressed that social science, in addition to discovering general laws, must concern itself with interpretation and criticism. In this sense, Cooley's work clearly parallels a critical sociology-of-knowledge position. All in all, a part of his writings provide a good basis for the development of a critical sociology of knowledge in relation to the role of sociology and sociologists.

9 / On the Cognitive Superiority of The Sociology of Knowledge

Introduction

It can be indicated that early American sociologists produced styles of thought which were related to both critical-emancipatory and social-technological themes in the sociology of knowledge. The specific tasks of this chapter are (1) to clarify the similarities and differences between these thinkers—this will be done both in relation to each other and in relation to the two themes (social-technological and critical-emancipatory) formulated in chapter 1; (2) to present an analysis of the politics of structure and consciousness in early American sociology; and (3) to suggest that the cognitive claim of superiority advanced by these two traditions in the sociology of knowledge cannot be secured from criticism. Moreover, I will go on to argue that since assumptions are an inevitable part of the sociological enterprise, we must be explicit about those assumptions and the reasons for holding them. As I see it, assumptions cannot be grounded in the practice of sociology itself, but must rest on moral, political, and aesthetic claims which are external to the domain of sociology. At this point, a brief analysis of critical theory will be undertaken to show that its claim to cognitive superiority is based on a moral stance toward the social world but not on a moral absolutist position. As such, it provides an appropriate grounding for the practice of sociology and of the sociology of knowledge.

A Summary and a Comparison

In relation to the themes formulated earlier in this work (chapter 1), we must stress that the guiding cognitive interests of early

American sociologists was *predominantly* social-technological in nature. All of these thinkers, with the sole exception of Cooley, held that men had certain emotional, irrational impulses. However, there are some important variations among them. Sumner, Ward, and Ross probably held the most pessimistic views of man, while Giddings, Cooley, and Small were more optimistic. Although Giddings stressed the plasticity of the species and Small the higher psychic qualities of humans, it was Cooley who emphasized the basic sociality of man. Yet even Cooley suggested that there were certain modes of behavior which existed at all times and developed from primary groups. These human traits (e.g., love, hostility, sympathy, emulation) performed positive functions for the social order. They were the ground floor of social interaction. The five other sociologists disagreed only about the intensity and nature of these impulses, not about their existence. Concomitantly, they were more prone to stress the idea that man was a creature of tradition and habit, and therefore less open to radical change. In this sense, then, the early American sociologists do come close to the social-technological tradition.

These early American sociologists argued that society had *moral* priority over the individual, but not *historical* or *logical* dominance. As they viewed it, the *individual* was, in part, the origin of most social activities. Of course, Cooley, from his idealistic framework, stressed the dual nature of man and society. The primacy of one over the other was simply dependent upon which of the two was to be analyzed. For early American sociologists, the evolutionary framework was predominant. For them, the institutions of society had developed to *serve* and *satisfy* the basic wants of man. These early sociologists also argued that society was necessary for *controlling* the impulsive nature of man. Even Cooley argued that institutions were the products of universal human needs. They gave moral priority to society or some basic unit of it. They tended to view society as an organic whole which was incredibly complex. Their emphasis on structural complexity meant that for an accurate analysis, research could not emphasize one dimension (e.g., economic interests). It also meant that reform—when desirable—must be approached circumspectively. In their assessment, hierarchy and inequality were inevitable corollaries of the modern division of labor. Some men were congenitally deficient and others did not deserve equal shares of the wealth. Competition, in principle, was good. None of these men attacked property as a basic value. Further, they argued that the basic institutions (i.e., family, religion, government, science) emerged as pragmatic controls for the impulsive behavior of man.

In addition, they stressed that authority relations were necessary for transference and formation of basic values. Society was subject to organic growth but not to radical transformation. In their analyses, people were not alienated under capitalism, but actually gained their humanity from it. The superiority of America lay in its industrial growth. They did not seek new modes of *particularism* (repression) in the developing industrial state. Rather they assumed that industrialization—in its capitalist form—was the harbinger of *universalism*. Men would be judged on merit alone.

Following the social-technological tradition, their paramount concern was for social order. This view, in part, stemmed from their ascription of *universal* impulses to all men. The social order was maintained only by controlling these drives. In short, people had to be protected from their own appetites. All of these academic theorists believed that men were *objects* whose behavior was law-like. Men, in essence, were not different from natural phenomena (only Cooley did not share these beliefs). However, there are many nuanced differences between these theorists' views of human nature. Sumner, for example, gave primacy to economic institutions, while Ward suggested the importance of educational organizations. In sum, however, because they did not give logical and historical priority to society, they do not fit perfectly our conception of the social-technological tradition. Yet, their views also do not correspond to the critical image of man and society.

These academic sociologists chose to concentrate on the societal totality as the generating unit of knowledge. They avoided what they termed monocausal or particularistic explanations. Some, like Giddings and Ross, focused on national or racial minds. Even Ward, Cooley, Small, and Sumner suggested something like a national mind in their own writings. Although Sumner suggests the importance of economic conditions for generating knowledge (mores), he also argues that these two elements worked together to produce a kind of cultural ethos. Cooley, on the other hand, comes closest to an idealistic framework, stating that knowledge is generated by the ideas we have of one another. In a materialistic-idealistic framework, these American authors are displaced over the whole continuum.[1] However, from the framework set out in chapter 1 of this work, they do tend toward a social-technological sociology of knowledge position. They do argue that knowledge is generated by cultural or societal totalities. In addition, their writings on the genesis of knowledge suggest an unanticipated element for this author. In their avoidance of monocausal explanation, they developed a pluralist thesis of causality.[2] This meant that men developed their ideas, beliefs, and values from a multitude of agents (public opinion, church, school, family, etc.). It is interesting to note that the pluralist thesis, which does not fit our conception of the social-technologist, does fit well with the idea of societal complexity. These theorists argued that the individual was subject to a whirlwind of social influences. In particular, the modern division of labor created a simultaneous division of knowledge. The lacuna in their theories, from a critical-emancipatory point of view, centered on the idea that no one group held decisive power or influence over others. The development of ideas and their distribution and consumption could not be explained on the basis of capitalist development alone.

These early American sociologists also tended toward the social-technologist position in terms of the type of knowledge analyzed. Again, however, there is not a perfect correspondence with that theme. The sociologists discussed here did not tend to analyze past social theories as repressive or as the reflection of dominant class interests. Yet Small, Ross, and Sumner do suggest in various places that control over the intellectual means of production has been important for the production and distribution of knowledge. Small devoted more energy than the others to analyzing the history of sociological theory, but even he does not view the development of knowledge as a product of class interests alone. Moreover, even Ward, Giddings, and Cooley took verbal swipes at the perceived inadequacy of other social theories. In this sense, they do not fit the social-technologist position. For the most part, however, all of them believed that the history of sociological theory was evolutionary and cumulative in its development. They analyzed the commonsense knowledge—both past and present—of the everyday world; in addition, they scrutinized the collective conscience of various types of groups. In a word, they accepted the recipe knowledge of the everyday world as given. There is a sense in which they took ideas seriously; however, it was mainly their own ideas that received due consideration. They criticized other ideas from their own grounding in scientific (positivist) rational procedures. There was very little emphasis on differential socialization. The social world was reified. Man was considered a social-biological creature who internalized norms and values. In principle, it did not matter what the nature of the social world was like. Whatever the society, it was a necessary and sufficient condition for the existence of humankind. In general, all societies simply developed mechanisms (i.e., institutions) which controlled individual impulsiveness. Almost all ideas, then, were viewed as functional requisites for the maintenance of order. Ideas, in general, were adaptive instruments which aided social control through internalization. In their analyses only their own ideas were differentially handled,

In particular, these theorists claimed that other ideas about the social world were wrong because organic complexity was not stressed. They were critics of socialism, of metaphysics, and (except for Sumner) of Herbert Spencer. They believed that the social sciences should imitate the natural sciences. Social science was to formulate laws and generalizations based on accumulated facts. They proclaimed their theories to be objective and universal in application, unlike other social theories. With differing degrees of intensity, all of these men felt that sociology should be of practical benefit. They were not proponents of knowledge as something good in itself. The guiding cognitive interest of their work was decidedly utilitarian. Sociology could bring about a better social order. If only other groups would heed the sociologist, a more satisfying experience could be brought about.

There are, of course, numerous differences between these theorists. Sumner, for example, was not particularly optimistic about the discovery of social laws, and Cooley often discussed the detection of the essential in social relationships, and discovery of the essential does not easily translate into the notion of laws. Ward, Small, Ross, and Giddings argued that the discovery of such social laws would allow man to intervene in the social process. In one sense, all of these theorists (except Sumner) do not fit the social-technological perspective. They were critics of the existing society, but the basis of their criticism is more liberal than radical in orientation.[3]

The primary role of the sociologists, as they viewed it, was to discover laws or regularities of human behavior. The secondary role was technical advising for government and other professional agencies. Small, Ward, and Ross, for example, argued that social scientists should have intimate connections with governmental agencies. Giddings also thought educated elites were necessary for leading the country. Sociologists could fulfill this role, in part, by providing a scientific analysis of society for students at the modern university. These students, it was assumed, would be the future leaders. Sumner and Cooley held slightly different positions. Sumner did not think it possible for any one group to direct society, because of the power of the mores. Therefore, the best we could expect from social scientists was a deepened understanding of past cultures. Cooley saw the sociologist as one among many possible social critics. These critics, in principle, could indicate the course of action for the whole of society, not just for some of its members.

Once again, it must be emphasized that Ward, Sumner, Giddings, Small, and Ross tend toward a social-technological sociology-of-knowledge position, while Cooley, in this aspect, tends more toward a critical-emancipatory framework. From a critical perspective, Cooley's work contains too much idealism; yet he was quite aware that men did not make their own history according to their wishes. In contrast, the other American social theorists were naturalists. They stressed the idea that man was a hunk of nature that had happened to become conscious. They, therefore, tended to look at ideas as adaptive instruments for social control. Truth or reason was defined in the context of success or failure in the social world. Reason became totally instrumentalized in their conceptions. Cooley, however, held on to the idea that the uses or abuse of nature had to be evaluated in the larger context of the social mind. Even if only vaguely, Cooley seemed to be suggesting that values could not be reduced to mere instrumental use alone.

For the most part, then, these early American sociologists do fit our conception of the social-technologist outlined earlier in chapter 1. They were critics of society, but the assumptive base from which they criticized belongs more to the social-technological tradition then to the critical one, even though radicalism, in its various forms, did exist, in part, in their writings. Their position in society had not been clearly outlined for them, and they had to construct their own view of the possibilities of sociology. Early American sociologists did develop a conception of the relationship between social structure and the production and distribution of ideas. Moreover, their view of this relationship had a distinctively political flavor to it in the context of their times.

The Politics of Structure and Consciousness

There is an interesting tension in the works of these early sociologists. They defended the idea of democracy, yet they believed in the necessity of elites. This tension, in part, originated from the tension within their own role in society. As intellectuals, they could not, in principle, argue that their theories were equivalent to those of others. This would obviously undermine their own position. Therefore, they stressed their own superiority and sought to justify it in the context of an ostensible democracy. One of the ways to cement their own claim was to argue that other ideas were not necessarily false, but were partial or fragmented. They and they alone saw society as it really was. This position was absolutely necessary; otherwise there could not be an argument for the existence of sociology. If they had a claimed that all other theories were false, however, they would be attacked as obvious elitists, a position untenable for a group of men struggling for recognition. Therefore, they chose what today is called the doctor-patient model for their role analogy. There is an interesting sociological dimension to this analogy. One can claim superiority on the basis of specialized knowledge and yet provide a rationale for that same knowledge. The ideological argument, among specialists, is to serve the public directly or indirectly. Knowledge then, it is claimed, is for the benefit of the people—not just an esoteric exercise for the intellectuals.

The early American theorists also were concerned with the impact of industrialization. Their writings indicate a concentrated attention to this theme. Their evolutionary theoretical perspective showed that industrialism had brought a division of labor but no concomitant philosophy or ideology to explain the divisiveness of modern society. It was obvious to them that an industrial nation had many benefits. It was efficient, and productivity was greatly increased. However, they also were aware that the division of labor created individualist philosophies of life, and from their perspective, these philosophies were inadequate. Sociology, they claimed, saw life as organically connected. Society was more than the sum of its individual parts. The attitude of individualism would tear the country apart. Therefore, one of their claims to superiority was based on seeing social life correctly. Yet their claim is merely an assertion. They continually reiterate the notion of totality but rely on everyone's common sense to prove it. Their claim really rests on the idea that everyone can, in principle, see that their argument is correct. Socialism made a similar claim about the totality of social relations. However, these early sociologists argued that the socialists were confused about the nature of man. Consequently, their theories were not workable. In essence, this disagreement was not a scientific dispute, but an ideological one. The argument centered on what man was really like in some ultimate sense. Metaphysical debates cannot be resolved on empirical grounds—yet this is exactly what was attempted. In part, the sociologists arguments were supported by the emerging university system. The university, in turn, was legitimated by its ability to train people for the liberal corporate state. It is not surprising that, in the long run, the academics won the debate over the nature of man. Their own arguments about the impulsive aspects of human behavior paralleled the corporations attempts to maximize human efficiency and, consequently, productivity.

Another common concern of the early sociologists was immigration. They were aware that immigrant laborers were utilized in the mines, factories, and railroads. However, they rarely evaluated the impact of immigration on the level of labor power. They stressed rather the immigrants' contributions in terms of cognitive power—that is, in accordance with the academicians' interests. Given diversity of the immigrants, one of the easiest ways to classify them was on the basis of national or racial thinking. This analytic mode certainly permits parsimony. Moreover, from the sociologists' perspective, only immigrants from those societies which espoused democratic, industrial, and/or scientific thinking were considered an asset. It was more than just understanding other cultures that was sought. Indeed, differential evaluation of the immigrants' contribution—on the cognitive level—was the aim. It was on this basis that the early sociologists evaluated other cultures. In short, the sociologists' right to evaluate others was based on their own concerns for the development of a corporate-industrial America. Their own thinking was part and parcel of an industrial society which needed certain types of people and concomitantly certain modes of thinking to justify its existence.

This analysis, then, shows that it is difficult, if not impossible, to analyze ideas apart from their social background. Ironically, part of the concern of this work was to show that the sociology of knowledge was itself subject to ideological influences. There is not "a" sociology of knowledge tradition but at least two political axes around which discussions take place about the relationship between structure and consciousness. In part, the sociology of knowledge is itself historically conditioned.

The sociology of knowledge, which, in part, claims to explain the social conditions or origins of ideas, implicitly—sometimes explicitly—undermines the autonomy of ideas. There is a sense in which to understand the social origin of an idea is to better understand the idea itself. It might be said that: (1) understanding the "strange" ideas of another culture or time and place may be enhanced through a study of social origins—really an appeal to the idea that as reasonable men in the same circumstances, we might hold the same beliefs; and (2) given the situation, one could not hold beliefs other than the ones available—one can do no other (e.g., it is difficult to imagine how a thirteenth-century European would have conceptualized the technical-belief system of a twentiety-century computer engineer).

Interestingly enough, the sociology of knowledge as a subdiscipline of sociology has been and continues to be, for the most part, tied into political analyses. It has constantly tried to establish the superiority of its own intellectual vision on the basis of showing what the origins of other ideas have been. Both the social-technological tradition and the critical one share this belief. However, even as theorists were making this claim, there was a simultaneous awareness of the precariousness of their own position. Mannheim, for example, argued not only for the theoretical import of a "free-floating" intelligentsia but for the practical necessity of it as well. Yet it is difficult for us to theoretically imagine the cognitive superiority of this group, even if it were possible for an intellectual to be a member of many different groups. It is difficult to think that there could be no social ground to ideas. Yet, given the first idea, it is harder to imagine what thinking simultaneously (i.e., a synthesis) from many positions would look like. On the other hand, some theorists have argued for the superiority of a proletarian cognitive vision. That is, because of historical necessity, this class must see social life correctly, and the proof of its vision will be self-evident in the revolutionary event. Again, we can only wonder whose historical necessity is involved. It is as if history were the hidden hand that caused men to think and act in certain ways. The idea of historical necessity suggests something *of this world* but *out of* human control. Better yet, what if, after the revolution, we do not see either the necessity or the transparency of our action? Will we, the new critics, be classified as reactionaries?

Some, like Lucien Goldmann, have argued that there is an objective criteria for distinguishing ideological statements. In short, ideological statements are not relatively the same. Goldmann writes: "Some value-judgments permit a better understanding of reality than others. When it is a question of determining which of two conflicting sociologies has the greater scientific value, the first step is to ask which of them *permits the understanding of the other as a social and human phenomenon, reveals its infrastructure, and clarifies, by means of an immanent critical principle, its inconsistencies and limitations.*"[4] However, Goldmann's formulation of the problem, while accurate, does not give us a clue of whether to choose a social-technological or critical-emancipatory position. Indeed, his formulation of the question in terms of "infrastructure," "immanent," and "critical" belies his own values. The problem of values enters even the question formulation. The moment the question was asked, it had already been answered. The issue of which political position is superior turns on the cognitive claim of superiority held by the opposing schools of thought. It is to the issue of superiority that the argument now turns.

The Claim of Cognitive Superiority

The differences in the two sociology of knowledge traditions were outlined earlier in this work (chapter 1). At this point, it is imperative to discuss which of the two traditions is cognitively superior, if either. The sociology of knowledge, in whatever political form, initially sought to evaluate other theories from a cognitively superior stance. This, I believe—in both vulgar Marxist and positivistic formulations—has proved impossible. The sociology of knowledge only raises anew the questions that appeared on more mundane social-theory levels. One could conclude, of course, that we should no longer worry about the assumptions of social theory and get on with other considerations. Because modern thinking is no longer grounded in authoritative criteria, however, we cannot pretend this is the case (the ostrich syndrome). On the other hand, we can no longer pretend to step outside of our skins—the positivistic split between subject and object—and claim that kind of cognitive superiority (visitor-from-another-planet syndrome). And finally, we cannot fantasize that what is *immanently* a critical theory will not be turned into a repressive (history or some other agency syndrome) praxis.

Although the sociology of knowledge has been stripped of its claim to cognitive superiority, it seems to me, at any rate, that it can still perform a useful role for those of us not willing to become doctrinaire Marxists or intellectual technicians for corporate capitalism. When combined with a critical theory of society, the sociology of knowledge can become the major agent for criticizing criticism itself. At this point, however, we need to take a closer look at critical theory.

The best place to begin summarizing the critical school[5] is with its analysis of the subject-object split that had permeated traditional social and philosophic thought. The critical school rejected the positivist emphasis on man as object—that is as a passive agent controlled mainly by the whims or laws of nature and history. On the other hand, it rejected the subjectivist emphasis on man's inward uniqueness, which denied real material forces and led to a glorification of the individual's autonomy. For the critical school: "A true epistemology must end the fetish of knowledge as such, which...leads to abstract schematizing. The truth was not what was 'left over' when a reduction of subject to object or vice versa took place. It resided instead in the 'force field' between subject and object."[6] The critical school emphasized to a greater or lesser degree the following points:[7]

A. There are no ultimate, secure starting points for an analysis of society. Science itself presupposes the existence of a prescientific (commonsense) world. If this is the case, then the best image we can begin with is one that emphasizes man as a reasoning and partially autonomous actor who is at the same time an "object" acted upon.

B. There are three types of science with distinct purposes. These sciences condition, and are conditioned through, the mediums of work, language, and power.
    1. exact sciences stress certainty and control.
    2. hermeneutical sciences emphasize the extention of intersubjective understanding.
    3. critical sciences have an emancipatory interest.

C. The specific tasks of critical science are:
    1. to reflect on system interest and cognition, since knowledge and interest are one;
    2. to illuminate history and science as self-forming processes;
    3. to indicate through the power of speculation and reflection the objective possibilities of a given society through a critique of what has been called necessary development;
    4. to cultivate speculation which plays an important role in holding the goal up to view, although the goal is not clearly specified;
    5. to use reason to grasp self-forming processes, rather than explanation;
    6. to develop a community of critical scientists;
    7. to align with progressive forces in society.

If I read critical theory correctly, it seems to me that its claim to cognitive superiority is based on a very straightforward principle with complex ramifications. It refuses and negates any social theory which stresses the passive political nature of the human species. It is not so much interested in what man is presently like, but focuses on the political potential of the species. This is not to say that the world has no determinate structure, but rather that the world is man-made and therefore can be altered in many ways.

In its analyses, the potentiality of man is emphasized. Let us look at this principle in light of Schroyer's summary of the critical school.

One of the major tasks of critical theory was to undermine the claim of science to a privileged separation from the interests and activities of the everyday world. By continuously stressing the embeddedness of science in the commonsense world, it aimed to show that no science, including their own, can escape this linkage. The major weakness of the positivists' claim to objectivity was their inability to explain their own origins. The social scientist, in particular, brings with him into the research process certain valuational interests which influence the selection of the problem as well as the whole nature of the process itself. Interestingly enough, critical theorists draw certain conclusions from this criticism that are not unlike Kant's argument for moral autonomy. Kant argued that since we cannot know what man is in himself (noumenon) then for the sake of responsibility and moral autonomy, we must assume for practical reasons that he is a free actor. Kant had already determined that man's actions in the phenomenal realm were subject to the same laws as those of nature. Likewise, critical theory deduces that since science has no secure starting point for an analysis of society, the best image of man we can hold for practical (read political) reasons is one that emphasizes human potential rather than passivity or complete freedom (idealism). Other models of man indirectly contribute to emphasis on passivity or complete voluntarism. While one can applaud this attempt to return to Kant's formulation, a serious question arises. Given that one ought to act to further the realization of a rational community life, how can such a noble ideal "become impotent in the course of concrete history?"[8] Schroyer writes that Habermas believes "a self-consciousness of communication that is free from domination (that is presupposed by rational discourse) is held to be the model that can be used for the critique of power distortions of everyday communications."[9] It is questionable whether such a model of communicative competence is of universal value for emancipation. According to Bernstein, Habermas does not tell us what types of individuals or under what conditions humans will seek to overcome the distorted speech situation.[10]

In an attempt to distinguish their analysis and intent from other forms of social theorizing, critical theorists have striven to demarcate their work from others. This has led to the classification of the sciences along the line already mentioned—certainty and control in the exact sciences; cultural maintenance through intersubjective understanding (hermeneutics); and the critical sciences, which have an emancipatory interest. The positive sciences, which stress certainty and control, view man as an object to be manipulated. These sciences have no emancipatory interest. These types of perspectives are particularly relevant in an economy that needs to create demand for its products. A managed economy is extremely dependent on a manipulated consumer. In this view of man, there is a definite split between the manager and the managed—the social scientist and the object of his research. Ironically, this current conservative image of man is not a traditional conservatism. It assumes that new needs can be created—that man is, to some degree, plastic. The real distinction occurs between those who create the needs for the public and the public itself. Concommitant with this distinction is the idea of structural complexity. The system is too difficult for the average person to understand; therefore, the split between the managed and the manager is inevitable. We all need specialists to interpret the movement of the modern world. This type of conservatism has venerable religious roots. It is the view that only those properly trained can indicate the values to be held and what proper action should be. It is the view of the elites, who have their own interests to protect. If understanding is to be had by everyone, then there is obviously no need for the specialists. That special distinction is eliminated for the positive scientist.

The hermeneutical sciences, which emphasize intersubjective understanding, also have some particular problems. In the desire to repair broken communicative traditions, hermeneutics stresses understanding, not change. This concern for understanding can go in two different directions. In the first view, understanding can lead to a certain form of passivity, in which it is felt that all cultures are equally close to the truth. It makes no sense to criticize another culture from some superior point of view, because all are relatively equal. This perspective tends to deny, in part, the idea that mankind can move toward a truly rational society. Even more bizarrely, the interpretation of texts can also lead to sheer mass manipulation. One can read anything into the texts for one's own purposes. It is clear that critical theory at this point is rejecting doctrinaire interpretations, such as Stalin's version of Marx. Indeed, this kind of interpretation may deliberately block criticism and move toward sheer propaganda.

Critical science, unlike the others, emphasizes neither the extension of intersubjective understanding nor certainty and control. This is not to say that critical theory is not unaware of the forces that determine man's behavior or the importance of understanding, only that *that is not enough.* Critical science has an emancipatory interest. Its goal is to make society rational. In addition to criticizing other theories, critical theory also has a body of maxims, or "ought" statements, about its own role in the world.

Again, we may congratulate critical theory for showing us the difference between the nonemancipatory sciences and itself. However, it is not clear how we judge among competing claims to truth in either the positive or the interpretive sciences. Assuming that we have emancipation as our interest, what knowledge should we operate with? This is not meant to imply that critical theory should legislate some formal criteria. It is quite clear to me that critical theory eschews formal logic. But what are the interpretations of the present world I should accept or act on for the sake of emancipation? At the very least, critical theory must begin to distinguish between those interpretations that are compatible with emancipation and those that are not.

The continuing role of critical theory is to reflect on system interest and cognition, since they are one. Only by a continued analysis of knowledge and the interests it serves can an emancipatory science flourish. This does not mean that science has immanent political implications, but it indicates that the consequences of various social theories must always be kept in mind. Critical theorists also argue that only an emancipatory science can view science and history as self-forming processes. Critical theory argues that there are no laws of history. History has taken place behind the backs of men and without the emergence of rationality. Again, the assumption is made that men make history, although not necessarily as they might like it. Any explanation which places the responsibility for history or science above the heads fo men is considered reification. The role of critical theory is to indicate the development possibilities of a given society through the power of speculation. This means that no matter what society is being analyzed, they all contain the potential for rational development—the basic enlightenment principle. Although fantasy is important in this speculation, such fantasy is not unencumbered by real objective possibilities. Fantasy not hinged on real possibilities may deteriorate into "rural idiocy" or bourgeois "1984s."

Unlike vulgar Marxists, critical theorists believe in holding the goal up to view, but theirs is not the Soviet Marxist goal of economic development. Critical theorists are rather vague about the goal. In part, this ambiguity is deliberate. In the past, men have coerced others for the sake of the goal. In the critical theorist's mind, this manipulation is something to be prevented. In a sense, one must give up all nationalistic ideologies and various social movements, for fear of having these theories become instrumentally coercive. The critical theorist must keep a certain distance from all commitments. This ambiguity about commitment is brought out aptly in Alvin Gouldner's discussion of critical theory and the communications revolution.

Critique thus vacillates between a rejection of the pseudodisinterestedness of positivistic social science, and a rejection of ideological mediations of the news, manifestly because critique cannot "burn its bridges," and must share certain tacit understandings with the world it aims to transcend, that there is 1) a dissonance between critique's call for demystification and its own labryinthianisms and elephantine opacity, as well as 2) a dissonance between critique's epic rhetoric of world "emancipation" on the one side, and, on the other, its essentially Fabian political practice—when it has any politics at all.[11]

Critical theory then is against explanatory or interpretive analyses of society when used alone. Critical theory argues that not only are these explanations not enough, they are also "false consciousness." The once potential revolutionary proletariat was transformed into an impotent collective state bureaucracy which reified Marx's analysis. This transformation of Marx was not accomplished alone. Marx's work contained implicitly positivistic elements which Albrecht Wellmer has recently analyzed in his *Critical Theory of Society.* Given that the proletariat are no longer a viable social force for the movement toward a rational society, critical theory aligns itself with various progressive forces in society without orthodox commitment—an unspecified praxis. "Rather than assume that a concept of emancipation can be derived deductively from theory, we must recognize it can be reconstructured only from the experience of the masses who have been trying to liberate themselves from industrial domination for centuries." Trent Schroyer also argues that certain general needs, "such as health, education, welfare, environment conditions—that can only be partially and inequitably met by the state—provide a social space for emancipatory movements."[12] Critical theory must also strive to create a critical intelligentsia—an intelligentsia which does not bind itself dogmatically to any social movement. Only in that way can it keep alive the power of negative thinking. Again, Gouldner summarizes critical theory and what it is about when it is at its best.

> This means that, when it is at its best, critical theory eschews all temptations to claims of moral elitism and superiority, as well as all posturings of innocence. It never imagines—when it is at its best—that its own self-understanding can be taken at face value, or that its commitments are lacking in ambiguities or contradictions. Critical theory makes a distinction between what it is and what it hopes to be. Affirming human emancipation as a goal, it never allows itself to intimate—when it is at its best—that it itself has already achieved that emancipation and never allows itself to forget that it, too, possesses a repressive potential. It knows that its own rationality, too, is limited by the world in which it exists and by the social positioning of those speaking for it. Knowing it will win no easy victories relying upon its continual work and struggle, as well as upon a sometime quiet capacity for "surrender," critical theory seeks to understand itself as well as the world, and it suspects—as self-serving and sycophantic—all offered conceptions of itself that bring it no painful surprises. When it is at its best.[13]

In conclusion, critical theory clearly operates both with a philosophical anthropology grounded in a philosophy of history and with human emancipation as its goal. Critical theory rejects any social theory which degrades humankind as a potential actor on the historical stage. It refuses to define rationality within the confines of positive science. Critical theory is clearly normative. It distinguishes itself from other social theories by not making otiose claims to objectivity and disinterestedness.

Although critical theory has not yet shown us what theories, if any, from the positive or hermeneutical sciences contribute to emancipation, the issue has been raised. Likewise, critical theory has not yet outlined how the noble ideal of a rational community has become butchered, but surely it is seeking this too. For critical theorists, the age of intellectual tranquillity is over, if it ever existed. There are no promissory notes to be delivered. It is, of course, reflexive without being nihilistic, empirical without the reification of facts, and speculative without being metaphysical. Unlike some aspects of early American sociology, the critical tradition claims cognitive superiority on the basis of the "assumed" practical potential of the species. It does not hide behind the idea of a positive science or a Marxist notion of immanent history. The assumptions of critical theory may be argued with, but they are not hidden. It alone, I believe, provides a foundation for a sociology of knowledge tradition which does not rely on pseudoscientific formulations to account for the relationship between social structure and consciousness.

Notes

Notes to Introduction

1. For an interesting view of the contemporary situation see Peter Berger, *The Sacred Canopy.*
2. Peter Berger, *Invitation to Sociology,* p. 29.
3. Frederick Copleston, *A History of Philosophy;* Bertrand Russell, *A History of Western Philosophy;* Wilhelm Windelband, *A History of Philosophy.*
4. Peter Berger and Thomas Luckmann, *The Social Construction of Reality;* Karl Mannheim, *Ideology and Utopia;* Pitirim Sorokin, *Social and Cultural Dynamics,* abridged ed.
5. Ernest Gellner, *Legitimation of Belief,* p. 31.
6. Göran Therborn, *Science, Class and Society,* p. 429.
7. Mannheim, *Ideology and Utopia.*
8. Don Martindale, *The Nature and Types of Sociological Theory,* pp. 3-27.
9. Guenther Roth, "Religion and Revolutionary Beliefs: Sociological and Historical Dimensions in Max Weber's Work—In Memory of Ivan Vallier."
10. Gunter Remmling, *Road to Suspicion;* Gunter Remmling, ed., *Towards the Sociology of Knowledge;* James Curtis and John W. Petras, eds., *The Sociology of Knowledge: A Reader;* Werner Stark, *The Sociology of Knowledge;* Peter Hamilton, *Knowledge and Social Structure: An Introduction to the Classical Argument in the Sociology of Knowledge.*
11. Robert W. Friedrichs, *A Sociology of Sociology;* Alvin W. Gouldner, *The Coming Crisis of Western Sociology.*
12. Albrecht Wellmer, *Critical Theory of Society.*
13. Alvin Gouldner, *Enter Plato;* Hermann Strasser, *The Normative Structure of Sociology.*
14. George Ritzer, *Sociology: A Multiple Paradigm Science.*
15. Therborn, *Science, Class and Society,* p. 222.
16. Kurt Wolff, Karl Mannheim, and Robert Merton have indicated some of the similarities and differences between American and European theoretical concerns. Kurt Wolff, "Notes Toward a Sociocultural Interpretation of American Sociology"; Robert Merton, "The Sociology of Knowledge and Mass Communications," in his *Social Theory and Social Structure,* pp. 439-55; Karl Mannheim, "American Sociology," in *Sociology on Trial,* ed. Maurice Stein and Arthur Vidich, pp. 3-11.
17. The still-classic work on the idea of class on this generation is Charles Page, *Class and American Sociology: From Ward to Ross.* On social change

see: Marjorie Sue Childers, "Social Change in American Sociology: The First Generation"; on politics: James Aho, "Sociology and Conflict"; Dusky Lee Smith, "Some Socio-Economic Influences on the Founding Fathers of Sociology, 1865-1917"; Leon Shaskolsky, "The Development of Sociological Theory in America—A Sociology of Knowledge Interpretation," in Larry and Janice Reynolds, eds., *The Sociology of Sociology*, pp. 6-30. A number of writers have alluded to an American contribution to the sociology of knowledge: Norman Birnbaum, *Toward a Critical Sociology*, p. 15; Roscoe C. Hinkle, "Basic Orientations of the Founding Fathers of American Sociology," p. 121 n. 8. More recently Hermann and Julia Schwendinger have placed this generation squarely in the stream of Western liberal thought in their *The Sociologists of the Chair*.

Notes to Chapter 1

1. Gunter Remmling, *Road to Suspicion*, and Remmling, *Towards the Sociology of Knowledge*.
2. Robert Merton, "The Sociology of Knowledge," in his *Social Theory and Social Structure*, pp. 510–42.
3. Thelma Lavine, "Knowledge as Interpretation: An Historical Survey."
4. Franz Adler, "The Range of the Sociology of Knowledge," pp. 396-423 in *Modern Sociological Theory in Continuity and Change*, ed. H. Becker and A. Boskoff; Jacques J. Maquet, *The Sociology of Knowledge—Its Structure and Its Relation to the Philosophy of Knowledge: A Critical Analysis of the System of Karl Mannheim and Pitirim A. Sorokin;* Werner Stark, *The Sociology of Knowledge: A Reader*, ed. James Curtis and John W. Petras.
5. Karl Mannheim, *Ideology and Utopia*, p. 220.
6. Herman Strasser, *The Normative Structure of Sociology*, pp. 16-17. I also borrow the terms critical-emancipatory and social-technological from Strasser's work.
7. I am following Merton's earlier formulation, in part, with the express purpose of drawing out the politics of these varying traditions in the sociology of knowledge. See Merton, "The Sociology of Knowledge."
8. Immanuel Kant, *Critique of Pure Reason*.
9. Leszek Kolakowski, *Toward a Marxist Humanism*, p. 66.
10. Karl Marx and Frederick Engels, *The Communist Manifesto*, p. 87; Marx and Engels, *The German Ideology* (Part 1).
11. Karl Marx, *The Poverty of Philosophy*, p. 189.
12. Herbert Marcuse, *Soviet Marxism*, pp. 151, 154; Marcuse, *One-Dimensional Man*, p. 9.
13. Edward Schaub, "A Sociological Theory of Knowledge," p. 335.
14. Emile Durkheim, *The Elementary Forms of the Religious Life*, p. 476; Durkheim, *Sociology and Philosophy*, p. 89; Durkheim, *Elementary Forms*, p. 28.
15. Otto Dahlke, "The Sociology of Knowledge," in *Contemporary Social Theory*, ed. Barnes, Becker, and Becker, pp. 66-67.

16. Durkheim, *Elementary Forms*, p. 484.

17. Ibid., pp. 492, 493.

18. George Lichtheim, "The Concept of Ideology," in his *The Concept of Ideology and Other Essays*, p. 18.

19. Georg Lukács, *History and Class Consciousness*, pp. 10, 55-59.

20. Trent Schroyer, "Toward a Critical Theory for Advanced Industrial Society," p. 214.

21. See Trent Schroyer, *The Critique of Domination;* William Leiss, *The Domination of Nature.*

22. Jurgen Habermas, *Knowledge and Human Interests.*

23. Georges Gurvitch, *The Social Frameworks of Knowledge*, pp. 35-36.

24. Ibid., p. 10.

25. Raymond Aron, *Main Currents in Sociological Thought*, 1:99.

26. Auguste Comte, *System of Positive Polity*, 1:7, 2:78, 3:290, 1:25-26.

27. Ibid., 1:25-26.

28. Ibid., 2:346.

29. Aron, *Main Currents*, 1:75.

30. Leszek Kolakowski, *The Alienation of Reason*, p. 20. Positivisim in most cases is simply identified as the imitation of the natural scientists by the social scientists. In short, the belief that the social sciences should follow the *methods* of the natural sciences. However, I find Kolakowski's treatment far more interesting and comprehensive. For this reason, I have relied on his analysis.

31. Ibid., pp. 3-10.

32. Lukács indicates that bourgeois thinking goes in two different directions. "As a result of its incapacity to understand history, the contemplative attitude of the bourgeoisie becomes polarized into two extremes; on the one hand, there were the 'great individuals' viewed as the autocratic makers of history; on the other hand, there were the 'natural laws' of historical environment" (*History and Class Consciousnsess*, p. 158). These two views were held simultaneously by a number of early American sociologists.

33. Marcuse, *One-Dimensional Man*, pp. 215, 214 n. 9.

34. Alvin W. Gouldner, "The Two Marxisms," in his *For Sociology*, p. 427.

35. Marcuse, *One-Dimensional Man*, p. x.

36. Jurgen Habermas, *Toward a Rational Society.*

37. Habermas, *Knowledge*, pp. 308, 312-15.

38. Robert Paul Wolff, *The Poverty of Liberalism*, p. 90.

39. Gouldner, "The Two Marxisms," p. 429.

40. Hans Peter Dreitzel, "Social Science and the Problem of Rationality: Notes on the Sociology of Technocrats," p. 173.

41. Robert Nisbet, "Conservatism and Sociology," in his *Tradition and Revolt* (New York: Vintage Books, 1970), pp. 73-89. See also John Horton, "Order and Conflict Theories of Social Problems as Competing Ideologies."

42. Russell Kirk, *The Conservative Mind*, p. 9. It also should be noted that the critical tradition *does not* emphasize democratic elitism. It is interested in democratic processes as both political method and ethical end. It stresses the equality of power, not equality of opportunity. It also views the elite struc-

ture of modern industrial societies as alterable. On this, see Peter Bachrach, *The Theory of Democratic Elitism,* especially p. 100.

43. There are three separate but related issues that must be discussed here concerning the cognitive status, appropriateness, and exhaustiveness of my two thematic formulations. First, these themes are only meant to be heuristic devices. Therefore, my interest was not in discussing the differences that exist between particular individuals within one theme. The value of the themes is determined by their usefulness. As will be illustrated later, these themes have only a limited usefulness. Second, are these themes appropriate for analyzing American sociologists, since they are formed primarily from my reading of selected European theorists? In a certain sense, this question also can be answered by demonstrating the usefulness or nonusefulness of these themes. In addition, however, it seemed appropriate to formulate these themes on the basis of European theorists, since, for the most part, the sociology of knowledge has been identified with European sociological thought. Finally, it could be argued that social-technological and critical-emancipatory themes do not exhaust the various political themes in the sociology of knowledge. Indeed, on this issue Werner Stark has already written an interesting essay, "The Conservative Tradition in the Sociology of Knowledge" (in Remmling, ed., *Towards the Sociology of Knowledge,* pp. 68-77). However, my goal was *not* to draw up a typology of all possible positions, but to indicate some heuristic framework for analyzing a group of writers who have not been examined from this perspective. The value of the framework rests on its ability to decipher other communications and is not meant as a formal inventory. Peter Hamilton has written insightfully about the various classical arguments in the sociology of knowledge in his *Knowledge and Social Structure.* Hamilton's work concerns itself with the Enlightenment, Hegel, Marx, Lukács, the Frankfurt School, Lucien Goldmann, Marx Scheler, Max Weber, Durkheim, Karl Mannheim, and phenomenological approaches (e.g., A. Schutz, Peter Berger, and Thomas Luckmann). Moreover, there is some foreknowledge available which indicates that early American sociologists were primarily liberal in their orientation. See Roscoe C. Hinkle and Gisela J. Hinkle, *The Development of Modern Sociology;* Don Martindale, "American Sociology Before World War II"; Charles Page, *Class and American Sociology: From Ward to Ross.*

44. The analysis of the early American sociologists' writings raises the issue of *how* to analyze texts. For the most part, I believe that the idea of an hermeneutical circle or spiral is the best theory-method for dialoguing with texts. The hermeneutical circle consists of a set of arguments that: (1) there is no development of knowledge without foreknowledge; (2) one must anticipate the global meaning of the text—that is, its overriding interest for being written; (3) the meaning of the various parts of the text are determined by the global concern; (4) there is a problem of how to get properly into the text. Hermeneutics has as its aim that more and more of the hidden assumptions become known and articulated. However, it also realizes that all assumptions cannot be made explicit at the same time. Further, it is a self-corrective process, in which the text operates as a check on our foreknowledge. In this sense, hermeneutics means that we need familiarity with the topics or subjects of texts more than we need biographical information about the author.

The model and structure of every hermeneutic event, then, is that of dialogue. This dialogue means, among other things, that: (1) we understand our dialogue partner when we can formulate his ideas in our own words; (2) we recognize the historicity of the dialogue partners; (3) human beings are not fully transparent to themselves; (4) the dialogue is to be analyzed by that which is ultimately at stake; (5) dialogues are always, in part, creative events; and (6) verification exists with the subject matter itself, in the sense that we understand better the subject matter at the end of our exploration. (Gerard Radnitzky, *Contemporary Schools of Metascience,* 3d ed., pp. 211-50. This style of hermeneutics suggests that we do not pretend to have no foreknowledge about the writers or the texts. One does start with an anticipation of what is to be discovered. In this light, the chapter outlining the various themes in the sociology of knowledge only serves to make explicit what had been implicit. Moreover, there is no neutral way to read a text. One always reads in terms of the categories available. The design of this method suggests that the texts will act as a check on our categories and that other scholars also will act to halt *any* kind of interpretation.

Notes to Chapter 2

1. Sammuel Hays, *The Response to Industrialism: 1885-1914,* p. 1.
2. Edward Kirkland, *A History of American Economic Life,* p. 380.
3. Constance Green, *The Rise of Urban America,* p. 105.
4. Seymour Lipset and R. Bendix, *Social Mobility in Industrial Society,* p. 75.
5. Colin Clark, "The Conditions of Economic Progress," in Lipset and Bendix, *Social Mobility,* p. 84.
6. Kirkland, *History,* pp. 382, 389, 495.
7. Richard Hofstadter, *The Age of Reform,* p. 188.
8. Kirkland, *History,* pp. 392–93.
9. Green, *Rise of Urban America,* p. 101.
10. Hays, *Response to Industrialism,* p. 51.
11. Hoffman quoted in Otis Graham, Jr., *The Great Campaigns: Reform and War in America,* p. 7.
12. Kirkland, *History,* p. 493.
13. Selig Perlman, *A History of Trade Unionism in the United States,* pp. 163, 164.
14. Hays, *Response to Industrialism,* p. 49.
15. Graham, *The Great Campaigns,* pp. 8, 9.
16. Burton Hendrick, *The Age of Big Business,* pp. 19, 85.
17. Hofstadter, *Age of Reform,* p. 136.
18. Graham, *The Great Campaigns,* p. 9.
19. Hofstadter, *Age of Reform,* p. 168; Samuel Eliot Morrison, *The Oxford History of the American People,* 3:157.
20. Hofstadter, *Age of Reform,* p. 169.
21. Robert Wiebe, *Businessmen and Reform: A Study of the Progressive Movement,* p. 160.

22. Richard Hofstadter and Michael Wallace, eds., *American Violence,* pp. 423, 425.

23. Gabriel Kolko, *The Triumph of Conservatism,* pp. 7-8.

24. Wiebe, *Businessmen and Reform,* pp. 210, 212.

25. Hofstadter, *Age of Reform,* p. 243.

26. Wiebe, *Businessmen and Reform,* p. 211.

27. James Weinstein, *The Corporate Ideal in the Liberal State, 1900-1918,* pp. ix-xii.

28. Hays, *Response to Industrialism,* p. 72.

29. Benjamin DeWitt, *The Progressive Movement,* p. 50.

30. Ibid., p. 49. This is DeWitt's comment and not Roosevelt's.

31. Henry Pelling, *American Labor,* p. 117.

32. DeWitt, *The Progressive Movement,* pp. 40-43.

33. Ibid., pp. 43-44.

34. Richard Hofstadter, *The Progressive Movement, 1900-1915,* pp. 2-3.

35. Ibid., p. 7.

36. Maldwyn Jones, *American Immigration,* p. 218.

37. Ibid., pp. 208-9. "The largest single foreign-born group in 1910 was from Germany; it contained more than two and a half million. But second and third places were occupied by natives of Russia and of Austria-Hungary, each of whom numbered well over a million and a half. Natives of Ireland and Italy came next, each with more than a million, three hundred thousand, while the Scandinavian countries, Great Britain, and Canada could each claim almost a million and a quarter."

38. Oscar Handlin, *The Uprooted,* pp. 49, 130.

39. Jones, *American Immigration,* p. 219.

40. Ibid., p. 321.

41. P. Taft, *The A. F. of L. in the Time of Gompers,* p. 41; J. R. Commons and associates, *History of Labor in the United States,* 2:396-402.

42. Pelling, *American Labor,* pp. 84-85.

43. Marc Karson, *American Labor Unions and Politics, 1900-1918,* p. 31.

44. Quoted ibid., p. 32.

45. R. Berthoff, "The Working Class," in *The Reconstruction of American History,* ed. John Higham, p. 133.

46. Theodore Draper, *Roots of American Communism,* p. 20.

47. Commons et al., *History of Labor,* 3:8-9, 2:308.

48. Draper, *Roots of American Communism,* p. 22.

49. Patrick Renshaw, *The Wobblies,* p. 5.

50. Ibid., p. 37.

51. Ibid., pp. 123-24.

52. Ira Kipnis, *The American Socialist Movement, 1897-1912,* p. 64.

53. Ibid., p. 16.

54. Daniel Bell, *Marxian Socialism in the United States,* p. 56.

55. Sally Miller, *Victor Berger and the Promise of Constructive Socialism, 1910-1920.*

56. James Weinstein, *The Decline of Socialism in America, 1912-1925,* pp. 5-8.

57. Morris Hillquit, *Socialism Summed Up,* p. 61.

58. David Shannon, *The Socialist Party of America,* pp. 1-42.

59. Weinstein, *Decline of Socialism,* p. 182.

60. Ibid., p. 159.

61. Walter P. Metzger, *Academic Freedom in the Age of the University,* p. 5.

62. Ibid., p. 20.

63. Ibid., pp. 42-43.

64. Jurgen Herbst, *The German Historical School in American Scholarship,* p. 3.

65. Ibid., pp. 1, 9.

66. Ibid., p. 112.

67. Ibid., p. 188.

68. Christopher Jencks and David Riesman, *The Academic Revolution,* p. 13.

69. Lawrence R. Veysey, *The Emergence of the American University,* p. 264.

70. Metzger, *Academic Freedom,* p. 139; Veysey, *Emergence of the American University,* pp. 347-49.

71. Metzger, *Academic Freedom,* p. 145.

72. White's comment quoted from Veysey, *Emergence of the American University,* p. 83; see also p. 85.

73. Ibid., pp. 88-92.

74. Ibid., p. 109.

75. Edward Shils, "Tradition, Ecology, and Institution in the History of Sociology," p. 780.

76. Veysey, *Emergence of the American University,* p. 316.

77. E. Digby Baltzell, *The Protestant Establishment,* p. 162.

78. Jencks and Riesman, *The Academic Revolution,* p. 237.

79. Joseph Ben-David, "The Universities and the Growth of Science in Germany and the United States," pp. 14, 18-19.

80. Metzger, *Academic Freedom,* p. 104.

81. Hofstadter, *Age of Reform,* p. 163.

82. Martin J. Sklar, "Woodrow Wilson and the Political Economy of Modern United States Liberalism," in *For a New America,* ed. James Weinstein and David W. Eakins, p. 55.

83. Ibid., p. 91.

84. Ronald Radosh, "The Corporate Ideology of American Labor Leaders from Gompers to Hillman," in Weinstein and Eakins, eds., *For a New America,* p. 126.

85. Richard Hofstadter and DeWitt C. Hardy, *The Development and Scope of Higher Education in the United States,* p. 31.

86. Ibid., p. 36.

87. Metzger, *Academic Freedom,* pp. 142, 180.

Notes to Chapter 3

1. This sketch of Sumner relied on the following sources: A. G. Keller, *Reminiscences (Mainly Personal) of William Graham Sumner;* Albert Keller, "Sketch of William Graham Sumner," in William G. Sumner, *The Challenge of Facts and Other Essays,* ed. A. G. Keller; Luther Bernard Papers, box 30, file 6, Archives, Pennsylvania State University, University Park, Pa.

2. Luther Bernard Papers, Pennsylvania State University, box 30, file 6.

3. William G. Sumner, *Folkways,* p. 629.

4. William G. Sumner, *What Social Classes Owe to Each Other,* p. 27.

5. William G. Sumner, *War and Other Essays,* pp. 14, 149–50.

6. Sumner, *Challenge of Facts,* pp. 138–39.

7. William G. Sumner, *Collected Essays in Political and Social Science,* p. 98.

8. Sumner, *What Social Classes Owe,* p. 60.

9. William G. Sumner, *Folkways,* p. 4; Sumner, *Earth Hunger and Other Essays,* p. 156; Sumner and A. G. Keller, *The Science of Society,* 1:5.

10. Sumner and Keller, *Science of Society,* p. 90.

11. Ibid., pp. 4-8.

12. Charles Page, *Class and American Sociology: From Ward to Ross,* p. 80.

13. Sumner, *Earth Hunger,* p. 283.

14. Sumner and Keller, *Science of Society,* 1:2220.

15. Sumner, *Challenge of Facts,* p. 37.

16. Sumner and Keller, *Science of Society,* 1:10.

17. Ibid., p. 9.

18. Page, *Class and American Sociology,* p. 93.

19. Sumner, *Collected Essays,* pp. 99, 102.

20. Sumner, *What Social Classes Owe,* pp. 27-28, 89.

21. Richard Hofstadter, in his work *Social Darwinism in American Thought,* indicates some of the important differences between Edmund Burke's conservatism and Sumner's view of the status quo (pp. 8-9).

Where Burke is religious, and relies upon an intuitive approach to politics and upon instinctive wisdom, Sumner is secularist and proudly rationalist. Where Burke relies upon the collective, long-range intelligence, the wisdom of the community, Sumner expects that individual self-assertion will be the only satisfactory expression of wisdom of nature, and asks of the community only that it give full play to this self-assertion. Where Burke reveres custom and exalts continuity with the past. Sumner is favorably impressed by the break made with the past when contract supplanted status....

On this matter, see also Leon Bramson, *The Political Context of Sociology,* pp. 23-25.

22. Sumner, *Folkways,* p. 59.

23. Sumner, *War,* p. 205.

24. Sumner, *Folkways,* pp. 29, 38.

25. Sumner and Keller, *Science of Society,* 1:52; Sumner, *Folkways,* pp. 136–37.

26. Sumner and Keller, *Science of Society,* 1:54–55.

27. Ibid., p. 214.

28. Ibid., p. 60.

29. Sumner, *Folkways,* pp. 521, 84–85.

30. Ibid., p. 231.

31. Sumner, *War,* pp. 150, 135–36; Sumner and Keller, *Science of Society,* 2:847, 1457.

32. Sumner, *War,* p. 151, and *Folkways,* pp. 109–10.

33. Sumner and Keller, *Science of Society,* 3:1681.

34. Sumner, *Folkways,* p. 351.

35. Sumner, *Earth Hunger,* pp. 87–88.

36. Sumner, *War,* pp. 158–59.

37. Sumner, *Challenge of Facts,* pp. 304, 295.

38. Sumner and Keller, *Science of Society,* 1:731; Sumner, *Challenge of Facts,* pp. 392–93.

39. For Sumner's analysis of industrial, military, and educational mores see *Challenge of Facts,* pp. 348, 30–31, 369, and *Folkways,* p. 635.

40. Charles Page *(Class and American Sociology,* pp. 95–96) suggests that Sumner did not believe in the possiblity of class conflict because the middle classes possed no class consciousness. "Within the middle class exists a dominant economic mobility that robs it of its status-class nature. This mobility, plus the independence of the American worker gives him such strength in the labor market that trade-unionism is unnecessary.... Not only is the middle class economically emancipated, but ideologically unique. It is a class disciplined in terms of a sense of morality, of public feeling, and of responsibility."

41. Sumner and Keller, *Science of Society,* 1:30–31.

42. Sumner, *Folkways,* pp. 367–68.

43. Ibid., p. 607.

44. Werner Stark, *The Sociology of Knowledge,* p. 250.

45. Sumner, *Folkways,* pp. 609, 613.

46. Ibid., p. 627.

47. Sumner and Keller, *Science of Society,* 2:771.

48. Ibid., 2:858–59.

49. Ibid., 3:2114–15.

50. Sumner, *What Social Classes Owe,* p. 141.

51. Sumner, *War,* p. 197.

52. Sumner, *Earth Hunger,* pp. 339–40.

53. Sumner, *Challenge of Facts,* pp. 215, 244.

54. Sumner, *Collected Essays,* p. 26.

55. Sumner, *War,* pp. 204–6.

56. Sumner, *Collected Essays,* pp. 114, 136.

57. Sumner, *Challenge of Facts,* p. 245.

58. Sumner, *Earth Hunger,* pp. 75, 24–25.

59. Sumner, *War,* pp. 167–68.

60. Sumner and Keller, *Science of Society,* 1:xxx.

61. Ibid., 3:2163, 2175.
62. Sumner, *War*, pp. 170–71.
63. Sumner and Keller, *Science of Society*, 3:2165–66.
64. Sumner, *War*, p. 191; Sumner and Keller, *Science of Society*, 3:2224; Sumner, *War*, p. 239; Sumner and Keller, *Science of Society*, 3:2187.
65. Sumner, *Folkways*, p. 97.
66. William G. Sumner, *Essays of William Graham Sumner*, 1:467, 477.
67. Sumner, *Earth Hunger*, pp. 363, 341.
68. Sumner, *What Social Classes Owe*, p. 14.
69. Sumner, *Earth Hunger*, pp. 74–75.
70. Sumner, *War*, p. 210.
71. Sumner, *Challenge of Facts*, p. 207.
72. Sumner, *What Social Classes Owe*, pp. 24, 75.
73. Sumner, *Earth Hunger*, p. 184.
74. Sumner, *War*, p. 184, and *Earth Hunger*, pp. 175–76.
75. Sumner, *Challenge of Facts*, pp. 18, 19.
76. Sumner and Keller, *Science of Society*, 3:2247.
77. Sumner, *What Social Classes Owe*, p. 138.

Notes to Chapter 4

1. This biographical portrait is based on the following sources: Howard W. Odum, *American Sociology*; Luther Bernard Papers, Pennsylvania State University Archives, University Park, Pa.; Luther Bernard Papers, University of Chicago, Special Collections; Samuel Chugerman, *Lester F. Ward: The American Aristotle*.
2. Emily P. Cape, *Lester F. Ward*, pp. 24–25.
3. Henry S. Commager, *The American Mind*, p. 208.
4. Chugerman, *Ward*, pp. 34–35.
5. Charlotte G. O'Kelley and John W. Petras, "Images of Man In Early American Sociology, Part 2: The Changing Concept of Social Reform," p. 319. The statements quoted are by O'Kelley and Petras about Ward.
6. Don Martindale, "American Sociology Before World War II," p. 126.
7. Fred H. Matthews, *Quest For an American Sociology: Robert E. Park and the Chicago School*, p. 93; Harry Elmer Barnes, "Lester Frank Ward: The Reconstruction of Society by Social Science," in *An Introduction to the History of Sociology*, ed. Barnes, p. 129.
8. Lester F. Ward, *Dynamic Sociology*, 1:ix, 11, 2:111.
9. Lester F. Ward, *Pure Sociology*, pp. 569, 101.
10. Ward, *Dynamic Sociology*, 1:472.
11. Ibid., 1:20, 25; 2:155.
12. Ward, *Pure Sociology*, p. 102.
13. Ibid., p. 122.
14. Ibid., p. 261.
15. Ward, *Dynamic Sociology*, 2:178.

16. John W. Petras, "Images of Man In Early American Sociology, Part 1: The Individualistic Perspective In Motivation," p. 232.

17. Lester F. Ward, *Outlines of Sociology*, pp. 91-92; Ward, *Dynamic Sociology*, 1:394; 2:220.

18. Ward, *Dynamic Sociology*, 1:35.

19. Ibid., 1:466.

20. Ward, *Pure Sociology*, p. 268.

21. Ward, *Outlines*, pp. 172-73.

22. Ward, *Dynamic Sociology*, 1:451.

23. Ibid., 2:214-15, 225; Lester Ward, *The Psychic Factors of Civilization*, p. 303; Ward, *Pure Sociology*, p. 555.

24. Ward, *Pure Sociology*, pp. 267, 271.

25. Ward here used the terms *protosocial* and *metasocial* much like Durkheim's idea of unsegmented and segmented societies. Ward, *Pure Sociology*, pp. 274, 277.

26. Ward, *Dynamic Sociology*, 1:492.

27. Lester F. Ward, *Applied Sociology*, pp. 132-33, 91.

28. Ward, *Dynamic Sociology*, 2:538.

29. Ward, *Applied Sociology*, pp. 93-95, and *Dynamic Sociology*, 2:89.

30. C. B. MacPherson, *Democratic Theory: Essays in Retrieval*, pp. 27-28. See the first two essays in this book for a lucid account of democracy in the context of capitalism: "The Maximization of Democracy" and "Democratic Theroy: Ontology and Technology."

31. Ward, *Applied Sociology*, pp. 45, 47.

32. *Mind* is an undefined term for Ward. He uses it in the context of brain physiology as well as for civilizations.

33. Ward, *Dynamic Sociology*, 2:471.

34. Ibid.; Ward, *Psychic Factors*, p. 156; Ward, *Dynamic Sociology*, 1:490.

35. Ward, *Dynamic Sociology*, 1:198.

36. Ward, *Pure Sociology*, p. 187.

37. Ward, *Outlines*, pp. 131, 133-34.

38. Ward, *Dynamic Sociology*, 2:420, 424-45.

39. Ibid., p. 427.

40. Ibid., 2:427, 431, 439-40.

41. Ward, *Psychic Factors*, p. 93.

42. Ward, *Dynamic Sociology*, 2:616, 437-49. For a Marxist critique and analysis of Ward's position on women, see Herman and Julia Schwendinger, *The Sociologists of the Chair*, pp. 311-13, 319-22.

43. Ward, *Dynamic Sociology*, 2:27, 417-19.

44. Ward, *Pure Sociology*, p. 46.

45. Ward, *Dynamic Sociology*, 1:66, 381, 50.

46. Ward, *Outlines*, p. 25.

47. Ward, *Psychic Factors*, p. 70.

48. Ward, *Applied Sociology*, pp. 85, 65, 75.

49. Ward, *Dynamic Sociology*, 2:516, and *Pure Sociology*, pp. 142-43.

50. Ward, *Outlines*, p. 29.

51. Ward, *Dynamic Sociology*, 2:273, 305–6.
52. Ward, *Psychic Factors*, pp. 177, 178.
53. Ward, *Outlines*, p. 9.
54. Ward, *Applied Sociology*, pp. 11, 21, 10.
55. Ibid., p. 15; Ward, *Dynamic Sociology*, 2:602; Ward, *Psychic Factors*, pp. 240–45.
56. Ward, *Dynamic Sociology*, 2:459–69.
57. Ibid., 1:45, 2:247; Ward, *Outlines*, pp. 203–4.
58. Ward, *Outlines*, pp. 161, 162, 163.
59. Ward, *Dynamic Sociology*, 2:335, 1:xxvii, 54, 2:14, 155.
60. Ward, *Psychic Factors*, pp. 290, 71–74.
61. Ward, *Dynamic Sociology*, 1:518, 2:359, 43–44.
62. Ward, *Pure Sociology*, p. 452.
63. Ward, *Outlines*, pp. 292–93.
64. Ibid., pp. 282, 205; Ward, *Pure Sociology*, p. 49.
65. Ward, *Dynamic Sociology*, 2:503–4, 407, 1:78.
66. Ward, *Applied Sociology*, p. 339.
67. Ward, *Psychic Factors*, p. 25, *Outlines*, p. 269, and *Applied Sociology*, pp. 332–33.
68. Ward, *Applied Sociology*, p. 328.
69. Ward, *Dynamic Sociology*, 1:22.
70. Ward, *Outlines*, p. 281.
71. Ward, *Applied Sociology*, pp. 299–302, 281.
72. Ward, *Dynamic Sociology*, 2:538.
73. Charles Page, *Class and American Sociology: From Ward to Ross*, p. 41.

Notes to Chapter 5

1. This sketch relied mainly on the following sources: Luther Bernard Papers, box, 1, folder 4, and box 30, University of Chicago, Special Collections; Luther Bernard Papers, box 23, file 2, Archives, Pennsylvania State University, University Park, Pa.; John L. Gillin, "Franklin Henry Giddings," in Howard W. Odum, ed., *American Masters of Social Science*, pp. 191-230; Howard W. Odum, *American Sociology*, pp. 86-94.
2. Odum, *American Masters*, p. 196.
3. Wright later headed the sociological department at Clark University during the first decade of the twentieth century. Wright was firmly committed to the idea that firm statistical methods must be used for accurate sociological inductions. This was particularly apt, since Wright believed that social science was characterized by loose, unchecked generalizations from random observations. Giddings also was enamored of statistical methods, and he was probably influenced by Wright in this regard.
4. Luther Bernard Papers, box 1, folder 4, University of Chicago, Special Collections.
5. Ibid.

6. Franklin H. Giddings, *The Principles of Sociology*, p. 327.

7. Franklin H. Giddings, *Studies in the Theory of Human Society,* Giddings, *Principles,* p. 226.

8. Franklin H. Giddings, *The Elements of Sociology*, pp. 45–47.

9. Franklin H. Giddings, *Civilization and Society*, pp. 46–47, 270–71.

10. Giddings, *Elements,* pp. 100–101, and *Principles,* pp. 123–24, 225

11. Franklin H. Giddings, *Inductive Sociology,* p. 99; Giddings, *Princi* p. 137.

12. Giddings, *Principles,* pp. 73–75.

13. Giddings, *Elements,* p. 242, and *Principles,* pp. 299–302.

14. Giddings, *Elements,* p. 229.

15. Franklin H. Giddings, *Democracy and Empire,* p. 315.

16. Franklin H. Giddings, *Readings in Descriptive and Historical Sociolc* pp. 6–7.

17. Giddings, *Civilization and Society,* pp. 32–33, and *Principles of S* *ology,* p. 420.

18. Giddings, *Readings,* pp. 8–9. Some interpreters have suggested that G dings's idea of society is primarily nominalist in orientation. Ultimately, "t group is little more than an instictively bound collection of discrete units (John W. Petras, "Images of Man In Early American Sociology, Part I: The I dividualistic Perspective In Motivation," p. 235.) However, Charles Page su gests that Giddings cannot be accused of a strictly individualist interpretatior "Pluralistic reactions to common stimuli rule out a strictly individualistic in terpretation of social life, for pluralistic behavior has its own laws, conditions and forms." (*Class and American Sociology: From Ward to Ross,* p. 167.) also believe that Giddings's idea of society cannot be reduced to a strictly nominalist orientation.

19. Giddings, *Inductive Sociology,* p. 47.

20. Giddings, *Principles,* pp. 124–31, and *Elements,* pp. 105–12.

21. Giddings, *Elements,* pp. 108–9.

22. Ibid., pp. 110–11.

23. Giddings, *Democracy and Empire,* p. 126, and *Civilization and Society,* p. 34.

24. Franklin H. Giddings, *The Responsible State,* p. 9; Giddings, *Principles,* p. 178.

25. Giddings, *Studies,* p. 145.

26. Giddings, *Readings,* p. 272.

27. Giddings, *Principles,* pp. 121–22, 133, and *Elements,* p. 77.

28. Giddings, *Principles,* pp. 104, 101.

29. Giddings, *Studies,* pp. 43–56.

30. Ibid., pp. 43, 48.

31. Ibid., pp. 55–56.

32. Giddings, *Elements,* p. 96.

33. Giddings argued the American Indian was more intelligent than the ne-gro, but less capable of adaptation to changing social conditions. The Indian yielded too easily to environmental influences. "Deprived of the support of

stronger races, he still relapses into savagery, but kept in contact with the whites, he readily takes the external impress of civilization, and there is reason to hope that he will yet acquire a measure of its spirit" (*Principles of Sociology*, pp. 328-29).

34. Giddings, *Inductive Sociology*, p. 176.

35. Giddings, *Principles*, p. 146, and *Elements*, p. 156.

36. Giddings, *Elements*, p. 86, and *Principles*, pp. 139–49.

37. Franklin H. Giddings, "Pluralistic Behavior," p. 394.

38. Giddings, *Civilization and Society*, pp. 209–13, and *Readings*, p. 411.

39. Giddings, *Principles*, p. 333.

40. Ibid., p. 5.

41. Giddings, *Studies*, p. 116.

42. Giddings, *Responsible State*, p. 42, *Principles*, p. 195, and *Democracy and Empire*, p. 70.

43. Giddings, *Studies*, p. 97.

44. Giddings, *Inductive Sociology*, pp. 121-22, *Studies*, p. 180, and *Readings*, pp. 391-92.

45. Giddings, *Studies*, p. 41, and *Principles*, p. 290.

46. Franklin H. Giddings, "The Quality of Civilization," p. 587, and *Civilization and Society*, p. 33.

47. Franklin H. Giddngs, "Are Contradictions of Ideas and Beliefs Likely to Play an Important Group-Making Role in the Future?" p. 794.

48. Giddings, *Democracy and Empire*, p. 338.

49. Franklin H. Giddings, "A Provisional Distribution of the Population of the United States into Psychological Classes," p. 338.

50. Giddings, *Inductive Sociology*, p. 63.

51. Ibid., pp. 86, 285. Table 2, which follows, is from Giddings, p. 86. See also Giddings, "A Provisional Distribution," p. 347, for the figures cited.

52. Giddings, "A Provisional Distribution," pp. 343-44.

53. Giddings's reply to a questionnaire sent out by Luther Bernard, reprinted in Luther Bernard, "The Teaching of Sociology," p. 196.

54. Giddings, *Elements*, p. 351.

55. Giddings, *Studies*, p. 127, and *Inductive Sociology*, p. 12.

56. Giddings, *Principles*, p. xvi.

57. Giddings, *Studies*, p. 130, *Democracy and Empire*, pp. 46–47, and *Studies*, p. 98.

58. Giddings, *Principles*, pp. 421, 20, 16, 10.

59. Giddings, *Studies*, p. 291.

60. Giddings, *Democracy and Empire*, pp. 64–65.

61. Giddings, *Civilization and Society*, pp. 266–82.

62. Ibid., pp. 217–18.

63. Giddings, *Elements*, pp. 113–18.

64. Giddings, *Principles*, p. 341, and *Inductive Sociology*, p. 230.

65. Giddings, *Democracy and Empire*, p. 53.

66. Giddings, *Inductive Sociology*, p. 245.

67. Giddings, *Principles*, p. 397; John B. Clark and Franklin H. Giddings, *The Modern Distributive Process*, p. 63.

68. Giddings, *Civilization and Society*, pp. 362–63.

69. Giddings, *Principles*, p. 322.
70. Giddings, *Democracy and Empire*, 357.

Notes to Chapter 6

1. This biographical portrait is based on the following sources: Howard W. Odum, *American Sociology*, pp. 94-96; Howard Becker, "Albion W. Small," pp. 320-22; H.E. Barnes, "The Place of Albion Woodbury Small in Modern Sociology"; Thomas W. Goodspeed, "Albion Woodbury Small."

2. Luther Bernard Papers, box 21, file 20, Pennsylvania State University, Archives, University Park, Pa.

3. Ibid.

4. Ibid.

5. Albion Small, *General Sociology*, pp. 4-5, 92.

6. Ibid., pp. 73-74.

7. Albion Small and George E. Vincent, *An Introduction to the Study of Society*, p.88.

8. Small quoting Schaeffle in Albion Small, *Introduction to the Science of Sociology*, p. 6.

9. Small and Vincent, *Introduction to the Study*, pp. 237-38.

10. Small, *General Sociology*, p. 570; Albion Small, "The Scope of Sociology," 6:507-8.

11. Albion Small, "A Decade of Sociology," p. 8.

12. Small, "The Scope of Sociology," 6:178, 64.

13. Small, *General Sociology*, pp. 472, 480. Vernon K. Dibble, in his work *The Legacy of Albion Small*, argues that "interests are Small's version of instincts" (p. 111), although the interests were not simply physical or biological. In Small's analysis, the interests were meant to represent a total human nature. Dibble argues that, "Small required a more unitary conception of human nature, in which the material elements are integrated with, but remain in dignified subordination to 'attention, valuation, and choice'" (p. 114). In short, Small did not hold a Pauline conception of human nature as fallen or depraved.

14. Albion Small, "Socialism in the Light of Social Science," p. 813.

15. Albion Small, *Between Eras from Capitalism to Democracy*, p. 28; Small, *The Meaning of Social Science*, p. 88; Small, *Introduction to the Science*, pp. 6-7; Small, *General Sociology*, pp. 619-20.

16. Small, *General Sociology*, pp. 325, 245.

17. James A. Aho, "Sociology and Conflict," pp. 240-41.

18. Herman and Julia Schwendiger, *The Sociologists of the Chair*, pp. 250-51.

19. Dibble, *Legacy of Small*, p. 26.

20. Some commentators of Small have suggested that he did develop a "quasi-socialistic thesis that nature and labor are the sole ultimate factors in productivity."

He showed the ethical bankruptcy of the profit economy and thoroughly exposed the wastes, inefficiency, and injustices of capitalistic exploitation. He attacked the whole conception of the immense fortunes, carrying with them extensive financial and industrial control. He made clear the fictitious nature of the divine-right theory of unlimited private property, which was the veritable cornerstone of our American *Politik* and economic system. In the place of the profit economy he would substitute the conception of production for human service under state supervision. Inheritance should be severely limited and labor given its just share in the contol of industrial enterprise and social policy.

(Harry Elmer Barnes, "Albion Woodbury Small: Promoter of American Sociology and Expositor of Social Interests," in Barnes, *An Introduction to the History of Sociology,* p. 418.)

21. Albion Small, *Origins of Sociology,* p. 283.

22. Small, *General Sociology,* pp. 659–60.

23. Small, *Between Eras,* pp. 105–6.

24. Ibid., pp. 28–29.

25. Ibid., p. 47.

26. Small, *Between Eras,* pp. 129–31.

27. Ibid., pp. 157–58.

28. Ibid., pp. 78–79, 83–85.

29. Ibid., pp. 383–84. (This is my paraphrasing of Small's argument.)

30. Small, *Introduction to the Study,* pp. 23–53.

31. Ibid., pp. 73, 74.

32. Albion Small, *Adam Smith and Modern Sociology,* pp. 112–13.

33. Albion Small, *The Cameralists: The Pioneers of German Social Polity,* p. viii.

34. Ibid., pp. 1–10.

35. Albion Small, "Technique as Approach to Science—A Methodological Note," p. 646; Small, *Introduction to the Science,* p. 5; and Small, *Meaning of Social Science,* pp. 9–10.

36. Albion Small, "The Scope of Sociology," 5:638, and *General Sociology,* p. 367.

37. Small, *Adam Smith,* p. 237, and *Cameralists,* p. 1.

38. Albion Small, "The Era of Sociology," pp. 1–2.

39. Albion Small, "Sociology and Plato's Republic."

40. Ibid., p. 533.

41. Albion Small, "The State and Semi-Public Corporation," p. 408.

42. Albion Small, "Sanity in Social Agitation," p. 350.

43. Albion Small, "The Present Outlook of Social Science," p. 436.

44. Small, "Socialism in the Light of Social Science."

45. Ibid., p. 816; Small, "Sanity in Social Agitation," p. 342.

46. Small and Vincent, *Introduction to the Study,* pp. 76–77.

47. Small, *Origins,* p. 28.

48. Ibid., pp. 41, 53.

49. Ibid., p. 66.

50. Ibid., p. 88.

51. Ibid., pp. 132–33, 154–66.

52. Ibid., pp. 177, 194, 199.

53. Ibid., p. 238.

54. Ibid., pp. 297, 302.

55. Small, "The Scope of Sociology," 6:42–66.

56. Small and Vincent, *Introduction to the Study,* pp. 18-19.
57. Ibid., p. 85.
58. Small, *General Sociology,* pp. 28-29, 32, 663.
59. Ibid., pp. 339, viii.
60. Albion Small, "Private Business a Public Trust," pp. 280-81.
61. Small, *Meaning,* p. 30.
62. Ibid., p. 115.
63. Ibid., pp. 230-37, 239.
64. Ibid., pp. 242, 227.
65. Small, *Origins,* p. 334.
66. Albion Small, "Fifty Years of Sociology in the United States."
67. Albion Small, "Some Structural Material for the Idea of Democracy,"
p. 272; see also pp. 405-44.
68. Ibid., p. 444.
69. Ibid., p. 417.
70. Small, "Sanity in Social Agitation," p. 350.

Notes to Chapter 7

1. This biographical portrait was drawn from the following sources: Edward Ross, *Seventy Years of It* (N.Y.: D. Appleton-Century Co., 1936); Luther Bernard Papers, box 34, file 16, Pennsylvania State University, University Park, Pa.
2. Luther Bernard Papers, Pennsylvania State University, box 34, file 16.
3. Ross, *Seventy Years,* pp. 64-65.
4. Edward Ross, *Principles of Sociology,* pp. 44, 605.
5. Ibid., pp. 51-58.
6. Ibid., p. 58.
7. Edward Ross, *Social Control,* pp. 41-48.
8. Ibid., pp. 7, 49, 51-52.
9. Ibid., p. 11.
10. Ibid., pp. 137-45, 110, 265.
11. Edward Ross, *Foundations of Sociology,* p. 272. E. A. Ross, *Social Psychology,* p. 322.
12. Ross, *Social Control,* p. 293, and *Social Psychology,* p. 351.
13. Ross, *Social Control,* p. 394.
14. Ross, *Foundations,* pp. 285-89.
15. Ross, *Principles,* p. 371; Edward Ross, "The Present Problems of Social Psychology," p. 472; Ross, *Principles,* p. 55; Ross, *Social Control,* pp. 64-65.
16. Ross, *Principles,* pp. 204-5.
17. Ross, *Social Control,* pp. 83-84.
18. Ross, *Principles,* p. 693.
19. Dibble points out, in an interesting comparison of Small and Ross, that the latter had been a fundamentalist and conservative Protestant about hu-

man nature. At an early point in Ross's career he had written an oration in which he denounced those atheists who did not believe that moral law was implanted in man's conscience. Not long afterwards, Ross read Darwin and Spencer. "By the beginning of the 1890's, the shock had set in. Ross abolished the moral law implanted in the human conscience, and instituted social control in its place." On the other hand, Small, a liberal Protestant, was not particularly shocked by Darwinism. (Vernon K. Dibble, *The Legacy of Albion Small*, p. 59.)

20. In his autobiography (1936), Ross wrote that he had overcome racial prejudice. *"Difference of race* means far less to me now than once it did starting on my explorations with the naive feeling that only my own Race is right, all other Races are more or less "queer." I gained insight and sympathy until my heart overleapt barriers of Race." (Ross, *Seventy*, p. 276.)

21. Ross wrote, for example, that the superiority of a given people is not necessarily racial. "Physical inferiorities that disappear as the peoples are equalized in diet and dwelling; mental inferiorities that disappear when the peoples are levelled up in respect to culture and means of education, are due not to race but to *condition*, not to blood but to *surroundings*," (My emphasis; "The Causes of Race Superiority," p. 67.)

22. Ibid., pp. 67–89.

23. Edward Ross, *The Changing Chinese*, pp. 51, 54.

24. Ibid., pp. 64, 102.

25. Ibid., pp. 315, 308–9.

26. Edward Ross, *Russia in Upheaval*, pp. 102, 108.

27. Edward Ross, *The Old World in the New*, preface, p. 14.

28. Ibid., p. 44.

29. Ibid., pp. 65–66.

30. Ibid., pp. 113, 116–7, 138.

31. Ibid., p. 299.

32. Ross, *Foundations*, pp. 24-25, and *Principles*, pp. 68–69.

33. Ross, *Principles*, p. 283.

34. Ross, *Social Psychology*, pp. 189, 110.

35. Ross, *Social Control*, p. 150, and *Social Psychology*, pp. 181, 58, 86.

36. Edward Ross, *Changing America*, pp. 113–34.

37. Edward Ross, "Socialization," pp. 667–68.

38. Ross, *Foundations*, p. 40.

39. Ross, *Principles*, p. viii, and *Social Psychology*, pp. 1, 2, 10.

40. Ross, *Foundations*, p. 42; Reinhard Bendix, *Nation-Building and Citizenship*; Ross, *Foundations*, p. 61.

41. Ross, *Social Control*, p. 300.

42. Ross, *Principles*, pp. 546–48.

43. Ibid., p. 41; Edward Ross, *Sin and Society*, pp. 3, 16.

44. Ibid., pp. 41, 90-91, 109–10.

45. Ibid., pp. 148–49.

46. Ross, *Changing America*, pp. 89, 124.

47. Ross, *Principles*, p. 506.

48. Ibid., p. 181.
49. Ross, *Social Control*, pp. 218–19.
50. Ross, *Principles*, p. 253.
51. Ross, *Social Psychology*, pp. 196, 198–99.
52. Ibid., pp. 192, 285, 286.
53. Ross, *Principles*, p. vii.
54. Ross, *Foundations*, p. ix.
55. Ross, *Principles*, pp. 631–32.
56. Ibid., p. 650.
57. Ross, *Social Control*, p. 304.
58. Ross, *Principles*, p. 647.
59. Ross, *Foundations*, p. 126, and *Changing America*, p. 207.
60. Ross, *Social Control*, p. 9; and *Principles*, p. 23.
61. Marjorie Sue Childers, "Social Change in American Sociology: The First Generation," p. 216.
62. Ross, *Social Control*, pp. 417–31, and *Principles*, pp. 149–54.
63. Ross, *Principles*, p. 554.
64. Edward Ross, "Estrangement in Society," pp. 358-59.
65. Ross, *Social Control*, pp. 363, 350-51.
66. Ross, *Changing Chinese*, p. 309, and *Principles*, 565-66.
67. Edward Ross, "The Diseases of Social Structures," pp. 139–58.
68. Edward Ross, "Social Decadence," p. 620.

Notes to Chapter 8

1. I have relied mainly on the following sources for the bibliographical information: Howard Odum *American Sociology*, pp. 109-12; Edward C. Jandy, *C.H. Cooley: His Life and His Social Theory;* Robert C. Angell, "C.H. Cooley"; Luther Bernard Papers, box 3, file 8, Pennsylvania State University, Archives, University Park, Pa.
2. Jandy, *Cooley*, p. 17. (This statement is Cooley's, quoted in Jandy.)
3. Luther Bernard Papers, box 3, file 8, Pennsylvania State University.
4. Angell, "C. H. Cooley," p. 378.
5. Charles H. Cooley, *Human Nature and the Social Order*, pp. 36, 38.
6. Charles H. Cooley, *Social Process*, p. 44.
7. Ibid., pp. 45, 47, 50.
8. Cooley, *Human Nature*, pp. 11, 16, 184.
9. Ibid., p. 119.
10. Ibid., pp. 185.
11. Ibid., pp. 71-72.
12. Ibid., p. 32.
13. Charles H. Cooley, *Social Organization*, p. 32.
14. Ibid., p. 27.
15. Cooley, *Human Nature*, p. 50, and *Social Organization*, p. 113.
16. Cooley, *Social Process*, p. 246.

17. Cooley, *Social Organization*, pp. 93, 111-12.
18. Ibid., p. 328; Charles H. Cooley, "The Process of Social Change," p. 81; Cooley, *Social Process*, pp. 8-10.
19. Charles H. Cooley, *Life and the Student*, p. 50.
20. Charles H. Page, *Class and American Sociology: From Ward to Ross*, p. 205; Roscoe C. Hinkle, "Charles Horton Cooley's General Sociological Orientation," pp. 13-14. Hinkle goes on to point out, quite rightly in my judgment, that Cooley's work can be characterized as "romantic idealism." In Cooley's work, this means a configuration of the following ideas: idealism, organicism, diversitarianism, nonrationality, pervasiveness of conflict, and constancy of change.
21. Cooley, *Social Organization*, pp. 64, 75, 117.
22. Cooley, *Social Process*, p. 19.
23. Cooley, *Human Nature*, pp. 392, 75, 295.
24. Cooley, *Social Organization*, pp. 313, 320, 313-14.
25. Cooley, *Social Process*, pp. 329-30, 283, 287, 330.
26. Cooley, *Social Organization*, p. 270, and *Social Process*, p. 335.
27. Cooley, *Social Organization*, p. 209, 241, 302.
28. Ibid., pp. 291, 304, 229.
29. Ibid., p. 270.
30. Cooley, *Human Nature*, p. 322, and *Social Organization*, p. 163.
31. Cooley's position here is close, if not parallel, to that of Edmund Husserl's in *Phenomenology and the Crisis of Philosophy*.
32. Cooley, *Life*, pp. 121-22.
33. Ibid.; Thomas Kuhn, *The Structure of Scientific Revolutions*.
34. Quoted in Jandy, *Cooley*, p. 238.
35. Charles H. Cooley, *Sociological Theory and Social Research*, pp. 292, 291-92; and *Life*, pp. 148-49.
36. Cooley, *Sociological Theory*, pp. 292, 333, 308, 290.
37. Ibid., p. 290.
38. Cooley, *Social Process*, pp. 55-56.
39. Cooley, *Sociological Theory*, p. 252.
40. Ibid., pp. 253, 254.
41. Ibid., p. 254-55.
42. Ibid., p. 257.
43. Ibid., p. 297.
44. Cooley, *Life*, pp. 159-60, and *Sociological Theory*, pp. 251-52.
45. Cooley, *Social Process*, p. 358, and *Sociological Theory*, pp. 258-59.
46. Cooley, *Social Organization*, p. 199, and *Human Nature*, p. 288.
47. Cooley, *Social Organization*, p. 117.
48. Cooley, *Social Process*, p. 348.
49. Cooley, *Social Organization*, pp. 53, 51.
50. Ibid., pp. 48-49, 51.
51. Cooley, *Social Process*, pp. 393, 368.
52. Cooley, *Life*, pp. 145, 143, and *Social Process*, p. 344.
53. Cooley, *Social Process*, pp. 383, 408.
54. Ibid., p. 403.

Notes to Chapter 9

1. See Roscoe Hinkle's excellent discussion of these aspects in his "Basic Orientations of the Founding Fathers of American Sociology," especially the discussion of the dualistic character of early American sociology (pp. 111-13).

2. C. W. Mills has written about the conservative political implications of the pluralist thesis in "The Professional Ideology of Social Pathologists," pp. 525-52 in his *Power, Politics, and People,* "The liberal 'multiple factor' view does not lead to a conception of causation which would permit point of entry for broader types of action, especially political action.... If one fragmentalizes society into 'factors,' into elemental bits, naturally one will then need quite a few of them to account for something, and one can never be sure they are all in" (pp. 536-37).

3. There is no doubt that they also participated in the *revolt against formalism* described by Morton White in *Social Thought in America.* They did reach back in time and across disciplines for explanations about the origins and development of society. At the same time, they rejected "mere history" in favor of the discovery of laws which is described in the European context by Carlo Antonio, *From History to Sociology.* On the liberalism of early American sociologists, see Leon Shaskolsky, "The Development of Sociological Theory in America—A Sociology of Knowledge Interpretation," and Dusky Lee Smith, "Sociology and the Rise of Corporate Capitalism," pp. 6-30, 68-84, in Larry and Janice Reynolds, eds., *The Sociology of Sociology.*

4. Lucien Goldmann, *The Human Sciences and Philosophy,* p. 52.

5. Critical theory here refers to the following works, although this is not meant to be a comprehensive list: Max Horkheimer, *Eclipse of Reason;* Max Horkheimer, *Critical Theory;* Max Horkheimer, *Critique of Instrumental Reason;* Max Horkheimer and Theodor W. Adorno, *Dialectic of Enlightenment;* Theodor W. Adorno, *Negative Dialectics;* Herbert Marcuse, *Negations;* Herbert Marcuse, *One-Dimensional Man;* Herbert Marcuse, *Soviet Marxism;* Jurgen Habermas, *Knowledge and Human Interests;* Jurgen Habermas, *Theory and Practice;* Jurgen Habermas, *Legitimation Crisis.* For a series of interesting works which analyze the historical and contemporary importance of critical theory, see: Martin Jay, *The Dialectical Imagination;* Göran Therborn, "The Frankfurt School"; Phil Slater, *Origin and Significance of the Frankfurt School;* Zoltan Tar, *The Frankfurt School;* Susan Buck-Morss, *The Origin of Negative Dialectics;* and E. R. Fuhrman, "Critical Theory and the History of Social Theory," "The Normative Structure of Critical Theory."

6. Jay, *Dialectical Imagination,* p. 69.

7. I am using Trent Schroyer, "Toward a Critical Theory for Advanced Industrial Society," to summarize critical theory here. See also Schroyer, "The Need for Critical Theory," and *The Critique of Domination.*

8. Richard J. Bernstein, *The Restructuring of Social and Political Theory,* p. 225.

9. Schroyer, "Need for Critical Theory," p. 37.

10. Bernstein, *Restructuring,* pp. 223-24.

11. Alvin Gouldner, *The Dialectic of Ideology and Technology*, p. 117.
12. Schroyer, *Critique of Domination*, pp. 25-51.
13. Gouldner, *Dialectic of Ideology*, pp. 293-94.

Bibliography

Adorno, Theodor W. *Negative Dialectics.* Translated by E. B. Ashton. New York: Seabury, 1973.

Aho, James A. "Sociology and Conflict." Ph.D. dissertation, Washington State University, 1971.

Allen, P. J., ed. *Pitirim A. Sorokin in Review.* Durham, N.C.: Duke University Press, 1963.

Angell, Robert C. "C. H. Cooley." *International Encyclopedia of the Social Sciences,* ed. David L. Sills. Vol. 3. New York: The Free Press, 1968.

Antonio, Carlo. *From History to Sociology.* Translated by Hayden V. White. Westport, Conn.: Greenwood Press, 1976.

Aron, Raymond. *German Sociology.* New York: The Free Press, 1964.

——. *Main Currents in Sociological Thought.* Translated by Richard Howard and Helen Weaver. 2 vols. New York: Doubleday and Co., 1968.

Bachrach, Peter. *The Theory of Democratic Elitism.* Boston: Little, Brown, and Co., 1967.

Baltzell, E. Digby. *The Protestant Establishment.* New York: Random House, 1964.

Barnes, Harry E. "The Place of Albion Woodbury Small in Modern Sociology." *American Journal of Sociology* 32 (July 1912-May 1913):15-44.

——, ed. *An Introduction to the History of Sociology.* Abridged ed. Chicago and London: University of Chicago Press, 1966.

——; Becker, Carl; and Becker, Howard, eds. *Contemporary Social Theory.* New York: A. Appleton-Century Co., 1940.

Becker, Howard. "Albion Small." *International Encyclopedia of the Social Sciences,* ed. David L. Sills. Vol. 14. New York: The Free Press, 1968.

——, and Barnes, Harry. *Social Thought From Lore to Science.* 3 vols. New York: Dover Publications, 1961.

——, and Boskoff, A., eds. *Modern Sociological Theory in Continuity and Change.* New York: Dryden Press, 1957.

——, and Dahlke, Helmut. "Max Scheler's Sociology of Knowledge." *Philosophy and Phenomenological Research* 2 (March 1942):309-22.

Bell, Daniel. *Marxian Socialism in the United States.* Princeton, N.J.: Princeton University Press, 1952.

Ben-David, Joseph. "The Universities and the Growth of Science in Germany and the United States." *Minerva* 7 (autumn 1968–winter 1969):1-35.

Bendix, Reinhard. *Embattled Reason.* New York: Oxford University Press, 1970.

——. *Nation-Building and Citizenship.* Garden City, N.Y.: Doubleday and Co., 1969.

Berger, Peter. *Invitation to Sociology: A Humanistic Perspective*. Garden City, N.Y.: Doubleday and Co., 1963.

——. *The Sacred Canopy*. Garden City, N.Y.: Doubleday and Co., 1969.

——, and Luckmann, Thomas. *The Social Construction of Reality*. Garden City, N.Y.: Doubleday and Co., 1967.

Berlin, Isaiah. *Karl Marx*. New York: Oxford University Press, 1959.

Bernard, Luther. "The Teaching of Sociology." *American Journal of Sociology* 8 (July 1909–May 1910):190–230.

Bernstein, Richard J. *The Restructuring of Social and Political Theory*. New York: Harcourt, Brace, Jovanovich, 1976.

Birnbaum, Norman. *Toward a Critical Sociology*. New York: Oxford University Press, 1971.

Bottomore, Thomas. *Critics of Society*. New York: Vintage Books, 1979.

——. *Elites and Society*. Middlesex, England: Penguin Books, 1964.

——. *Karl Marx*. Translated, with an introduction, by Thomas Bottomore. New York: The Free Press, 1964.

Bramson, Leon. *The Political Context of Sociology*. Princeton, N.J.: Princeton University Press, 1961.

Buck-Morss, Susan. *The Origin of Negative Dialectics*. New York: The Free Press, 1977.

Cape, Emily P. *Lester F. Ward*. New York: G. P. Putman's Sons, 1922.

Childers, Marjorie Sue. "Social Change in American Sociology: The First Generation." Ph.D. dissertation, New School for Social Research, 1973.

Chugerman, Samuel. *Lester G. Ward: The American Aristotle*. New York: Octagon Books, 1965. This book was first published in 1939 by Duke University Press.

Clark, John B., and Giddings, Franklin. *The Modern Distributive Process*. Boston: Ginn and Co., 1888.

Commager, Henry S. *The American Mind*. New York: Bantam Books, 1970.

Commons, J. R., and associates. *History of Labor in the United States*. 4 vols. New York: The Macmillan Co., 1936.

Comte, Auguste. *System of Positive Polity*. 4 vols. New York: Burt Franklin, 1877.

Cooley, Charles H. *Human Nature and the Social Order*. Introduction by Philip Rieff; foreword by G. H. Mead. New York: Schocken Books, 1964. This book was first published in 1902.

——. *Life and the Student*. New York: Alfred A. Knopf, 1931.

——. "The Process of Social Change." *Political Science Quarterly* 12 (March 1897):63–81.

——. *Social Organization*. Introduction by Philip Rieff. New York: Shocken Books, 1962. This work was first published in 1909.

——. *Social Process*. Introduction by Roscoe Hinkle. Carbondale, Ill.: Southern Illinois University Press, 1966. This book was first published in 1918.

——. *Sociological Theory and Social Research*. Introduction by R. C. Angell. New York: Kelley Publishers, 1969.

Copleston, Frederick. *A History of Philosophy.* 8 vols. Garden City, N.Y.: Image Books, 1962.

Coser, Lewis. *The Functions of Social Conflict.* New York: The Free Press, 1956.

——. *Masters of Sociological Thought.* New York: Harcourt, Brace, Jovanovich, 1971.

——. *Men of Ideas.* New York: The Free Press, 1965.

Crick, Bernard. *The American Science of Politics.* Los Angeles: University of California Press, 1967.

Curtis, James, and Petras, John W., eds. *The Sociology of Knowledge: A Reader.* New York: Praeger Publishers, 1970.

Debs, Eugene. *Debs: His Life, Writings and Speeches.* Girard, Kans.: The Appeal to Reason, 1908.

——. *Walls and Bars.* Chicago: Socialist Party, 1927.

——. *Writings and Speeches of Eugene B. Debs.* New York: Hermitage Press, 1948.

DeWitt, Benjamin. *The Progressive Movement.* Seattle and London: University of Washington Press, 1915.

Dibble, Vernon K. *The Legacy of Albion Small.* Chicago and London: University of Chicago Press, 1975.

Draper, Theodore. *Roots of American Communism.* New York: Viking Press, 1957.

Dreitzel, Hans Peter, ed. *Recent Sociology No. 2.* New York: The Macmillan Co., 1970.

——. "Social Science and the Problem of Rationality: Notes on the Sociology of Technocrats." *Politics and Society,* winter 1972, pp. 165–82.

Durkheim, Emile. *The Division of Labor in Society.* Translated by G. Simpson. New York: The Free Press, 1933.

——. *The Elementary Forms of the Religious Life.* Translated by Joseph Swain. New York: The Free Press, 1965.

——. *The Rules of Sociological Method.* Translated by Sarah Solovay and John Mueller. New York: The Free Press, 1938.

——. *Sociology and Philosophy.* Translated by D. F. Pocock. New York: Cohen and West, 1951.

Friedrichs, Robert. *A Sociology of Sociology.* New York: The Free Press, 1970.

Fuhrman, E. R. "Critical Theory and the History of Social Theory." *Humboldt Journal of Social Relations* 5 (spring-summer 1978):1–25.

——. "The Normative Structure of Critical Theory." *Human Studies* 3 (July 1979):209-28.

Gellner, Ernest. *Legitimation of Belief.* Cambridge: Cambridge University Press, 1974.

Giddings, Franklin H. "Are Contradictions of Ideas and Beliefs Likely to Play an Important Group-Making Role in the Future?" *American Journal of Sociology* 23 (July 1907–May 1908):784–810.

——. *Civilization and Society.* Edited by Howard Odum. New York: Henry Holt and Co., 1932.

——. *Democracy and Empire.* New York: The Macmillan Co., 1900.

——. *The Elements of Sociology.* New York: The Macmillan Co., 1925. This work was first published in 1898.

——. *Inductive Sociology.* New York: The Macmillan Co., 1901.

——. "Pluralistic Behavior." *American Journal of Sociology* 25 (July 1919–May 1920):385–404, 539–61.

——. *The Principles of Sociology.* New York: The Macmillan Co., 1900. This work was first published in 1906.

——. "A Provisional Distribution of the Population of the United States into Psychological Classes." *The Psychological Review* 8 (1901):337–49.

——. "The Quality of Civilization." *American Journal of Sociology* 17 (July 1911–May 1912):581–89.

——. *Readings in Descriptive and Historical Sociology.* New York: The Macmillan Co., 1923. This work was first published in 1906.

——. *The Responsible State.* New York: Houghton Mifflin Co., 1918.

——. *Studies in the Theory of Human Society.* New York: The Macmillan Co., 1922.

Ginger, Ray. *Eugene V. Debs: A Biography.* New York: Collier Books, 1973.

Goldman, Lucien. *The Human Sciences and Philosophy.* Translated by Hayden White and Robert Anchor. London: Chaucer Press, 1969.

Goodspeed, Thomas W. "Albion Woodbury Small." *American Journal of Sociology* 32 (July 1912–May1913):1–14.

Gouldner, Alvin W. *The Coming Crisis of Western Sociology.* New York: Basic Books, 1970.

——. *The Dialectic of Ideology and Technology.* New York: Seabury Press, 1976.

——. *Enter Plato.* 2 vols. New York: Harper Torchbooks, 1965.

——. *For Sociology.* New York: Basic Books, Publishers, 1973.

Graham, Otis, Jr. *The Great Campaigns: Reform and War in America.* Englewood Clifffs, N.J.: Prentice-Hall, 1971.

Green, Constance. *The Rise of Urban America.* New York: Harper and Row, 1965.

Gross, Llewlyn, ed. *Symposium in Sociological Theory.* Evanston, Ill.: Row, Peterson, 1959.

Gurvitch, Georges. *The Social Frameworks of Knowledge.* Translated by Kenneth and Margaret Thompson. New York: Harper and Row, 1971.

——, and Moore, Wilbert, eds. *Twentieth Century Sociology.* New York: Philosophical Library, 1945.

Habermas, Jurgen. *Knowledge and Human Interests.* Translated by Jeremy Shapiro. Boston: Beacon Press, 1971.

——. *Legitimation Crisis.* Translated by Thomas McCarthy. Boston: Beacon Press, 1975.

——. *Theory and Practice.* Translated by John Viertel. Boston: Beacon Press, 1974.

——. *Toward a Rational Society.* Translated by Jeremy Shapiro. Boston: Beacon Press, 1968.

Hamilton, Peter. *Knowledge and Social Structure: An Introduction to the Classical Argument in the Sociology of Knowledge.* Boston and London: Routledge and Kegan Paul, 1974.

Handlin, Oscar. *The Uprooted.* Boston: Little, Brown and Co., 1951.

Hays, Samuel. *The Response to Industrialism: 1885-1914.* Chicago: University of Chicago Press, 1957.

Hendrick, Burton. *The Age of Big Business.* New Haven, Conn.: Yale University Press, 1919.

Herbst, Jurgen. *The German Historical School in American Scholarship.* Ithaca, N.Y.: Cornell University Press, 1965.

Higham, John, ed. *The Reconstruction of American History.* New York: Harper and Row, 1962.

Hillquit, Morris. *Socialism Summed Up.* New York: H. K. Sly, 1912.

Hinkle, Roscoe C. "Basic Orientations of the Founding Fathers of American Sociology." *Journal of the History of the Behavioral Sciences* 11 (April 1975):107-22.

——. "Charles Horton Cooley's General Sociological Orientation." *Sociological Quarterly* 8 (winter 1967):5-20.

——, and Hinkle, Gisela. *The Development of Modern Sociology.* New York: Random House, 1954.

Hoffer, Eric. *The Ordeal of Change.* New York: Harper and Row, 1952.

Hofstadter, Richard. *The Age of Reform.* New York: Random House, 1955.

——. *The Progressive Movement, 1900-1915.* Englewood Cliffs, N.J.: Prentice Hall, 1963.

——. *Social Darwinism in American Thought.* Boston: Beacon Press, 1944.

——, and Hardy, DeWitt C. *The Development and Scope of Higher Education in the United States.* New York: Columbia University Press, 1952.

——, ed. *Great Issues in American History, From Reconstruction to the Present Day, 1864-1969.* New York: Vintage Books, 1969.

——, and Wallace, Michael, eds. *American Violence.* New York: Random House, 1971.

Holsti, Ole R. *Content Analysis for the Social Sciences and Humanities.* Reading, Mass.: Wesley Publishing Co., 1969.

Hopper, Stanley, and Miller, David, eds. *Interpretation: The Poetry of Meaning.* New York: Harcourt, Brace and World, 1967.

Horkheimer, Max. *Critical Theory.* Translated by Matthew J. O'Connell and others. New York: Herder and Herder, 1972.

——. *Critique of Instrumental Reason.* Translated by Matthew J. O'Connell and others. New York: Seabury Press, 1974.

——. *Eclipse of Reason.* New York: Seabury Press, 1974.

——, and Theodor W. Adorno. *Dialectic of Enlightenment.* Translated by John Cumming. New York: Herder and Herder, 1972.

Horton, John. "Order and Conflict Theories of Social Problems as Competing Ideologies." *American Journal of Sociology* 71 (May 1966):701-13.

Hughes, Everett C. *The Sociological Eye.* Chicago: Aldine-Atherton, 1971.

Husserl, Edmund, *Phenomenology and the Crisis of Philosophy.* Translated by Quentin Lauer. New York: Harper and Row, 1965.

Huszar, George, ed. *The Intellectuals.* New York: The Free Press, 1960.

Jandy, Edward C. *C. H. Cooley: His Life and His Social Theory.* New York: Dryden Press, 1942.

Jay, Martin. *The Dialectical Imagination.* Boston: Little, Brown and Co., 1973.

Jencks, Christopher, and Riesman, David. *The Academic Revolution.* Garden City, N.Y.: Doubleday and Co., 1969.

Jones, Maldwyn. *American Immigration.* Chicago: University of Chicago Press, 1960.

Kant, Immanuel. *Critique of Pure Reason.* Translated by Norman Kemp Smith. New York: St. Martin's Press, 1965.

Karsner, David. *Debs: His Authorized Life and Letters.* New York: Boni and Liverright, 1919.

Karson, Marc. *American Labor Unions and Politics, 1900-1918.* Boston: Beacon Press, 1958.

Keller, A. G. *Reminiscences (Mainly Personal) of William Graham Sumner.* New York: Henry Holt and Co., 1925.

Kipnis, Ira. *The American Socialist Movement, 1897–1912.* New York: Columbia University Press, 1952.

Kirk, Russell. *The Conservative Mind.* Chicago: Henry Regnery Co., 1953.

Kirkland, Edward. *A History of American Economic Life.* New York: Appleton-Century-Crofts, 1951.

Kolakowski, Leszek. *The Alienation of Reason.* Translated by Norbert Guterman. Garden City, N.Y.: Doubleday and Co., 1969.

——. *Toward A Marxist Humanism.* Translated by Jane Peel. New York: Grove Press 1968.

Kolko, Gabriel. *The Triumph of Conservatism.* Chicago: Quadrangle Books, 1963.

Kuhn, Thomas. *The Structure of Scientific Revolutions.* 2d ed. Chicago: University of Chicago Press, 1970.

Lasch, Christopher. *The New Radicalism in America.* New York: Vintage Books, 1965.

Laslett, John, and Lipsett, Seymour, eds. *Failure of a Dream?* Garden City, N.Y.: Anchor Press, 1974.

Lavine, Thelma. "Knowledge as Interpretation: An Historical Survey." *Philosophy and Phenomenological Research* 10 (June 1950):526–40; 11 (Sept. 1950):88–103.

Leiss, William. *The Domination of Nature.* Boston: Beacon Press, 1974.

Lichtheim, George. *The Concept of Ideology and Other Essays.* New York: Random House, 1967.

Lipset, Seymour, and Bendix, R. *Social Mobility in Industrial Society.* Berkeley: University of California Press, 1959.

Lukács, Georg. *History and Class Consciousness.* Translated by Rodney Livingstone. Cambridge, Massachusetts: MIT Press, 1972.

MacPherson, C. B. *Democratic Theory: Essays in Retrieval.* London: Oxford University Press, 1973.

Mannheim, Karl. *Essays on the Sociology of Knowledge.* Edited with an introduction by Paul Kecskemeti. London: Routledge and Kegan Paul, 1952.
———. *Ideology and Utopia.* Translated by Edward Shils. New York: Harcourt, Brace and World, 1936.
Maquet, Jacques, J. *The Sociology of Knowledge: Its Structure and Its Relation to the Philosophy of Knowledge—A Critical Analysis of the System of Karl Mannheim and Pitirim A. Sorokin.* Translated by John Locke. Boston: Beacon Press, 1951.
Marcuse, Herbert. *Negations.* Boston: Beacon Press, 1969.
———. *One-Dimensional Man.* Boston: Beacon Press, 1964.
———. *Soviet Marxism.* New York: Random House, 1961.
Martindale, Don. "American Sociology Before World War II." Pp. 121-43 in *Annual Review of Sociology.* Vol. 2. Edited by Alex Inkeles, James Coleman, and Neil Smelser. Palo Alto, California: Annual Reviews, 1976.
———. *The Nature and Types of Sociological Theory.* Boston: Houghton Mifflin Co., 1960.
Marx, Karl, and Engels, Fredrich. *The Communist Manifesto.* Translated by S. Moore. Revised edition. New York: Washington Square Press, 1964.
———. *The German Ideology.* Part 1. Edited with an introduction by C. J. Arthur. New York: International Publishers, 1970.
———. *The Poverty of Philosophy.* New York: International Publishers, 1963.
Matthews, Fred H. *Quest for An American Sociology: Robert E. Park and The Chicago School.* Montreal and London: McGill-Queen's University Press, 1977.
McCloskey, Robert. *American Conservatism in the Age of Enterprise, 1865-1910.* New York: Harper and Row, 1951.
Merton, Robert. *Social Theory and Social Structure.* 1st rev. ed. New York: The Free Press, 1957.
Metzger, Walter P. *Academic Freedom in the Age of the University.* New York: Columbia University Press, 1955.
Miller, Sally. *Victor Berger and the Promise of Constructive Socialism, 1919-1920.* Westport, Conn.: Greenwood Press, 1973.
Mills, C. W. *Power, Politics, and People.* Edited with an introduction by Irving Louis Horowitz. New York: Oxford University Press, 1967.
Mitzman, Arthur. *Estrangment and Sociology.* New York: Alfred A. Knopf, 1973.
Morrison, Samuel Eliot. *The Oxford History of the American People.* 3 vols. New York: New American Library, 1965.
Nisbet, Robert. *Tradition and Revolt.* New York: Vintage Books, 1970.
Odum, Howard. *American Sociology.* New York: Longmans, Green and Co., 1951.
———, ed. *American Masters of Social Science.* New York: Henry Holt and Co., 1927.
O'Kelley, Charlotte G., and John W. Petras. "Images of Man in Early American Sociology, Part II: The Changing Concept of Social Reform." *Journal*

of the History of the Behavioral Sciences 6 (October 1970):317–34.

Ortega y' Gasset, Jose. *Concord and Liberty.* New York: W. W. Norton and Co., 1946.

Page, Charles. *Class and American Sociology: From Ward to Ross.* New York: Schocken Books, 1969. This work was first published in 1940.

Palmer, Richard E. *Hermeneutics.* Evanston, Ill.: Northwestern University Press, 1969.

Pelling, Henry. *American Labor.* Chicago: University of Chicago Press, 1960.

Pennsylvania State University, Archives. Luther Bernard Papers, University Park, Pa.

Perlman, Selig. *A History of Trade Unionism in the United States.* New York: Augustus M. Kelley, 1950.

Petras, John W. "Images of Man In Early American Sociology, Part I: The Individualistic Perspective in Motivation." *Journal of the History of the Behavioral Sciences* 6 (July 1970):231–40.

Radnitzky, Gerard. *Contemporary Schools of Metascience.* 3d ed. 2 vols. Chicago: Henry Regnery, 1973.

Radosh, Ronald, ed. *Debs.* Englewood Cliffs, N.J.: Prentice-Hall, 1971.

Reiss, Albert J. "Sociology: The Field." *International Encyclopedia of the Social Sciences,* ed. David L. Sills. New York: The Free Press, 1968.

Remmling, Gunter. *Road to Suspicion.* New York: Appleton-Century-Crofts, 1967.

——, ed. *Towards the Sociology of Knowledge.* London: Routledge and Kegan Paul, 1973.

Renshaw, Patrick. *The Wobblies.* Garden City, N.Y.: Doubleday and Co., 1967.

Reynolds, Larry, and Reynolds, Janice, eds. *The Sociology of Sociology.* New York: David McKay Co., 1970.

Rieff, Philip, ed. *On Intellectuals.* New York: The Free Press, 1970.

——. *The Triumph of the Therapeutic.* New York: Harper and Row, 1968.

Ritzer, George. *Sociology: A Multiple Paradigm Science.* Boston: Allyn and Bacon, 1975.

Ross, Edward. "The Causes of Race Superiority." *Annals: American Academy of Political and Social Sciences* 28 (July 1901):67–89.

——. *Changing America.* New York: Chautauqua Press, 1915.

——. *The Changing Chinese.* New York: The Century Co., 1912.

——. "The Diseases of Social Structures." *American Journal of Sociology* 24 (July 1918–May 1919):139–58.

——. "Estrangement in Society." *American Journal of Sociology* 23 (July 1917–May 1918):620–32.

——. *Foundations of Sociology.* 5th ed. New York: The Macmillan Co., 1920. This work was first published in 1905.

——. *The Old World in the New.* New York: The Century Co., 1914.

——. "The Present Problems of Social Psychology." *American Journal of Sociology* 10 (July 1904–May 1905):456–72.

——. *Principles of Sociology.* New York: The Century Co., 1920.

——. *Russia in Upheaval.* New York: The Century Co., 1918.

——. *Seventy Years of It.* New York: Appleton-Century Co., 1936.

——. *Sin and Society.* New York: Houghton, Mifflin, and Co., 1907.

——. *Social Control.* New York: The Macmillan Co., 1914. This work was first published in 1901.

——. "Social Decadence." *American Journal of Sociology* 23 (July 1917–May 1918):620–32.

——. "Socialization." *American Journal of Sociology* 24 (July 1918–May 1919):652–71.

——. *Social Psychology.* New York: The Macmillan Co., 1919. This work was first published in 1908.

Roth, Guenther. "Religion and Revolutionary Beliefs: Sociological and Historical Dimensions in Max Weber's Work—In Memory of Ivan Vallier." *Social Forces* 55 (December 1976):257–72.

Russell, Bertrand. *A History of Western Philosophy.* New York: Simon and Schuster, 1945.

Schacht, Richard. *Alienation.* Garden City, N.Y.: Doubleday and Co., 1971.

Schaub, Edward. "A Sociological Theory of Knowledge." *Philsophical Review* 20 (November 1954):333–42.

Scheler, Max. "The Future of Man." *The Monthly Criterion,* February 1928, pp. 110–24.

——. *Philosophical Perspectives.* Boston: Beacon Press, 1958.

——. "Problems with a Sociology of Knowledge," translated by Ernest Banly. *Philosophy Today* 12 (1968):42–70.

Schroyer, Trent. *The Critique of Domination.* Boston: Beacon Press, 1975.

——. "The Need for Critical Theory." *Insurgent Sociologist* 3 (1973):29–40.

——. "Toward a Critical Theory for Advanced Industrial Society." pp. 210–234 in *Recent Sociology No. 2,* ed. H. P. Dreitzel. New York: The Macmillan Company, 1970.

Schwendinger, Herman, and Schwendinger, Julia. *The Sociologists of the Chair.* New York: Basic Books, 1974.

Scott, Andrew M. "The Progressive Era in Perspective." *The Journal of Politics* 21 (1959):685–701.

Shannon, David. *The Socialist Party of America.* New York: The Macmillan Co., 1955.

Shils, Edward. *The Intellectuals and the Powers and Other Essays.* Chicago and London: University of Chicago Press, 1972.

——. "Tradition, Ecology, and Institution in the History of Sociology." *Daedalus* 99 (fall 1970):760–825.

Slater, Phil. *Origin and Significance of the Frankfurt School.* Boston: Routledge and Kegan Paul, 1977.

Small, Albion. *Adam Smith and Modern Sociology.* Chicago: University of Chicago Press, 1907.

——. *Between Eras From Capitalism to Democracy.* Kansas City, Inter-Collegiate Press, 1913.

——. *The Cameralists: The Pioneers of German Social Polity.* Chicago: University of Chicago Press, 1909.

———. "A Decade of Sociology." *American Journal of Sociology* 11 (July 1905–May 1906):1–10.

———. "The Era of Sociology." *American Journal of Sociology* 1 (July 1895–May 1896):1–15.

———."Fifty Years of Sociology in the United States." *American Journal of Sociology* 21 (July 1915–May 1916):721–864.

———. *General Sociology.* Chicago: University of Chicago Press, 1905.

———. *Introduction to the Science of Sociology.* Waterville, Me.: The Mail Office, 1890.

———. *The Meaning of Social Science.* Chicago: The University of Chicago Press, 1910.

———. *Origins of Sociology.* Chicago: University of Chicago Press, 1924.

———. "The Present Outlook of Social Science." *American Journal of Sociology* 18 (July 1912-May 1913):433-69.

———. "Private Business A Public Trust." *American Journal of Sociology* 1 (July 1895–May 1896):276–89.

———. "Sanity in Social Agitation." *American Journal of Sociology* 4 (July 1898–May 1899):355–51.

———. "The Scope of Sociology." *American Journal of Sociology* 5 (July 1899–May 1900):506–26, 617–47, 778–813.

———. "Socialism in the Light of Social Science." *American Journal of Sociology* 17 (July 1911–May 1912):804–19.

———. "Sociology and Plato's Republic." *American Journal of Sociology* 30 (July 1924–May 1925):513–33, 683–702.

———. "Some Structural Material for the Idea of Democracy." *American Journal of Sociology* 25 (July 1919–May 1920):257–97, 405–44.

———. "The State and Semi-Public Corporation." *American Journal of Sociology* 1 (July 1895–May 1896):398–410.

———. "Technique as Approach to Science—A Methodological Note." *American Journal of Sociology* 27 (July 1921–May 1922):646–51.

———, and Vincent, George E. *An Introduction to the Study of Society.* Dubuque, Iowa: Brown Reprints, 1971. This work was first published in 1894.

Smith, Dusky Lee. "Some Socio-Economic Influences on the Founding Fathers of Sociology, 1865-1917." Ph.D. dissertation. State University of New York at Buffalo, 1970.

Sorokin, Pitirim. *Social and Cultural Dynamics.* 4 vols. New York: American Book Co., 1937.

———. *Social and Cultural Dynamics.* Abridged by the author. Boston: Porter Sargent 1957.

———. *Social Mobility.* New York: Harper and Brothers, 1927.

Southern, David. *The Malignant Heritage: Yankee Progressives and the Negro Question, 1901-1914.* Chicago: Loyola University Press, 1968.

Stark, Werner. *The Sociology of Knowledge.* London: Routledge and Kegan Paul, 1958.

Stein, Maurice, and Vichich, Arthur, eds. *Sociology on Trial.* Englewood Cliffs, N.J.: Prentice-Hall, 1963.

Strasser, Herman. *The Normative Structure of Sociology.* Boston and London: Routledge and Kegan Paul, 1976.

Sumner, William. *The Challenge of Facts and Other Essays.* Edited by A. G. Keller. New Haven: Yale University Press, 1914.

———. *Collected Essays in Political and Social Science.* New York: Henry Holt and Co., 1885.

———. *Earth Hunger and Other Essays.* New Haven: Yale University Press, 1913.

———. *Essays of William Graham Sumner.* 2 vols. Edited by A. G. Keller and Maurice R. Davie. New Haven: Yale University Press, 1934.

———. *Folkways.* New York: Ginn and Co., 1940. This work was first published in 1906.

———. *War and Other Essays.* Edited by A. G. Keller. Freeport, N.Y.: Books for Libraries Press, 1970. These essays were first published in 1911.

———. *What Social Classes Owe to Each Other.* Caldwell, Idaho: Caxton Printers, 1966. The first edition of this work appeared in 1883.

———, and Keller, A. G. *The Science of Society.* 4 vols. New Haven: Yale University Press, 1927.

Taft, P. *The A. F. of L. in the Time of Gompers.* New York: Harper and Brothers, 1957.

Tar, Zoltan. *The Frankfurt School.* New York: John Wiley and Sons, 1977.

Taylor, Stanley. "Social Factors and the Validation of Thought." *Social Forces* 41 (October 1962):76–82.

Therborn, Göran. "The Frankfurt School." *New Left Review* 63 (1970):65–96.

———. *Science, Class and Society.* London: NLB, 1976.

Tiryakian, Edward, ed. *The Phenomenon of Sociology.* New York: Appleton-Century-Crofts, 1971.

University of Chicago, Special Collections, Luther Bernard Papers.

Veysey, Lawrence R. *The Emergence of the American University.* Chicago and London: University of Chicago Press, 1965.

Ward, Lester. *Applied Sociology.* New York: Ginn and Co., 1906.

———. *Dynamic Sociology.* 2 vols. New York and London: D. Appleton and Co., 1910. This work was first published in 1883.

———. *Outlines of Sociology.* New York: The Macmillan Co., 1923. This book was first published in 1897.

———. *The Psychic Factors of Civilization.* 2d ed. New York: Ginn and Co., 1906. This book was first published in 1892.

———. *Pure Sociology.* New York: Augustus M. Kelley, 1970. This book was first published in 1903.

Weber, Max. *The Methodology of the Social Sciences.* Translated and edited by Edward Shils and Henry Finch. New York: The Free Press, 1949.

Weinstein, James. *The Corporate Ideal in the Liberal State, 1900–1918.* Boston: Beacon Press, 1968.

——. *The Decline of Socialism in America, 1912–1925.* New York: Vintage Books, 1969.

——, and Eakins, David W., eds. *For A New America.* New York: Vintage Books, 1970.

Wellmer, Albrecht. *Critical Theory of Society.* Translated by John Cumming. New York: Herder and Herder, 1971.

White, Morton. *Social Thought in America: The Revolt Against Formalism.* Boston: Beacon Press, 1957.

Wiebe, Robert. *Businessmen and Reform: A Study of the Progressive Movement.* Cambridge, Mass.: Harvard University Press, 1962.

Wilson, Edmund. *To the Finland Station.* Garden City, N.Y.: Doubleday and Co., 1953.

Windelband, Wilhelm. *A History of Philosophy.* 2 vols. New York: Harper and Row, 1958.

Wittgenstein, Ludwig. *On Certainty.* Translated by Denis Paul and G.E.M. Anscombe. New York: Harper and Row, Publishers, 1972.

Wolff, Kurt. *"Notes Toward a Sociocultural Interpretation of American Sociology." American Sociological Review* 41 (October 1946):545–53.

——, ed. *Essays on Sociology and Philosophy.* New York: Harper and Row, 1960.

Wolff, Robert Paul. *The Poverty of Liberalism.* Boston: Beacon Press, 1968.

Index